Allegra, Claudia Roden, and Fred in the garden, 2002

Leon

Ingredients & Recipes

By
Allegra McEvedy

CONTENTS

Leon was founded on the principle:
that food can be both lovely and good for you...

Allegra, Henry, and John, Ludgate Leon, March '08.

Our Story

Leon was begun by Henry, John, and me some time around the early part of the new millennium.

Henry had had a spell as a chef before moving into management consultancy, which is where he met John; my and Henry's family had known each other for ages—our big sisters have been bestest of friends since they were 11—and we younger siblings bonded in our teenage years through a love of food.

John and Henry were traveling a lot around the country and were increasingly frustrated by the limited menus on offer for people without much time to eat—particularly if they care about their food. Knowing what was in the food and how they would feel an hour or so later didn't make them happy.

I was coming at it from a parallel point of view, having already rebelled against the notion that fine dining was the only way for a chef to make a difference. I became convinced that good, seasonal food was something that should be available to everybody—a right, not a privilege.

So there were huddled meetings after we'd all finished our day jobs, and over a couple of years our ideas distilled into some kind of clarity, then one by one we chucked in our jobs, committing ourselves completely to the idea of changing the face of fast food.

On June 26, 2004, the first Leon opened on Carnaby Street, in London, and six months later we won Best New Restaurant in Great Britain from the *Observer Food Monthly*. By the start of 2008 we had nine Leons, and had just picked up an award for Best Restaurant Concept in Europe.

But back when we only had one restaurant, what really made us believe we were on the right track were our customers; it wasn't all plain sailing, but the overriding message we got from them was that they were glad we were around.

So a massive Leon Lovers' Love-in to each and every one of you—and at the moment that's tens of thousands every week—for all your support, patience, and, above all, for coming back. And to the people who haven't eaten with us yet, we're really looking forward to showing you what we do.

The Leon Food Principles

It took us a long time to clarify exactly what we do, but now we seem to have distilled it down: food that tastes good and does you good. At our seasonal tastings, if most of us don't make an instinctive yummy noise when we taste something new then it doesn't go through to the next round. Even then it's got a way to go before getting onto the menu, including those times when we have regulars in for what are usually quite boisterous sunset tastings. We all love food and are fiercely protective, passionate, and proud of the menu at Leon.

That's the big picture, but all these words like "passionate" and "delicious" have been hijacked by just about everyone in the food industry, bandied about by folk who wouldn't know passion if they stood in the middle of a Bogart–Bergman kiss. For us, it's about flavors that get your taste buds working.

We love ingredients so much we've given them their own book. Superfoods—the collective term for ingredients with strong health-giving properties—have a special place for us, but really they are just ingredients with bonus points attached to them. And we try to steer clear of anything that's too high on the glycemic index, so that you feel invigorated for hours after you've eaten with us, rather than needing a nap.

Seasonality just makes sense.

Finally, most important in life and in food, is the right to treat yourself without guilt. There is this perception out there that in order to look after your body you have to deny yourself, and we hope that our food never feels like that. The health thing should seem no more than incidental to our customers, who come for the good food, not a holistic aromatherapy moment. We all have our naughty pleasures, and a little bit of pure fun is a necessary part of life and love. So that's why our chocolate mousse feels deliciously wicked, why our prize-winning Catalan chorizo is lip-smacking with piggy fat, and why most Leons have a booze license. We're not obsessive about health, but want a long, happy, and fun life, and part of the balancing act has to be giving yourself a little something that makes you happy inside.

As well as changing the menu with the seasons, we also like to mark the passing of time as the day drifts by, and so you can go into the same Leon for breakfast, lunch, supper, and have a different kind of menu, service, and feel each time. It's all about loving the change that we live through.

Our aim with this book is to give you everything you need to make the most of what's out there. When the three of us first got together to talk book, we quickly realized that it was not only the recipes from the restaurants that we wanted to write about, but ingredients, seasonality, and sourcing—basically everything that has a bearing on what goes on in our kitchens.

So this book is a game of two halves: the first is the Ingredients Book, so you can learn about the building blocks, and the second is the Recipe Book, to give you some ideas of what you can build with them. This way you can read up on curly kale, for example, before finding out about how to use it.

We've included a pull-out guide to ingredients through the seasons in the middle, and also in the Appendix there are buying tips—things to look for to make sure you're getting good produce. For us, that pretty much takes care of the whole journey: sourcing, shopping, knowledge, and cooking, and we hope this helps you steer your way through the huge array of choices that face a cook in our times.

THE INGREDIENTS BOOK

Everybody knows that good food, and food that's good for you, is all about starting with the right basic building blocks. Ingredients are everything to us, not only the use of nature's finest at the right time of year, but also the pure joy that quality brings, from an egg with a properly yellow yolk, to a piece of fish still slippery from the sea. This first book is all about bringing the importance of ingredients back to the forefront of our minds. The choices we make as we shop are the overriding factors that will affect the way our food tastes.

The entries have been based around the ingredients that we use at Leon, with others mentioned that we just couldn't imagine life without. We've also put in special mentions for

and

for those desert island ingredients (the foods that you would be happy to live with only and forever) that are fundamental to us.

We hope the Ingredients Book will be a good read for anyone who cares about what they put into their body: people who get excited when they see the color of a blood orange bursting through its skin; or for whom the world stops for a second when they taste an exceptional slice of bacon. Our book is for anyone who loves food, and couldn't contemplate an existence without raspberries.

SUNS

is essential for Life—both

HINE

for us and our Ingredients

FRUIT

Some apples we like

Variety	Look	Taste	Use
Bramley *(v)*	One of the biggest apples out there, mid-green, often with a knobbly part where the stalk goes in.	Too sour to eat raw, due to more malic acid than sugar; but with some heat and sugar becomes the undisputed champion for cooking.	From apple sauce to dried apples. Bramleys have 20% less dry matter than eating apples, hence the lovely mush that happens when cooked.
Chivers Delight	By eating standards a big apple. Greenish-yellow skin, ripening to golden; red blush.	Superbly hard and crunchy; flavor not immediate but just gets better and better.	A very good eater, bred by Stephen Chivers near Cambridge, in the UK, in the 1920s.
Cox's Orange Pippin *(ii)*	A smallish round apple, orange/greenish/yellow, streaked with red.	This midseasonal is the oldest of the best-known eating varieties (1825); crisp, juicy, and aromatic.	Raw, just like that, but sautéed slices are also good with pork dishes. Known as a dessert apple in the UK.
Discovery	A white-fleshed, rosy-red apple with a pink tinge below the skin.	Crisp, juicy, and slightly perfumed in a lovely way.	Traditionally the first apple of the season (late August) and is best enjoyed raw.
Granny Smith *(i)*	Perfect supermarket apple. All-over green to the point of looking cloned.	Crisp. And rather tart.	Their uniformity is their appeal to the supermarkets and their weakness for us.
Jonagold *(iv)*	Nice sharing of muted green and almost rusty red. Usually quite a big apple.	Good bite to the skin, with a pure, rich flesh. Sweet and juicy, close to Cox's Orange Pippin.	Eating apple—also one of the best for storing.
Royal Gala *(iii)*	Medium-sized, predominantly red, with green showing through.	Good, bouncy crunch and the perfect texture.	Derived from Golden Delicious and Pippin. Best for eating.
Spartan	Looks like Snow White's apple: clear flesh, shiny skin.	Aromatic and almost floral. Very sweet and juicy.	Cultivated in Canada in the early 20th century as an eating apple.

BRITISH FRUIT

Apples

Where do they grow? Sidestepping the facetious answer, "In orchards," the answer is almost anywhere with a mid-mild climate. Apple trees need soil that can drain well, and are fine anywhere except at either extreme end of the temperature scale. The earliest of the British grown apples to be ready tend to be Discovery (what a nice bite) in late summer. Harvesting carries on through to the first frosts of winter.

How do I use them? Well, it all depends on what variety you have. Some are best for cooking, others that naturally ferment are better for cider-making, but of course the majority are good to go straight from the bough. The aim is to try to get specific about your apple, rather than just generically using a supermarket hybrid for all your apple needs. For a really good show of varieties go to your local farm stand in fall, or take a drive through apple-growing regions near you.

What's in it for me? The old adage about an apple a day comes from the fact that they really do have a little bit of just about everything in them, from vitamin A to zinc.

Anything else? Calvados. And the Saxon Christmas tradition of wassailing was born from the blessing of the apple harvest.

....

☛ **Friends pork, cinnamon, pastry …**
Relations pears, quince … Recipes Good Morning Muffin p.150; Autumn Slaw p.266; Apple & Blackberry Juice p.287; Apple, Ginger & Goji Berry Juice p.287; Hot Apple Mull p.288

Pears & Quince

Where do they grow? Both these trees like full sun and a sheltered position. They grow happily in the UK's climate, and Worcestershire is England's most famous pear-producing county. Sitting slightly at odds with that are the beginnings of pears over eastward, with Kashmir, the Middle East, and China all having referenced them some thousands of years ago.

Quinces are equally ancient (it is thought that the "apples" mentioned in the Song of Solomon were actually quinces) and also grow well all over the Middle East and the Med. Pears have literally hundreds of varieties, but the "streamlining" of producers that supermarket purchasing execs love to do means we rarely see different kinds: Comice, William, Conference—that's about all the average urban British cook has on offer.

How do I use them? Pears can be anything from the juiciest, sweetest, dribble-down-your-chin Comice, right through to the also pleasurable, crisp, hard, and refreshing Conference (the squatter the pear, the juicier it will be when fully ripe). Williams sit somewhere between the two, being tallish and pretty juicy, and are worth a mention because they give us the excellent and intense liqueur Poire William. A good pear is best just eaten raw; in contrast quinces are usually cooked, but quinces are most famous for the gorgeous preserve they make due to their huge pectin content. Historically this was a forefather of jams and marmalades, though now is most commonly seen as the Spanish cheese accompaniment *membrillo*. And speak to the people in Worcestershire about making perry, which is to pears as cider is to apples.

What's in it for me? Similar to apples in that they have a little bit of quite a lot: zinc, iodine, and sulfur, along with vitamins A and C. Famously good for your digestion (plenty of fiber), and the uric acid is good for the old waterworks.

Anything else? Babycham, popular in the UK in the 60s and 70s, is actually perry (just not a very good one). Pears are the least allergenic of all foods. Pyriform means "pear-shaped." Pear wood is a favorite for making woodwind instruments.

....

☛ **Friends cheese, cinnamon, pastry, partridge (in a…) … Relations apples**

Pears & Quince (above right); *i.* Conference; *ii.* Quince; *iii.* Comice; *iv.* William

Plums (left); *i.* Gaviota, more commonly known as Golden Plum; *ii.* Victoria; *iii.* Pioneer

Plums

Where do they grow? In moist and sunny climates, which in Britain means down south, with some of the best varieties coming out of Sussex, Devon, and Kent. The Asians are keen on a plum, as shown by the first mention of them being by Confucius in 479 B.C.E. They spread west to the Med, and were also found already growing happily in America when the Europeans landed. The plum varieties we have in Europe are descendants of trees uprooted from Damascus in Syria. The most common variety in Britain is Victoria, which was found as a seedling in a garden in Sussex during her reign. Plums are now the second most-cultivated fruit in the world.

How do I use them? If you can find a plum with flavor (not as easy as it sounds), just cram it into your mouth as quickly as possible, closely followed by another one. For when this fruit is great, it is so great, and when it's not, well, frankly we'd rather suck on a floorboard. They like being cooked, so crisps, jams, pies, and the like are a fitting destination. Or you can go all Balkan and make them into the lethal Slivovitz—a plum moonshine, which must be quite something: 70% of all plums grown around there are sent to the distillery.

What's in it for me? Big in minerals, so they're good for the blood and, like most fruit, contain plenty of vitamin A. And then there's all that "keeping you regular" thing.

Anything else? Christmas pudding used to be called plum pudding even though it never had any plums in it—in the 17th century people were a bit loose with their dried-fruit terminology and the "plums" were actually raisins. More than 100 plum pits were found on Henry VIII's ship *Mary Rose* when she was raised from the bottom of the sea four and a half centuries after she sank.

☛ **Friends** sweetness, red game, spices, booze … **Relations** damson plums, greengages, sloe berries, apricots, and cherries … **Recipes** Dittisham Plum Ice Cream p.264

Rhubarb

Where does it grow? Left to its own devices rhubarb is an early summer fruit (well, technically it's a stem, not a fruit), but the massive forced rhubarb industry based in Yorkshire (known as the Rhubarb Triangle, and I'm not kidding) gives us this fine beast as early as February. Forced rhubarb is grown in sheds by candlelight, and famously you can hear it creaking as it grows. Requires plenty of moisture in the soil, whether forced or not, which is why wild rhubarb is often found next to rivers.

How do I use it? By the yard when it's available. Look beyond rhubarb crisp or pies, and let its fruity sharpness lead you in other directions — as in chutney, or a compote to go with rich meats. Would work anywhere you were going to have cranberry sauce. In Norway they make both savory and sweet soups out of it. In desserts, rhubarb that is cooked and still keeps its stem shape is more refined than a stringy, wet pile.

What's in it for me? Plenty of iron and vitamin C, but don't go near the leaves because they are poisonous and will corrode your kidneys.

Anything else? In February 2010, the European Commission's Protected Food Name scheme awarded Yorkshire Forced Rhubarb Protected Designation of Origin (PDO) status. This means it enjoys the same status as Parma ham or Greek feta. Irish giant rhubarb grows to be as thick as a man's arm.

☛ **Friends** custard, foie gras (and ducks and poultry in general), pastry … **Relations** dock leaves, sorrel, and buckwheat … **Recipes** James's Rhubarb & Ginger Jam p.146; Rhubarb Compote p.149; What-Joey-Wants-Joey-Gets Rhubarb Crisp p.268; Rhubarb & Vanilla Smoothie p.282

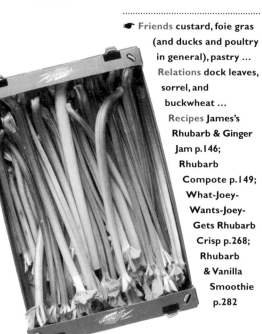

MEDITERRANEAN FRUIT

Apricot

Where does it grow? First noted in Pakistan's Hunza valley in 2000 B.C.E., apricots then headed west (and, to a lesser extent, east to China, where smoked apricots are a delicacy) and are now widely associated with Middle Eastern and Mediterranean cooking. Current top exporters are Iran and the US. A good harvest is not all about the heat of the sun—apricots need a cold winter too. Season-wise they are the earliest of the stone fruit (like peaches, cherries, and plums), which makes them early summer. It was originally thought that they were a member of the plum family, so they were given the name *Prunus armenaica*, but actually it turns out they are more closely related to peaches and almonds. The error in their grouping, however, was never corrected.

How do I use it? The season for fresh is short, but luckily they dry well, keeping nearly all their flavor, natural sugars, and nutrients (just be careful to avoid the overly orange ones treated with sulfur dioxide (E220), though this practice is banned in the US. If you find yourself with an abundance of fresh apricots, once you're bored with smoothies head for a spot of jam-making to really motor through them. The dried are indispensable in many savory dishes, particularly from the Muslim world. Also works with many of game birds and, of course, anything to do with lamb. The Japanese put an *umeboshi* (a very pickled and salty baby apricot) on top of their breakfast bowl of rice… truly a much more effective wake-you-up than a double espresso.

What's in it for me? Equal parts of vitamin A, iron, and beta-carotene make this bustlingly full of goodness. Vitamin A is good for your eyes, iron obviously is strength-building, and the last is a strong free-radical fighting antioxidant.

Anything else? Immortalized by the Cowardly Lion in *The Wizard of Oz*: "What puts the ape in apricot?" to which, of course, the answer is… "COURAGE!"

☛ **Friends** lamb, rosemary, pâtisserie … **Relations** all the stone fruit, and almonds … **Recipes** Moroccan Chicken Tagine p.236; Apricot Madeira Cake p.263

Cherries

Where do they grow? Nowadays most of the global export market in this fruit is handled by North America, with Michigan declaring itself the "Cherry Capital of the World." There is still a decent European and Middle Eastern season in the height of summer, and in good hot years we can even produce some here in the south of Britain. Testament to this is that 15th-century markets in London were flooded with them, though they may not have been quite as sweet and juicy as our taste buds now demand.

How do I use them? By the handful if you find a good batch, but something slightly magical happens to them as they cook, which makes them one of our favorite fruits for baking. Black Forest gateau is, or maybe was, a worldwide staple, and if you've never eaten a cherry clafoutis straight from the oven you're missing out. There's also a tendency, as with most fruit, to push them duckward, and if you're feeling adventurous you can always make your own kirsch, which probably isn't a bad investment of time and money to pleasure. A woman who can't bake a cherry pie isn't really worth marrying, according to the old song.

What's in it for me? Being so sweet, cherries have quite a lot of fruit sugar in them, but it's the natural kind so it is absorbed slowly into your system and therefore is a great way to keep your energy levels up. Cherries contain melatonin, a powerful antioxidant that is particularly linked to your sleeping and restfulness, and are considered good for cell rejuvenation.

Anything else? *Hanami* in Japan is the "viewing of the cherry blossom," which sends the entire country into a frenzy in the days leading to its arrival in springtime. They take it very seriously and, my God, it's breathtaking when it comes.

☞ Friends **champagne, picnics, pâtisserie, cough syrup, tropical cocktails ... Relations plums, greengages, and all that gang; see also Sour Cherries, p.125**

Figs

Where do they grow? *The* fruit of the Med, originally from Asia Minor. Fig trees can also be seen bearing fruit in Britain, but they basically thrive on sunshine so our natives never quite seem to hit the dizzy flavor heights that their Med cousins do. Green and purple are the most common varieties, and they are best left until the end of summer for maximum sweetness. Tearing open a ripe fig is one of nature's special treats for all the senses.

How do I use them? The best way is straight off the branch, but if you feel like cooking them, cut them in half, sprinkle them with sugar, give them a quick broil, and devour with mascarpone and a glass of vin santo. Once the season's done, dried figs liven up a bowl of oatmeal, or stew slowly with any rich game.

What's in it for me? Good poops!

Anything else? Figs get 27 mentions in the Bible, second only to grapes in the biblical fruit chart. Carbon dating has identified some figs found near Jericho in the West Bank as being 11,400 years old. Best way to tell if a fig is really ripe is not by smelling or squeezing but by looking for a slight stickiness to the skin, where the sweetness inside is literally bursting to get out.

☞ Friends **the Israelites ... Relations figs are hermaphrodites so they have no immediate relations**

BAG OF CHERRIES

They say that life is like a bowl of cherries but we find it easier to carry round in a bag.

out £2.00 (in £2.35)

powell's books

503.228.4651 / 800.878.7323 / powells.com

powell's
city of books
1005 w burnside st
downtown portland
daily: 9am - 11pm

powell's books at
cedar hills crossing
3415 sw cedar hills blvd
mon - sat: 10am - 9pm
sun: 11am - 7pm

powell's books
on hawthorne
3723 se hawthorne blvd
mon - thurs: 9am - 10pm
fri - sat: 9am - 11pm
sun: 9am - 9pm

powell's books
for home & garden
3747 se hawthorne blvd
mon - sat: 9am - 9pm
sun: 9am - 8pm

powell's books
at pdx
at portland int'l airport
(call or check website
for hours)

Grapes

Where do they grow? Most high-quality wine is grown in one of two belts that circle the globe: the first, in the Tropic of Cancer, runs through Europe and California, while the second, in the southern Tropic of Capricorn, swings all the way around the planet, taking in South Africa, Australia, and Chile. Wine is one of the oldest alcoholic drinks in the world, and not only the Romans were known to imbibe—the Persians were producing wine some 6,500 years ago. When American-grown grapes are not in season, the US imports table grapes (as opposed to grapes for winemaking) from Chile or Mexico. In France they grow some stunning little white Muscat grapes for eating, while in Italy the diametrically opposite big, purple, almost plum-sized ones from Puglia ripen to bursting by the scorching southern Italian sun. The flavor of the grapes has a lot to do with soil and climate too, but that in itself is a whole other book.

How do I use them? Well, grapes are good but wine wins. And from the wine we can make vinegar (see page134), a total kitchen staple. Grape jelly is popular in America, too.

What's in it for me? Red is much better for you than white (during his fasts Gandhi lived on grape juice), with plenty of antioxidants in the skin (rough rule of thumb is the darker the color the more goodness it has in it). Grape seed oil is very high in HDLs (high-density lipoproteins), which are good for your skin, hair, and nails.

Anything else? In 1863 a nasty little bug from the US, called phylloxera, wiped out all the European vines, so the roots in vineyards around in Europe are descended from grafts brought over from the States once the epidemic had passed. Grapes get more mentions than any other fruit in the Bible.

....

☛ Friends food (for wine), cheese (for grapes) …
Relations thousands of different kinds of grape varieties means there's not much room for other family members

Melons

Where do they grow? Like mankind, melons came out of Africa and have achieved nearly the same success in global domination: almost anywhere in the world that we would consider hot (roughly three months of sunshine above 82°F) can grow some variety of this adaptable fruit. Don't stick with the one kind but explore others—they're all good at certain times. If you have a bad one, that's all it is, just a bad one, and go in search of a better example.

How do I use them? You know how to use them so our time is better spent helping you find really good ones: avoid supermarkets and go to stores that specialize in food from hot countries, such as Turkish, Iranian, or Thai, etc. A ripe melon should feel heavy relative to its size. Put your nose right up against its root end and inhale; the aroma should be heady and rich. If you're lucky enough to be looking at a melon with a stem (which is a good sign in itself), a gentle tug should release it if it's good to go. Once you have your ripe melon in hand, either eat it just like that or blend the flesh with ice and a little lime and mint for a great summer cooler.

What's in it for me? All melons contain the same kinds of enzymes that are in our stomach, so are easy to digest. Potassium, which at cell level is good at repairs, is combined here with vitamin A, which makes this a supple skin winner. The seeds are a common snack at Arabic tables, and good for digestion and urinary function.

Melons (Clockwise from top); Watermelon, Honeydew, Muskmelon, Galia

Anything else? Alexander Dumas left his entire collection of 300 books to his local village, Cavaillon, on the proviso that they gave him twelve melons a year for life.

☞ **Friends Parma ham, mint … Relations** the *Cucurbitaceae* family is a huge and far-reaching one, with squash, zucchini, pumpkins, gourds, and cucumbers among their number … **Recipes Melon, Mint & Pomegranate p.142; Melon & Mint Juice p.287**

Know your melons:

Muskmelon:	Strong netting, green segmenting, and fragrant orange flesh. Juicy.
Charentais:	Waxy, greeny-white skin with darker stripes. Similar inside to a muskmelon but milder.
Honeydew:	Thick yellow skin, football-shaped with light green flesh. Clean, crisp, and refreshing.
Watermelon:	Dark green outside, red flesh, big black seeds.
Santa Claus melon:	Lemon yellow to dark green froggy skin; whitish. Crunchy like honeydew.
Galia:	Muted yellow skin with light white netting, whitish flesh. Hybrid of muskmelon and h'dew.
Ogen melon:	Smooth orangey yellow skin with very light green flesh. Juicy and crisp.

Peaches & Nectarines

Where do they grow? Ideally they like it neither too hot (as in tropical) nor too cold and wet, but they do need lots of sun to reach their stunning flavor potential. The hotter parts of the US and southern Canada do very well for them, but so does continental Europe during summer. All varieties fall into one of three categories: clingstone, freestone, or semifreestone, which describes exactly what you would think it does.

How do I use them? The great Southern author Alice Walker wrote, "Life is better than death, I believe, if only because it is less boring and … has fresh peaches in it." A little depressing, but certainly a big appreciation of the fruit of her childhood. Ripe peaches are best eaten raw, but hard or insipid ones can be improved with cooking. The Italians like to broil them, the French to flambé, while those Southern belles from the time of the Civil War took to preserving them in brandy and serving them with their famous Virginia ham. Harry's Bar in Venice would never have reached its legendary status without millions of white peaches donating their juice for Bellinis (not to be confused with blinis, which are little yeasty buckwheat pancakes for caviar and smoked salmon). People fall into two categories on peach fur—love or hate—and the joy of nectarines is simply the fruit without any of the fuzz. Their name comes from "nectar of the gods" and their skin is more akin to a plum than a peach.

What's in it for me? Vitamins A, B, and C all bounce around together wrapped up in a beautiful skin. Peach juice and oils (in the kernel) are good for your complexion, testament to this is the phrase "She's a peach."

Anything else? Escoffier named that classic dessert of the 20th century, Peach Melba, after Dame Nellie Melba, the Australian soprano (as well as the toast). And in a completely different culture, the Japanese believe that Momotaro, one of their most noble heroes, was born from a peach.

☞ **Friends booze, ice cream, opera singers … Relations apricots**

TROPICAL FRUIT

Bananas

Where do they grow? Almost all bananas eaten in the United States come from Latin America, with Costa Rica and Ecuador being the largest suppliers. The banana's origins, however, were in Malaysia. From there they drifted west to India, where they were noted in Pali Buddhist writings in the 6th century B.C.E. Some folk have rechristened Alexander the Great "the Great Banana," since he is credited with bringing them to the Western world. Time and trade took bananas across Africa, and their big move across the Atlantic happened in 1516 when they were taken by a Portuguese Franciscan monk. Over the next few centuries the well documented account of intense plantation life ensured their mass production. The banana is now the world's most popular fruit.

How do I use them? Mostly raw if you're being good, though there is a time and place for a flambé/fritter and, of course, we blend them into our smoothies. The Fair Trade ones just do taste better, and often have a slight pinkness to them.

What's in it for me? Potassium, but, pound for pound they have more vitamin B_6 in them than liver. Serotonin is directly related to B_6, so somewhere inside, you smile each time you eat a banana. All the goodness comes into them as they ripen and soften. Plenty of fiber too.

Anything else? They're not actually trees, but herbaceous plants. All bananas used to be small (the little, squat ones are still my favorite), and the word "banana" comes from the Arabic for finger. The industry has been riddled with wrongness for many centuries: slavery, monopolies, price-fixing, nepotism, and bent governments have all contributed to making this fine fruit the center of much unhappiness. Buying Fair Trade is the only way to guarantee that its future is fairer.

☛ Friends **rum, dairy, dark brown sugar, spices** … Relations **plantains** … Recipes **Breakfast Power Smoothie p.141; Good Morning Muffin! p.150; Date & Banana Smoothie p.282**

Pineapple

Where do they grow? Columbus discovered them in Guadeloupe in the Caribbean archipelago; with all the to-ing and fro-ing across the Atlantic, some seeds made it over to Holland, but they didn't really take to the climate and still remained a very expensive royal treat until after World War Two. Nowadays the main worldwide producers are Hawaii and Malaysia.

How do I use them? A bit of suck and chew on the raw fruit is best. Turn the juice into a dairy-free smoothie using coconut milk. Also vital if you like piña coladas.

What's in it for me? As well as the usual vitamins you'd expect (A and C), there is a veritable all-star cast of minerals: top of the bill are calcium for strengthening bones and magnesium for muscular function. Also very good for aiding digestion, particularly of meat, so eat it after a heavy supper to give you a better night's sleep.

Anything else? Never keep your pineapple in the fridge. In 18th-century London you could hire pineapples for the equivalent of about $8,000 a night if you were having a party, but you weren't allowed to eat them.

☛ Friends **coconuts, rum, pig (arguably)** … Relations **weird rainforest plants, but no other fruit** … Recipes **Pineapple & Basil p.142**

i

ii

iii

SUPER FOODS

Kiwi

Where do they grow? Like so many of the exoticary, these were first noted in the Yangtze River area of China, hence their other name of Chinese gooseberries. Then, in 1906, a lady called Isabel Fraser, who was principal of Wanganui Girls' College, went on vacation to China, picked up some seeds, and took them back home to New Zealand, hence their future name, and where they were first grown commercially. NZ is still a major exporter, along with California, Chile, and Israel. The first shipment reached UK shores in 1953.

How do I use them? Really, raw is the way forward. Just cut the top off and dig into it with a teaspoon like a soft-boiled egg. Or blend it into a smoothie, but even that has a slightly odd texture.

What's in it for me? It has been said by nutritionalists that a kiwi fruit is the best, overall, most balanced way to start your day. Reputedly contains 10 times more vitamin C than a lemon, and actively promotes the release of energy from cells. Also, following the six months after they've been harvested they lose almost none of their nutritional value, as opposed to oranges, which suffer heavily in this department. They are so good for you that in Taiwan they're known as "wonderfruit." Move over, superfoods.

Anything else? New Zealanders named their favorite fruit after their national bird, and from there it just took off (the name, not the bird). You can freeze kiwis whole, just like that, without them losing any of their flavor, color, or good enzyme activity when thawed.

☞ **Friends** doesn't have any—
it's a breakfast thing ...
Relations named after the
native bird of New
Zealand, which is
like being
family ...

Mango

Where do they grow? Archeologists have found mangoes on digs in India that have been dated to 20 million years ago, and India is still the number one producer in the world. The two most commonly grown varieties are the particularly delicious Alphonse, which has a short early summer season that's eagerly awaited, and the less excitingly named Tommy Atkins, which is noted for its stability during traveling. There are many different species, varying in size from basketball to apricot, and there is as much variety in their sweetness and texture too.

How do I use them? The best way to prepare: cut in half like an avocado, going through the most rounded parts letting your knife follow the edges of the seed so the fruit falls into two halves. Remove the seed, then hold one half in the cup of your hand and score through to the skin in $\frac{1}{2}$-inch squares. Turn the skin inside out to make the flesh easily accessible and don't forget to suck on the seed. The problem being that the flesh loves its seed so much, the two just do not wish to be separated, and yet, in true Bollywood style, these ill-fated lovers must be torn apart. Also opens the door to a world of lassis, smoothies, and the charmingly named *barfis*, all blended drinks in which the mango may be used. And lastly my personal favorite— mango chutney, surprisingly easy to make— sugar syrup, spices, pieces of fruit, and a quick simmer.

What's in it for me? An ABC of all the usual fruity goodies (talking vitamins), great carotenes for your skin and free-radical battles, and natural sulfur, which is antibacterial.

Anything else? The Moghul ruler Akhbar reportedly had a mango orchard with more than 100,000 trees in the 16th century. A mango tree fruited in Kew, in west London, in 1818. One of the founders of Leon wrote a song when she was fifteen called "Where Did My Mango."

☞ **Friends** bananas, the blender, and most other fruit ... **Relations** pistachio nuts, cashews ...

iv

Tropical Fruit *i.* Pineapple; *ii.* Banana; *iii.* Mango; *iv.* Kiwi

BERRIES & CURRANTS

Black & redcurrants

The *Ribes* genus, which includes currants and their close cousin the gooseberry, are suited more to the climate of northern Europe than anywhere else in the world.

Massive amounts of vitamin C, hence the sharpness. When turned into a syrup and stored for a year they lose only 10–15% of their vitamins—tiny compared to most other fruits. Homeopathic medicine has long used it to ward off colds and the like.

The Ribena company currently uses more than 95% of the native British blackcurrant crop to make the beverage of the same name. Smells like a monopoly, and explains why those little cartons are so expensive. And what we Brits haven't made into Ribena, the French grab for their Kir. Love those Kir Royales though.

Redcurrants are more hype than helpful in the kitchen because they are unfeasibly tart. Perched on top of an unsuccessful dessert, with a dusting of powdered sugar, is a surefire way to garnish yourself out of a culinary fix, however.

Raspberries

These in England, but it's the Scots who really excel. Cool winter, damp spring, and a bit of summer sun make the eastern coast ideal. From around the turn of the 20th century the Scots started to get serious about their raspberry growing. In 1946, the Scottish Raspberry Investigation was set up at University College in Dundee to promote their production, and from there the industry went from strength to strength, until recent years when it has shown a decline as imports flood our market. The US is the largest importer of the raspberries, with most coming from Canada and Chile.

Raspberries have to ripen on the bush, so they count as a luxury fruit. Lots of antioxidants to keep your cells fit, and as with all berries, the more intense the color the more goodness inside.

Raspberries freeze particularly well, and their antioxidant count hardly deteriorates at all.

The nymph Ida picked them for the young Jupiter and turned them from white to red with her blood, and indeed for some centuries raspberries were known as Ida. The British can still get white raspberries in some heritage gardens, while you can get some funky yellow and purple ones in North America.

Raspberry vinegar (*vinaigre de framboise*) is a French favorite with foie gras and other fatty meats, while in Britain it was used as a cure for sore throats from the 17th century through to World War Two.

Watch out for the lethal raspberry-infused beer made by Belgian monks—delicious and dangerous in equal measures.

Strawberries

Don't eat them out of season—some things are supposed to be a treat, and there's no need to follow the instant gratification trend that has gripped our world; it only leads to disappointment in the long run.

The variety most commonly sold in the UK is the scarlet strawberry, which was brought over from Virginia, though it is now California that dominates American strawberry production.

Wild strawberries are mighty in their tininess, with a different and arguably more special flavor and texture than the cultivated ones.

B_3 is name of the star player in this fruit's make-up, which helps the skin's natural protection from the sun.

Strawberries are big in natural fruit sugars—fructose—so all the sweetness without the synthetic crash. Nothing heralds the arrival of the summer more than this really juicy fruit; she alone carries a nation's hope of sunshine on her shoulders. It is thought the name is derived from straw being used to insulate the soil around the plants, while also enriching it.

Gooseberries

One of Britain's oldest native fruits (the English classic mackerel with gooseberries is centuries old), most are now grown in East Anglia.

Really the first soft(ish) fruit of the year, they have a short, early summer season that is easily and often missed.

Like all the berries they are rich in potassium and vitamins A and C.

Called gooseberries because it was thought they went well with goose, which they do.

Look for the purple, red, yellow, and golden ones later in the season that can be eaten raw. Very special indeed in summer salads.

There is an annual gooseberry festival in Egton, North Yorkshire, that has been going since the 18th century. Gooseberries can often turn pinkish in cooking, as well as if they are left to ripen on the plant, which betrays their close botanical link to currants.

Blackberries

That deep color indicates goodness, and the goodness in these little beauties takes the form of vitamins C and D, as well as quercitin, a handy super-antioxidant (like a superfood but much, much smaller).

Folklore says don't pick them after Michaelmas (September 29), because the devil is supposed to have fiddled with them.

Blackberries cook better than any other berry. Like all the dark berries, it's an end-of-the-summer thing, Mother Nature making their season coincide with the start of their partner-in-fruit-crisp, the apple.

The best of England's hedgerows proffer us their berries, and every year picking while rambling magically blurs the boundaries between summer's last and fall's first.

Cranberries

These useful little berries grow on small evergreen shrub bushes in the northern hemisphere. Cranberry harvesting is an amazing spectacle: the fields they grow in are flooded and a machine rustles away under the water so that all the bazillions of berries are released from the bushes and float to the surface. The only thing left to do is open one of the dykes on the side and strain the berries off as they pour out.

These bitterest of berries are built on a solid foundation of vitamin C, and are generally beneficial for all things dermal and duodenal.

Along with whale blubber (which can't be *that* healthy), cranberries form a colorful part of the Inuit diet, and everyone knows they're famously long-living. Good for girls too.

Cranberries are harvested very late in the year, so they don't need any refrigeration, which makes them the greenest berry in the world.

Blueberries

Most of the ones over here are from the States, but we do have a short season, mostly from the south coast (the little bushes like sandy soil near the sea). The French are also admirers of *les myrtilles*.

The blueberry very much enjoys its superfruit status. Loads of antioxidants, antifungals, and digestion-benefiting parts all wrapped up in a beautiful, musky, dusty blue skin.

One of nature's only blue foods.

Beware getting your vit-kick at the expense of air miles. Only do it when they're bang in season and maxed up with good things (end of summer) to make it worthwhile for you and sustainable for your planet.

☛ **Friends** cream and all manner of dairy; vodka for cranberries ... **Relations** mulberry, dewberry, loganberry, tayberry, brambleberry, golden cloudberry (ahhh) ... **Recipes** **Summer Berry Compote p.149**; **Blackberry Compote p.149; Summer Berry Smoothie p.281; Blackberry & Apple Juice p.287**

Pommelo　　　**Grapefruit**　　　**Pink Grapefruit**　　　**Orange**

CITRUS

Where do they grow? It all started in the Far East, seemingly China but, of course, now the citrus family is familiar the world over. Like so many others among nature's fruits, their worldwide spread is down first to the Romans, and then, some centuries later, to Columbus and the conquistadors. Brazil and the US now produce more than 40% of the world's citrus. The only hint that remains of their Eastern origin is in names like mandarin and satsuma, the former being Chinese and the latter Japanese.

They need a lot of sun come the growing time, but a wintry sharpness in the air also does them good.

How do I use them? The all-round best way has got to be juice (one-third of the world's citrus production is turned straight into juice) but, be warned, because orange juice loses 90% of its nutritional value if left to stand for 24 hours. Grapefruit, one of the largest in the clan, make a lovely cholesterol-lowering breakfast, and string sacs of the smaller varieties are essential at Christmas.

Citrus zest is a vital ingredient to any cook, and lemon juice is the acid of choice in our House Dressing. All citrus are delicious, if sometimes a little surprising, when peeled and eaten raw. Last word: caipirinhas. And mojitos.

What's in it for me? 75–90% vitamin C deserves respect, and then there are the essential oils in the skin too, which are used in perfumes and aromatherapy. Handy for scurvy-staving as well.

Anything else? Because people are lazy and don't like spitting out the seeds, trees producing seedless fruit must be grown and grafted because they can't be grown from seed. The original seedless tree from which all subsequent cuttings have been taken was planted in Riverside County, California, and it's still going.

The coloring in blood oranges comes from the antioxidant anthocyanin.

The orange was featured on the coinage of ancient Judea in 142 B.C.E.

....

☛ **Friends** cakes, duck, almonds, olive oil …
Relations oranges, lemons, limes, citrons, satsumas, tangerines, mandarins, grapefruits, ugli fruits, pommelos, kumquats, blood oranges, clementines …
Recipes Sweet Potato Falafel p.153; House Dressing p.197; Chicken Superfood Salad p.203; Sumptuous Slaw p.207; Chicken, Asparagus & Fair Trade Lemon Cassoulet p.228; Black-eyed Peas, Spinach & Lemon p.256; Lemon, Ginger & Mint Quencher p.283; Leon Lemonade p.286; Allegra's Beautiful Juice p.286; Lemon & Ginger Coldbuster p.288

Ingredient we love

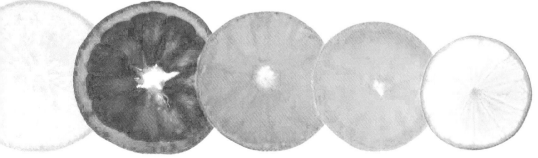

Lemon   Blood Orange   Satsuma   Clementine   Lime   Kumquat

PASSPORT

HERBS

Name: Basil
Aka: *Ocimum basilicum*
Age: 5,000+ years
Place of origin: India
Distinguishing features/flavor:
Slightly aniseed, sweet, tastes of raw summer
Seasonal residence: Summer
Closest living relative:
Holy (or Thai) basil (*Ocimum tenuiflorum*)

> **APROVED FOR THE FOLLOWING DESTINATIONS**
> • Pesto, and its French cousin *pistou*
> • Tomatoes
> • Pasta
> • Salads
> • Under the skin of a roast chicken

Name: Bay
Aka: *Laurus nobilis*
Age: As old as the hills
Place of origin: Mediterranean
Distinguishing features/flavor:
Sharp, pungent but mellowing; touch of juniper, aromatic spice
Seasonal residence: Year round
Closest living relative: The laurel (*Prunus laurocerasus*), which is glossy leaved, as opposed to bay's matt finish

> **APPROVED FOR THE FOLLOWING DESTINATIONS**
> • Court-bouillon /bouquet garni
> • Stews, Sauces, Pies, Bakes, Stocks … basically any dish where there is enough time and liquid to allow the bay to give a little of itself
> • Top of a terrine

27

Name: Chervil
Aka: *Anthriscus cerefolium*
Age: Before 1330 B.C.E. (evidence found in King Tutankhamun's tomb)
Place of origin: Middle East/southern Russia
Distinguishing features/flavor: Lightly aniseed, fresh, and a bit grassy
Seasonal residence: Spring /summer
Closest living relative: Hemlock (which is poisonous—Socrates was sentenced to death by hemlock by the Senate)

> **APPROVED FOR THE FOLLOWING DESTINATIONS**
> • *Fines herbes*
> • Egg dishes
> • Delicate things like poached fish
> • Creamy/buttery sauces
> • Summer salads

BISA — VISA

Name: Chives
Aka: *Allium schoenoprasum*
Age: Everything starts with an onion—the oldest vegetable family on record
Place of origin: Mediterranean
Distinguishing features/flavor: Mildly oniony, but greener; zippy and slightly sweet
Seasonal residence: Spring and summer
Closest living relative: The scallion, and the rest of the onion (allium) family

> **APPROVED FOR THE FOLLOWING DESTINATIONS**
> • Eggs (scrambled, omelet)
> • New potatoes
> • Floating in sauces
> • Finishing risottos
> • In salads
> • Anything warm and cheesy
> • Not gratuitous garnish

22

Name: Cilantro
Aka: *Coriandrum sativum*
Age: 2,000 B.C.E.
Place of origin: Egypt and the southern Med
Distinguishing features/flavor: fresh, bright, and zippy; see also Coriander Seeds, page 122
Seasonal residence: Spring, summer
Closest living relative: Parsley (*Petroselinum crispum*)

APPROVED FOR THE FOLLOWING DESTINATIONS
- Guacamole, salsa, and all things Mexican
- All manner of Asian dishes, including being an essential in Thai green curry, but never in Japanese cuisine
- Floating in Asian broths, like the delicious Vietnamese *pho*

22

Name: Dill
Aka: *Anethum graveolens*
Age: First noted in Russia in the 10th century
Place of origin: Central Asia, southern Mediterranean
Distinguishing features/flavor: Fortifyingly fennely, strongly herby, wafts of caraway and parsley
Seasonal residence: Spring to late summer
Closest living relative: Fennel (*Foeniculum vulgare*)

APPROVED FOR THE FOLLOWING DESTINATIONS
- Many things Baltic, like pickled herring and gravadlax
- Light summer fish dishes
- Potato & herb salad
- Pickles

DRIES WELL
WELL APPROVED · THIS · HERB · DRIES · WELL · THIS · HERB

23

Name: Flat-leaf parsley
Aka: *Petroselinum neapolitanum*
Age: First mentioned in early Roman times, so about 2,500 years
Place of origin: Southeastern Europe
Distinguishing features/flavor: A touch of celery and a bit dilly, strong with chlorophyll, minerals, and slightly sweet
Seasonal residence: Year round
Closest living relative: Curly parsley (*Petroselinum crispum*)

APPROVED FOR THE FOLLOWING DESTINATIONS
- The base for chopped herb sauces, e.g. salsa verde, chimichurri
- Finishing all manner of dishes, for a bit of fresh green
- Middle Eastern salads (tabbouleh)
- To finish fish dishes, especially *meunière*: lemon and parsley

26

27

Name: Marjoram
Aka: *Origanum majorana*
Age: 13th century B.C.E.
Place of origin: Middle East/Asia
Distinguishing features/flavor:
Strong and very perfumed; oily and pungent;
floral, with some of the fire of mint; piney
Seasonal residence: Summer
Closest living relative: Oregano
(*Origanum vulgare*)

APPROVED FOR THE FOLLOWING DESTINATIONS
- Marinades
- *Herbes de Provence*
- Middle Eastern *khoresh*
- Slow-cooks, Italian style
- *Kleftiko*
- Suits BBQ flavors

Name: Mint
Aka: *Mentha piperita*
Age: Mentioned in ancient Greek
mythology…
Place of origin: … but the Arabs have
also loved it for a long time
Distinguishing features/flavor:
Fresh and healing, strong and powerful
Seasonal residence: Spring/summer
Closest living relative: Spearmint
(*Mentha spicata*)

APPROVED FOR THE FOLLOWING DESTINATIONS
- Potato salad • Salsa verde
- Mints • Peas
- Lamb • Juleps
- Toothpaste • Tsatziki
- Mojitos
- Tea

Name: Oregano
Aka: *Origanum vulgare*
Age: Genesis
Place of origin: All around the Med
Distinguishing features/flavor: Piney,
evergreen, and powerful; slightly bitter
Seasonal residence: Summer/fall
Closest living relative: Marjoram
(*Origanum majorana*)

APPROVED FOR THE FOLLOWING DESTINATIONS
- Tomato sauce
- Pizza (use dried)
- Slow cooks
- Chimichurri
- Marinades

This passport contains 24 pages.
Ce passeport contient 24 pages.

27

Ce passeport contient 24 pages.
This passport contains 24 pages.

BISA — VISA

Name: Rosemary
Aka: *Rosmarinus officinalis*
Age: 5,000 years—found in the tombs of
ancient Egypt
Place of origin: Southern Med
Distinguishing features (flavor): Resinous,
pungent, tastes like fall, butchly perfumed
Seasonal residence: Fall/winter
Closest living relative: Lavender
(*Lavendula augustifolia*)

APPROVED FOR THE FOLLOWING DESTINATIONS
- Sweet things: sugar, chocolate, oranges, honey
- Roast meats, including stuffing
- Marinades
- White beans
- Roast potatoes (with goose fat)

22

Name: Sage
Aka: *Salvia officinalis*
Age: *Salvia* means wise and wisdom comes with age
Place of origin: All over the Med and North Africa
Distinguishing features/flavor: Woody and resinous, slightly bitter, oily, and robust
Seasonal residence: Fall and winter
Closest living relative: *Salvia divinorum*—a Mexican visionary herb

APPROVED FOR THE FOLLOWING DESTINATIONS
- Stuffing
- Melted butter (on pasta, liver, etc.)
- Fatty roast meats
- Legumes, nuts
- Christmas

Name: Tarragon
Aka: *Artemisia dracunculus*
Age: Bit wooly this one—sometime after the mammoths…
Place of origin: Siberia
Distinguishing features/flavor: Full-on aniseed, but still tastes green and fresh
Seasonal residence: Summer/fall
Closest living relative: Wormwood, as in absinthe (*Artemisia absinthium*)

APPROVED FOR THE FOLLOWING DESTINATIONS
- Béarnaise
- Creamy eggy dishes
- Poached fish/chicken
- Vinegar

Name: Thyme
Aka: *Thymus vulgaris*
Age: Older than Father Thyme
Place of origin: Europe, Asia, North Africa
Distinguishing features/flavor: Evergreen, camphor, mahogany, wild meadows
Seasonal residence: Summer, but sits well throughout the year
Closest living relative: Broad-leaved thyme (*Thymus pulegioides*)

APPROVED FOR THE FOLLOWING DESTINATIONS
- *Toutes les choses provençales*
- Marinade for meats (including Jerk chicken)
- Middle Eastern dishes like *za'atar*
- Bouquet garni/stocks
- Slow-cooks like cassoulet

HAND SELECTED
AND PACKED

50 LBS.
NET WEI◄

VEGETABLES

SHALLOTS, WHITE ONION, SHALLOTS, LEEK, GARLIC, SPRING ONIONS, PEARL ONION, SHALLOT, RED ONION, ONION (BROWN), CHIVES, WHITE ONIONS, RED ONION & LEEKS, NOVEMBER 2007

THE ALLIUMS

Probably the most important and ubiquitous vegetable dynasty on the planet. Flavor-wise, the onion is at the heart of an extraordinary amount of the world's cuisine, as well as being high in minerals. This collective looks after our blood and has been shown to have cholesterol-lowering properties.

All members contain varying amounts of the sulfurous volatile oil that brings tears to our eyes and is at the heart of their goodness; the ferocity of taste is directly linked to how much that member has in it, which is proportional to the amount of goodness they can do for you. As they lose their bite during cooking, so too do they lose some of their magic powers.

Brown Onion

People tend to think onions last for ever, which they do, but that doesn't mean there isn't a world of difference when you cook with a fresh one. This humble onion is the bedrock of the family, and every now and then it's worth getting some fresher, more local ones, preferably with a pink tinge, rather than the standard Spanish giants, just to remind yourself of the difference.

Red Onion

The Italian staple, usually smaller and sweeter than its whiter cousins. Just as happy heading for the oven along with some roast vegetables to get the sweetness out, or macerated in lime juice for a sharper finish. An excellent onion for stewing, grilling, or broiling, and, as well as taste, appreciate that attractive shade of purple—not really red at all.

White Onion

Milder in flavor than the brown-skinned onion, these are bigger in Asia, the US, and in continental Europe than elsewhere. Their slightly sweeter taste makes them ideal served raw or just cooked but still with a bit of bite.

Shallot

Brought back by the Crusaders from Palestine, this much milder-tempered cousin has the most subtle and mild flavor of all the roundish (as opposed to longish) onions.

The French have long been beside themselves over this elegant mauve allium. The regular ones are round, but banana shallots are torpedo-shaped and give you a better yield for the amount of peeling time; slightly different flavor, not quite so special, but markedly less hassle.

Scallion

This two-tone onion is extremely handy when it comes to finishing your dish with zip and fresh greenness. Instead of making a bulb, scallions (or green onions as some people call them) put all their energy into growing up with their chlorophyll-filled hollow shoots. Use all the onion, not just the white part.

Leek

The most intrinsically British (or is it Welsh?), member of the family, leeks generally like a longer cooking time, as befits someone of their size and stature. Does the same job of tasting like a scallion (but this time in a cooked situation) while also doing what this family is famed for—making a background flavor basis.

Chives

The tall, thin, and elegant one, there's not a lot to a chive. Bit of zing, bit of pretty, and that's about it.

Pearl Onion

Producers have understood how irritating they are to peel (soak them in hot water first to make your life easier), so the best use is to buy a 2-pound bag of frozen and grab a handful whenever your house is suffering from total fresh onion breakdown.

Garlic

SUPER FOODS

While the onion sits at the center of the family, garlic is surely the most revered. It's that volatile oil again, getting into your bloodstream and being excreted back out through your skin and lungs—hence the old breath issue.

When the new season's garlic arrives there is no need to peel them because the skin is still fresh and edible—slice through it and cook, just like that. As for the rest of the year, it tends to come in smaller bulbs that are annoying to peel and don't have as much bite.

As well as the bulb, there are two other parts of the plant worth a mention. Try to catch ramps season: it's quite brief, and if it's a very wet spring it hardly happens at all, but in your mind log it as the time when the first buds appear on the trees and you won't be far off. Ramps grow wild in the woods from Georgia to Quebec. Once you've got them, treat them like spinach.

And a couple of months later come the bulbils, which are tiny little buds that look like fresh green peppercorns. Bite one and it pops in your mouth to release a short, intense, but soft hit of garlic. Not often seen, but lots of fun when they are, and in terms of cooking think of them like samphire. Garlic: you either like it, or you're completely nuts about it.

Ingredient we love

Artichokes

Where do they grow? It's a Med thing, with the Italians clutching this thistly beast to their hearts, and those on the Maghreb (the run of countries on the northern coast of Africa) using its stalks as flavoring for stews and stocks. The young gourmande Catherine de' Medici was responsible for introducing them to France for her wedding, aged 14.

How do I use them? No two ways about it, if you're after the heart alone they are a bother to prep, but the best things in life take a little work, and this is no exception.

Or you can avoid all that and just cook them whole—steaming is much better nutritionally than simmering, so none of their potent goodness is lost to the water. Once the leaves around the very base come away with a gentle tug, let them cool a little upside down then serve with vinaigrette or melted butter. Suck on the leaves, loving their increased tenderness as you get closer to the heart; take out all traces of the aptly named choke and then devour the heart. A suitably noble prize for all that work.

Slice the small young ones off just above the waist and trim off any tough parts and then they're good to go; shaving them raw into salads is both excellent crunch and actually kind of sweet.

What's in it for me? A diet of artichokes will lower your cholesterol, because cynarin, their active enzyme, is a proper fat-cell buster. The liver loves artichokes for its fat metabolization.

Anything else? Operation Artichoke by the CIA in the early 1950s explored the use of opiates in interrogation. Always wash your hands with lemon juice before you start prepping them. They leave an astonishingly dirty and bitter residue on your hands if you don't.

☛ **Friends** olive oil, lemon, thyme, garlic … **Relations** cardoons, the common thistle; very distantly Jerusalem artichokes

Asparagus

Where does it grow? These tender shoots like a light kind of soil, and aren't that fussy really as long as it's well drained and, most importantly, weed-free.

Asparagus was first seen in the London markets in 1670.

Peru is currently the world's leading exporter, but it would be crazy to eat Peruvian when American-grown asparagus from California, Washington, and Michigan is available from January to June.

How do I use it? First the prepping: hold your spear in the middle between thumb and forefinger then, with your other hand on the stalky end, snap it; this will give you the natural point below which the asparagus is too tough to eat.

The easiest way to cook it is steaming or blanching in salted boiling water for a couple of minutes. Foodies say you are best to stand the bunches with the tips up, in just two inches of water. That way the tougher end gets some serious cooking action while the delicate tips steam lightly. Or you can grill or roast them—both are delicious and impart an otherwise hidden nuttiness.

The first pickings or "thinnings" are called sprue asparagus, and they are delicious raw.

What's in it for me? Low in calories, high in fiber and useful minerals. It's a real friend to the kidneys and blood, providing a general spring-clean of the urinary system, which is borne out and paid for by the smelly pee. Also contains folic acid, which helps with formation of new cells, and natural fluoride.

Anything else? The Anglo-Saxon medics mention asparagus in their up-beat sounding tome *Leechdoms*.

☛ **Friends** fat, be it butter or extra-virgin; salty cheese, chicken … **Relations** *asparagus densiflorus*—South African flowering plant … **Recipes** Chicken, Asparagus & Fair Trade Lemon Cassoulet p.228

Eggplant (right); *i.* Pea Eggplant; *ii.* Thai White Eggplant *iii.* Dutch Eggplant; *iv.* Black Beauty; *v.* Violetta di Firenza *vi.* Japanese Eggplant

Eggplant

Where do they grow? First seen in India, their popularity spread throughout Europe in the late medieval period, with the Italians leading the way in the 15th century. Their true season is July to September, but are considered year-round now.

Eggplants are the fruit of the least poisonous of the *Solanaceae* family, and the only nonpoisonous cousins—but safely distanced kissable cousins—are the tomato and the mighty potato.

How do I use them? First the salting business: this is by and large unnecessary now but remains in our minds as a hangover from a time when they were bred differently and were much more bitter. Nothing is more enjoyable than sticking them directly in the coals/on the BBQ/on the gas stove and watching their skin blacken and crackle. They're done when a gentle squeeze around their girth yields a soft, mushy flesh inside. Cool, peel, and chop roughly for the beginnings of moutabal, babaganoush, and other classic meze.

If you opt for the slice or chunk, you can choose from baking, braising, steaming (an Asian top tip), grilling, sautéing, or even deep-frying in batter, which is the true way to begin making the astounding *melanzane parmigiana*. It's also one of the quickest paths to a triple bypass.

Vital in caponata and its French exchange, ratatouille.

What's in it for me? There's potassium and calcium, which help stimulate the liver. Virtually fat-free.

Anything else? In the 1800s it was thought eating eggplant caused insanity and even leprosy.

☛ Friends **olive oil, garlic, zucchini, the Ottomans** … Relations **tomatoes, potatoes, deadly nightshade, chiles** …
Recipes **Leon Biyaldi p.158; Sicilian Grilled Vegetables p.166; Egyptian Eggplant & Tamarind Stew p.252**

Avocados

SUPER FOODS

Where do they grow? The majority come from South and Central America, specifically Chile, Peru, and Mexico, where they have been cultivated for more than 7,000 years. Most of those produced in the American subcontinent are the Fuerte variety, with the smooth green skin. There is a Spanish season for the Hass variety (with the knobbly skin) that runs from January to July.

How do I use them? Raw! Never try to cook them, no matter how delightful your '70s buffet cookbook tells you they are when stuffed and baked. Delicious in salads or just like that with a splash of vinegar and, of course, there's the mighty guacamole. Coat their flesh with lemon juice to avoid oxidization.

What's in it for me? From the misty depths of the Inca and Aztec jungles, via the Spanish to the courts of Europe, all around the Med, through to the Middle and Far Eastern civilizations, drifting south through India, Africa, and finally over to Australia, the avocado has and will continue to fill the cells of mankind with vitamins A, C, and E. Giving us glowing skin, easily digestible monounsaturated fats, and fighting the daily fight against free radicals, this is a true superfood.

Anything else? When stored with bananas, avocados will always ripen because of the ethylene gas the bananas release.

In Mexico the average person consumes 33 pounds of avocados each year—great skin, but they don't make you tall. George Burns said the only thing He did wrong when creating the world was to make the stone in the avocado too big.

☛ Friends **lime, chile, salt** … Relations **pretty much on its own out there, and related only in shape to a pear** …
Recipes **Leon Original Superfood Salad p.198; Lee's Hippy Farm Beans p.253**

Bare Asian Necessities (above); *i.* Galangal; *ii.* Lemongrass;
iii. Kaffir Lime Leaves; *iv.* Garlic (see Alliums); *v.* Ginger

BARE ASIAN NECESSITIES

Ginger

Zingiber officinale, is a rhizome that was indigenous to Southeast Asia before the Chinese made it world-popular. A natural remedy, specifically for warding off colds (see Lemon & Ginger Coldbuster, page 288) most of the power is concentrated in the outermost skin. So, best not to peel. Just give it a good wash and as long as it's good and fresh you can grate it just like that. Elizabeth David used to swear by keeping it in foil in the fridge, but I think our supply and fridges are better these days. Ferocious in its intensity, historically, ginger has been used in many ways, both medicinal and culinary, savory and sweet. A vital part of all Asian cooking, it was being ground and transported to Europe by the Romans, but more for health reasons. It wasn't for about another 1,000 years that it started to be used in cooking, but then things really took off (candied ginger became a favorite in medieval England.) Good for digestion and upset stomachs, as well as clearing the paths and passages in your body.

iv

Galangal

A knobbly little root like ginger, galangal is almost white in its paleness, with pinkish, sticklike protrusions. Native to China, but also important in a lot of northern Indian dishes. The Arabs came to love it too with its tarter taste. Often called Chinese ginger for obvious reasons, its flavor is slightly milder and more resinous. Used in authentic southeastern Asian curry pastes, including the international bestseller—Thai green. Has very beautiful, hyper-real, pink and orange flowers.

Garlic See Alliums, page 39.

Lime Leaves

The leaves of the kaffir lime tree impart a very special taste to soups, broths, and stocks, and are another essential ingredient in Thai green curry. They have the sharpness of the citrus clan, but with a heady, perfumed, exceptional flavor that is unachievable with any other ingredient. Lime leaves make your Asian food taste truly authentic, and are usually found in plastic food bags in the fridge at Thai and Asian grocery stores. They can be frozen for ages. Simply take them out a couple at a time, tear and inhale. They bounce back beautifully given a little liquid to work with.

Lemongrass

The most elegant of grassy-looking plants, a little like pampas. Grows in the tropics and has a strong volatile oil that perfumes our food or, alternatively, is made into a chemical-free mosquito deterrent. Fresh, zingy, and quite unlike anything else—a bunch of sticks lasts for up to a month in the fridge. Crush the tough, fibrous, fat end with the flat side of a knife blade and throw it into the pot for flavoring; the tenderer top end can be thinly sliced, eaten, and digested. Really likes coconut milk.

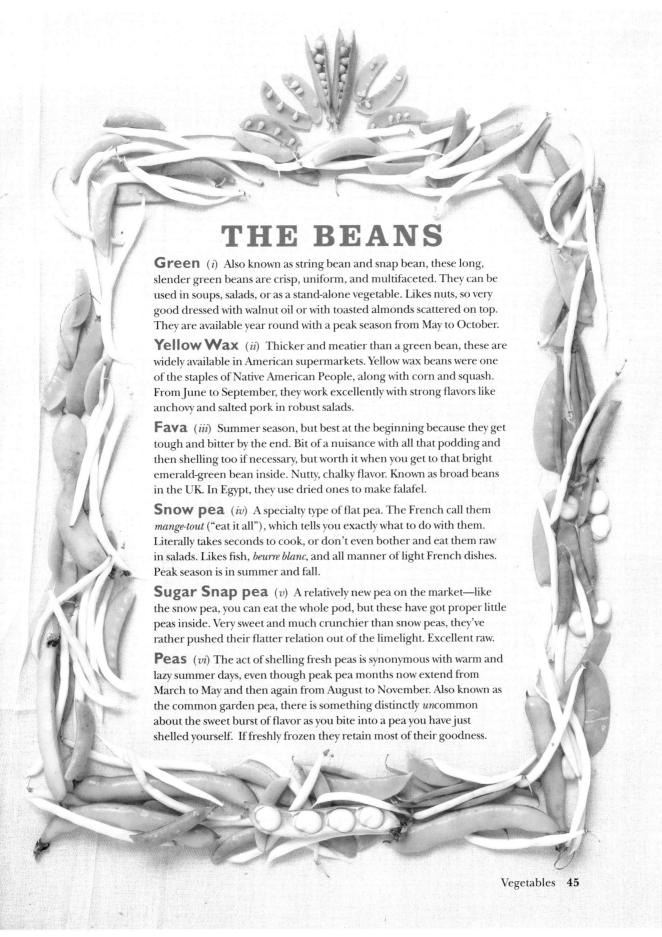

THE BEANS

Green (*i*) Also known as string bean and snap bean, these long, slender green beans are crisp, uniform, and multifaceted. They can be used in soups, salads, or as a stand-alone vegetable. Likes nuts, so very good dressed with walnut oil or with toasted almonds scattered on top. They are available year round with a peak season from May to October.

Yellow Wax (*ii*) Thicker and meatier than a green bean, these are widely available in American supermarkets. Yellow wax beans were one of the staples of Native American People, along with corn and squash. From June to September, they work excellently with strong flavors like anchovy and salted pork in robust salads.

Fava (*iii*) Summer season, but best at the beginning because they get tough and bitter by the end. Bit of a nuisance with all that podding and then shelling too if necessary, but worth it when you get to that bright emerald-green bean inside. Nutty, chalky flavor. Known as broad beans in the UK. In Egypt, they use dried ones to make falafel.

Snow pea (*iv*) A specialty type of flat pea. The French call them *mange-tout* ("eat it all"), which tells you exactly what to do with them. Literally takes seconds to cook, or don't even bother and eat them raw in salads. Likes fish, *beurre blanc*, and all manner of light French dishes. Peak season is in summer and fall.

Sugar Snap pea (*v*) A relatively new pea on the market—like the snow pea, you can eat the whole pod, but these have got proper little peas inside. Very sweet and much crunchier than snow peas, they've rather pushed their flatter relation out of the limelight. Excellent raw.

Peas (*vi*) The act of shelling fresh peas is synonymous with warm and lazy summer days, even though peak pea months now extend from March to May and then again from August to November. Also known as the common garden pea, there is something distinctly *un*common about the sweet burst of flavor as you bite into a pea you have just shelled yourself. If freshly frozen they retain most of their goodness.

BRASSICA GALACTICA

SUPER FOODS

White Raw or sauerkraut, steamed or souped, this humble member of the family quietly gets on with the job and lets others take the glory. The tightly packed nature of the leaves means it will last for ages; extremely good value for money.

Red Britain's favorite winter sport: braising red cabbage. Dried fruit and apples, goose fat, wine, vinegar, spices, bacon…you can put almost anything in there and the flavor will out. Clearly that way you are not up for many, if any, of the massive nutritious points available, so braise half and have the other half shredded raw with vinegar and golden raisins.

Napa Steam it for just a few seconds, chuck it into stir-fries at the last minute, or eat it raw. In Korea they pickle it and turn it into a fiery condiment called *kimchee*. Also known as Chinese cabbage, its light green puckered leaves are much more delicate than their Western cousins, which kind of fits with the people too.

Cabbages and the Brassica family have been heralded since Roman times for their healing properties, which is not surprising with chlorophyll, iron, sulfur, vitamins, minerals, and nutrients all rolled up inside them. Brassicas are one of the largest families of crops on the Earth and are an amazing source of goodness that grow happily right here in our fields. Here are some of their stars:

Savoy Takes a lot less cooking than you'd think; should still be a little crunchy around the stalk and stem. Thought to have descended from wild Roman cabbages, it was developed in Savoy during the Middle Ages, and was taken to the UK in the 17th century. Likes chestnuts, bacon, and is a friendly face to all cooks throughout the winter. Try it with mustard, a distant relative, and sour cream too.

Brussels sprouts These grow in lateral buds up the main stalk of the *gemmifera* variety of brassica. Most of the bitterness that turns so many people off is contained in the middle, so the old kitchen practice of crossing them on their bottoms is more than just to ensure even cooking—it actually helps to leach out any unpleasant flavor. Has the highest level of sulfur compounds than any of the other brassicas, which might have something to do with their world-famous affect on flatulence.

Green pointed Known as Sweetheart or Hispi cabbage in the UK, this pointy-headed cabbage has green leaves on the outside, graduating to yellow in the middle. The elongated bluish-green heirloom cabbage, Winningstadt, is a similar US variety. Use it raw in slaw, or shred it finely and add it at the last minute to soups of either the brothy or creamy variety. Contains vitamin K, which is important for blood-clotting. Very nice in chowders.

PLANET of the BRASSICAS

Clockwise from top left: Broccoli; Kale; Cauliflower; Greens; Purple Broccoli Rabe

Broccoli We love it, and it features in all our superfood salads. Blood-strengthening, antioxidant, stress-relieving, energy-boosting, and even supposed to have anticancerous effects. But you only get all that if you don't overcook it.

Kale Packed with phytochemicals that help us stave off colds. Activates enzymes that help the body eliminate free radicals. Needs proper cooking—15-ish minutes. There's a spectacular purple version as well if you feel like a change.

Cauliflower The whiter variety arrived with the Moors in Spain in the 12th century. It spread futher across Europe from Italy in the 16th century and reached North America with colonization. Folic acid, calcium, and useful iron. Delicious roasted. Try its space-age-looking cousin the Romanesco for a trip-the-light-fantastic kind of fractal-formed brassica.

Greens (spring and winter)
"Greens" is a suitably loose term for a kind of loose-headed cabbage. Firmly part of the large Brassica family, the spring variety is the best known. They are thought to be a close relative of the wild cabbage, and have a charming, irregular, floppy look to them.

Seasonal greens take a very light cooking, which in turn means that more of their family's magnificent innate goodness can be passed on to us.

As with all brassicas, greens have built in antifreeze, which makes them taste better as the mercury plummets, and is why they are most associated with the dark days of winter and the crisp first moments of spring.

Purple Broccoli Rabe People have been growing and selling it for years, but with all the carotenoids, iron, calcium, fiber, and vitamin A, the supermarkets have caught on lately and are promoting it as the new super-vegetable in town. Very yummy in early spring. Stems should be snappy, not bendy.

BULBS & HEADS

i　　　　*ii*　　　　*iii*

Radicchio (*i*)

is so much more than the red leaf in mixed salad bags; the taste in the leaves is both strong and bitter. When it gets tougher in the winter, cooking it becomes a better option, and it turns into a totally different, very special beast when grilled, braised with vinegar, or wilted into pasta or risotto.

Having what are called "bitter principles," its actions are especially helpful to the liver.

Romaine (*ii*)

This vegetable secured its place in the lettuce hall of fame in 1903 in Chicago, when an Italian immigrant threw together a salad and named it after his most famous countryman, Julius Caesar. Distant cousin to endive and dandelion but sweeter than both, like a big crisp Baby Gem.

Belgian endive (*iii*)

or chicory as it's known in the UK, has a bitterness that betrays the strength inside. Common chicory root can be ground up as a coffee substitute, and is added to some coffees as an "extender," so flavor clearly abounds.

Horace mentions it in the 1st century B.C.E. as a mainstay of sustinence, along with olives and, strewn beneath the bed, Belgian endive supposedly helped Cleopatra's seduction of Mark Antony.
A leaf with proper flavor, bite, and handsome looks, Belgian endive cooks to an interesting texture (the Flemish have a favorite way with them called *Witloof uit den Oven*). However, you'd have to go a long way to beat raw Belgian endive drizzled with a mustardy vinaigrette and scattered with a few toasted hazelnuts.

Butternut Squash

Where do they grow? This is one that Columbus brought back—maybe his wasn't exactly in this form, but the squash family in general came from the New World. They kept a reasonably low profile in Europe until the 1970s, when hippies embraced them (along with one another) and they became standard food for vegetarians.

How do I use them? They do roast very well (it enhances their natural sweetness), and if you want to make a purée you do it by roasting, then mashing/blending. Just boiling them in water is supremely uninteresting, but having said that, they are a natural in soups.

What's in it for me? That fierce orange color is a surefire sign of carotene, which is a big bodily preparer for winter. Bumper crop of minerals too.

Anything else? Along with beans and corn, squash completes what is the Hopi people call the "Three Sisters": between them they contain every essential amino acid that our bodies need. This three-way alliance, also called "the trinity" is one of the most famous nutritional legends on the planet.

☛ **Friends** piggy, pasta, Parmesan, sage ... **Relations** all the rest of the weird and wonderful world of squash (spaghetti, acorn, crookneck, ironbark, pattypan), as well as the extended family of pumpkin, zucchini, cucumber, and melon ... **Recipes** Rainbow Superfood Salad p.208; Butternut & Bacon Chowder p.187

Celery

Where does it grow? Celery is not as easy to grow as you might believe—it takes a long time to mature and likes it cool and wet, otherwise it gets very stringy and mean.

The Romans were keen on it—Apicius, their most famous celebrity chef, grew it in his garden and describes making a purée from it.

The shame of most heads of celery sold here in the UK is that so often they have been rudely lopped off just where the leaves start, yet those leaves are both full-on in flavor, very good for you, lovely in soups, stews, casseroles, and also delicious when thrown in with simmering meats.

How do I use it? Celery is the slightly forgotten part of the soup and stew Holy Trinity, the other two being onions and carrots, aka *le mirepoix* in France. There are lots of recipes for boiling/braising it in mainland and northern Europe, and most are then bathed in a béchamel type sauce, which is a real texture sensation to eat.

Much easier, less weird, and better for you is raw celery with cheese.

What's in it for me? Famously celery has a negative calorific value. Plenty of minerals and vitamins help to keep the kidneys and liver functioning healthily. This is why it has been used in medicine for much, much longer than it has been eaten.

Anything else? Remnants of celery were found in King Tut's funeral garland.

You can't even think about serving quail eggs without celery salt.

The fifth Doctor Who kept a piece of celery in his lapel, because he was allergic to certain gases in the Praxis range of the Spectrum.

Sound-effects people still use celery snapping for gory bone crunches.

☛ **Friends** onions, carrots, thyme, cheese, nuts ... **Relations** parsley, celeriac ... **Recipes** many, many soups and slow-cooked dishes

Chiles (left & right) *i.* Dutch Red; *ii.* Anaheim; *iii.* Habanero; *iv.* Bird's Eye; *v.* Thai Green; *vi.* Dutch Green; *vii.* Mulatto

Ingredient we love — Chiles

Wild chiles were being picked in Mexico around 7,000 B.C.E., but the West (shortly followed by the East) didn't meet them for eight and a half centuries, when the Portuguese brought them back from the New World. From there they spread, quite rightly, like wildfire along spice routes and through trading stations; now nearly every great global cuisine holds them close to their heart (which is fine because it's chile fingers into eyes that really hurts). And the reason for their huge worldwide success—surely only the onion tribe is as completely internationally adored?—is capsaicin, the active chemical component that gives them their heat and drives us crazy (and incidentally is insoluble in water so, even though you can't kill the heat with cucumber or yogurt, these do help soothe the pain.)

Chemically, thanks to a bit of funny wiring, when we eat capsaicin it not only blows our heads off but also triggers something in the pleasure part of our brain, which is confusing. As any chile-lover will tell you, it's addictive. And as anyone who's been in direct contact with it will also tell you, it really burns, which is why it's used in sprays for policing riots, and crowds and in self-defence sprays.

Luckily there's a world of chiles out there for us addicts to explore, and the differences in their taste and use are as varied as their size and shape. Little tiny bird's-eyes from Asia, smoked chipotles from Mexico, noras (essential for paella) from Spain, insanely hot Scotch bonnets from the West Indies, dark green ones in India, dried peperoncini flakes in Italy, and ground into fiery paprika in Hungary.

Versatile in their strength (from mild to dangerous), flavor (from bitter through to sweet with the occasional too bloody hot to taste anything) and usage, chiles are a seasoning to be well respected.

☛ **Friends** what's not to love? … **Relations** bell peppers … **Recipes** Chile Pumpkin & Wild Mushroom Soup p.181; Roast Tomato, Chile & Cumin Soup p.178; Chili con Carne p.212; Spicy Coconut Fish p.240; Leon Gobi p.251; Green Pea Curry p.254; Smokin' Chili Sauce p.261

Type of Pepper	Scoville Rating
Pure capsaicin	15,000,000—16,000,000
Nordihydrocapsaicin	9,100,000
Standard US Grade pepper spray	2,000,000—5,300,000
Naga Jolokia	855,000—1,041,427
Dorset Naga	876,000—970,000
Red Savina Habanero	350,000—577,000
Habanero Chile	100,000—350,000
Scotch Bonnet	100,000—350,000
Jamaican Hot Pepper	100,000—200,000
Thai Pepper; Malagueta Pepper; Chiltepin Pepper	50,000—100,000
Cayenne Pepper; Ají Pepper; Tabasco Pepper	30,000—50,000
Serrano Pepper	10,000—23,000
Tabasco Sauce (Habanero)	7,000—8,000
Wax Pepper	5,000—10,000
Jalapeño Pepper	2,500—8,000
Tabasco Sauce (Tabasco Pepper)	2,500—5,000
Rocotillo Pepper	1,500—2,500
Poblano Pepper	1,000—1,500
Tabasco Sauce (Green Pepper)	600—800
Anaheim Pepper	500—1000
Pimento, Pepperoncini	100—500
No heat, Bell Pepper	0

Zucchini

Where do they grow?
This standard Med vegetable is thought to be the result of cross-pollination from squash samples taken to Europe from the New World by Columbus. There is no definite mention of anyone eating them until the 19th century, when both the French and the Italians started to use them, albeit a slightly different-looking variety from the one we are familiar with.

Zucchini is a well-loved summer squash that grows very easily in most moderate climates, though it demands a lot of water. Fresh zucchini are available in most grocery stores throughout the year, with a peak time in late spring.

How do I use them? Starting with their beautiful and delicious flowers (because they do come first), pick them with the little baby zucchini still attached. Gently unfurl their petals and stuff them with something with a bit of bite to it: anchovies with ricotta is a classic. Then make the very lightest batter you know how and deep-fry for just a few minutes. One of the special delights of spring.

Zucchini is versatile, so once yours have grown to full size, it's up to you: there's never a wrong time for *zucchini fritti*, but for a healthier option, braising sends them into the most fabulous texture zone.

Healthiest of all are steaming and grilling, both of which they also handle very nicely, cooked with herbs, a good extra virgin, and their great love, garlic.

What's in it for me? Some helpful minerals like magnesium, phosphorus, zinc, and potassium. Good for digestion.

Anything else? The British didn't know about them until Elizabeth David mentioned them in her seminal books *Mediterranean Cooking* (1950) and *French Country Cooking* (1951). This is why they are known by the French name *courgettes* in the UK, while in North America they are known by the Italian name, *zucchini*.

....

☞ **Friends** garlic, olive oil, herbs, tomatoes, batter, and all things *provençale* ... **Relations** melons, cucumbers, pumpkins: the great *Cucurbitaceae* dynasty ... **Recipes** Sicilian Grilled Vegetables p.166; Chunky Vegetable & Chermoula Soup p.173; Sumptuous Slaw p.207; Jossy's Moorish Vegetable Tagine p.249

Cucumber

Where do they grow? For centuries cucumbers have been prolific from India to Italy, Egypt to England, reaching an early high point there during the reign of Edward III (1327–77), albeit in slightly different shapes and sizes. In the Middle East they tend to prefer the shorter, thinner varieties that are about one-third of the length boring, standard EU-endorsed ones sold in Britain. In the North America, English (hothouse) cucumbers are usually sold wrapped so tightly you have to peel the plastic back like a condom. However, such cucumbers can grow to 2 feet in length, lack the bitter seeds of older cucumbers, and have the added benefit of supposedly being burpless.

How do I use them? The English, of course, make cucumber sandwiches to serve at High Tea, while on the far side of the Med (Greece, Turkey, and Cyprus) cucumbers tend to get mixed with yogurt for meze, dips, and salads.

What's in it for me? Plenty of H_2O (96%) and plenty of crunch. Aside from that it's mostly about soothing puffy eyes.

Anything else? Brining and pickling smaller cucumbers with dill gives us dill pickles—a lifetime essential.

Most of the tiny little cucumbers, known as cornichons, come from the Caribbean.

Fennel

Where does it grow? Very native to the Med, and you can still see it growing wild around the temples in Sicily. In the 9th century Charlemagne passed one of his many horticultural edicts, stating that sweet fennel must be grown in the south, i.e. Provence. From there it gained popularity and wended its way through time, battles, and warm breezes to the Arab world, where it was traded with the Asians, who fell slightly in love with the flavor of its seeds.

How do I use it? Raw is both excellent and excellent for you, especially in salads with bitter leaves like radicchio and Belgian endive, which provide the perfect foil to its sweetness.

Fennel grills, roasts, and braises extremely well, and is more than happy to end up on a plate next to some pork. Its affinity for piggy is also borne out by the naming and presence of fennel seeds in the stunning fresh Italian sausage "*salsiccie al finocchio,*" often the one seen squeezed out of its skin on top of pizzas.

What's in it for me? The fennel and pig combo is one of those lovely foodie partnerships that does more than just taste good—fennel aids digestion, particularly of fat, which most pork has a healthy amount of.

It also stimulates the appetite, and helps to regulate blood fat levels.

Sweet fennel seed tea was given to babies suffering colic, and fennel is often an ingredient in gripe water, along with ginger and dill, which settles the stomach and eases stomach cramps.

Anything else? Fennel is thought to be one of the nine sacred Druidian herbs, along with mistletoe.

In Italy, *finocchio* is a derogatory slang name for a homosexual man.

Edward I (reigned 1272–1307) had eight and a half pounds of fennel seeds ordered every month.

☛ Friends **pig, olives, acidity** ... Relations **dill** ...

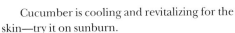

Cucumber is cooling and revitalizing for the skin—try it on sunburn.

☛ Friends **sharpness (lemon, vinegar— particularly malt vinegar), salt, mint, yogurt, and, slightly reluctantly, white sliced bread** ... Relations **all the melons, squashes, and that gang** ... Recipes **Gazpacho p.177; Leon Original Superfood Salad p.198; English Cucumber & Orange Quencher p.283**

LEAVES: THE DARK SIDE

Chard

There are many different varieties, from the foot-long Swiss chard to the cute baby red chard, which, in a salad, adds depth of flavor to any bowl of leaves. When baby red chard grows up it becomes rhubarb chard, so named for the vivid color of its stems. And for a real Technicolor explosion in your vegetable patch try rainbow chard, with its hyper-real hues.

Swiss chard is a two-for-one deal: you're getting the most out of this vegetable if you cook the stalks and the leaves separately. The stalks can be chopped and lightly sautéed with garlic, whereas use the leaves as you would treat spinach—but with a more textured and bolder result.

Chard is a powerhouse of iron, calcium, and vitamins A and B. It contains less oxalic acid than spinach, which is a good thing, because it means we are able to absorb more of the nutrients in it. Particularly good for the blood by helping the rejuvenation of red blood cells and therefore helping to regulate blood-fat levels.

In other words, it's like spinach, but better.

As you might have guessed from its botanical name, *Beta vulgaris*, it's part of the enormous Beet family. The Swiss prefix came about in the 19th century to distinguish it from French chard, which we now call cardoons.

Arugula

Also known as rocket, roquette, and rucola. (We prefer the name that sounds like it's going to take you to the Moon, but let's stick with arugula for now.) This most popular of leaves has exploded into our lives only in the last few decades—before that it was mostly used as a wild leaf in Italy. Never disappointing, arugula brings peppery bite to any salad, and wilts well to bring a bit of new life when stirred into pasta, etc., at the last minute.

Never far from a chunk of Parmesan, but too often weighed down with heavy balsamic when a lighter vinegar lets it sing.

Good with vitamin C and iron.

Chard

Baby Red Chard

BOROUGH OF CHARD

Rocket

Watercress

Not altogether surprisingly, this anciently loved British leaf grows in water. The darkness of the leaves tells you it's good for your liver and blood. A cousin of the nasturtium and sharing the strength of its bite, this was the leaf of the Middle Ages and features heavily in old cookbook recipes from soup to game.

Watercress is a leaf feeder, so keep it in the fridge with the leaves in a bowl of water and the stalks pointing up; yellows amazingly quickly if you don't look after it.

Spinach

The 12th-century Arabic writer Ibn-al-Awam called spinach "the prince of vegetables," and I think few would deny it's certainly up around there. First noted around Persia, but thanks to its excellent taste and nutritional value it was soon found all over medieval Europe replacing sour sorrel as the garden leaf of choice.

Adores a bit of nutmeg, and it's hard to think of a food it doesn't fit in with: dairy, salads, meat, soups, fish, for example.

Although there's definitely lots of goodness in those leaves, the legendary status Popeye bestowed on it is slightly inflated. Spinach also contains lots of oxalic acid, which can play havoc with our kidneys and stop us from maximizing the absorption of nutrients.

Best friends with garlic, and madly in love with olive oil.

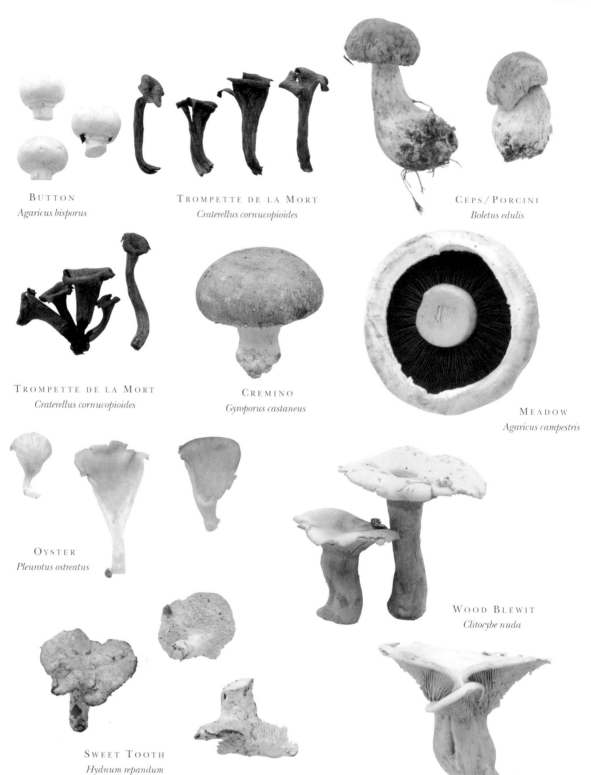

BUTTON
Agaricus bisporus

TROMPETTE DE LA MORT
Craterellus cornucopioides

CEPS / PORCINI
Boletus edulis

TROMPETTE DE LA MORT
Craterellus cornucopioides

CREMINO
Gyroporus castaneus

MEADOW
Agaricus campestris

OYSTER
Pleurotus ostreatus

WOOD BLEWIT
Clitocybe nuda

SWEET TOOTH
Hydnum repandum

MUSHROOMS

The ultimate in forager's food, these woodland beauties make up in flavor for what they lack in nutritional value. From one of the most prized ingredients in the world, the truffle, right down to the baby button mushrooms, fungi do a full range in flavor, visuals, and price. Mostly consisting of water, they love a little bit of fat to work with—olive oil and butter both have their time and place. Wild, with beech and oak trees as their guardians, the season starts at the end of summer with the orangey chanterelles and goes on until first frost.

Flat/Meadow/Portabella

These are not exactly the same, with Portabella being darker, Meadow being rounded at the edge of the cap, and Flat being, well, flat. However, in the large and wonderful forest there are so many types it's easier to group them together because they share common characteristics: big, meaty, not much shrinkage, earthy, and when cooked producing a lot of dark water that turns them black.

Cremino

This is a brown, chocolate-capped mushroom with a thick stalk that's very good in stocks. Like most mushrooms (apart from the year-round cultivated white ones) they look beautifully autumnal, and have a nuttiness that suits their season.

Button

The smallest and cheapest in the market but price isn't always related to flavor. There's good mushroom action locked inside their pristine bodies, particularly if you give them an extended sauté (with garlic, of course) to get all the water out.

Oyster

These straddle the divide between cultivated and wild, in that they look wild but are cultivated. Smooth on the top side and feathery underneath, this is what is called a bracket fungus because, in its natural habitat, it likes to grow directly out of the tree. Color varies from a steely grey to a warmer orangey yellow, and they are adored in China, where they are known as *ping gu*—sweet.

Wild

Apart from truffles, *ceps* (Fr.) or *porcini* (It.) are considered the highest prize. Soft and sexy, their season brings on a roadside frenzy in Italy at the stands where they're sold. Behind them is a wealth of romantic names, from wood hedgehog to *trompette de mort*—few other vegetables are quite so impressive in their natural state. Some are a real pain to clean, but as with most things in the kitchen, you get out what you put in. So, as long as you've got the time (and money), they are well worth the investment.

> Thousands of species of mushroom grow wild across North America (there are reportedly 2,000 species of mushrooms in Ohio alone). Many are posionous, and being able to identify these correctly could save your life. Exercise extreme caution when gathering wild mushroons for the table.

Bell Peppers

Where do they grow? The descendants of the Spanish conquistadors have totally naturalized them into their cuisine, as have their close neighbors Portugal, France, and Italy, but the deep roots of this most attractive of vegetables are still in the American subcontinent. On its travels around the world, the bell pepper (or sweet pepper), a member of the capsicum family, was particularly warmly welcomed in Africa, along with its hell-raising nephews and nieces, the chiles.

Seasonally they belong in late summer, the green ones (more bitter) coming first, followed by the yellow (getting sweeter but bland), and finally the red with their mature, ripe, and full-bodied sweetness.

There are now very few places on the planet where you won't find bell peppers in the market. **How do I use them?** Raw is good, but once you put them near the heat the classics just keep on coming: roasted, grilled, broiled, stuffed, and baked, these are a total Med staple.

Leon food heroine Claudia Roden's first rule is always to grill them over an open flame (a gas stove will do) until they are blackened all over. From there, put them into a bowl tightly covered with plastic wrap or place them in an airtight bag to sit and cool for a while. When you are able to handle them, peel them, but—and this is important—keep the juice (excellent flavor) and, tempting as it is, don't run the slimy peppers under cold water to get the last seeds off—massive flavor-loss potential. Keep the peeled bell peppers in their juice with a little herbage and garlic in a jar in the fridge for up to a week. A very handy vegetable to have around. **What's in it for me?** Surprising amounts of vitamins C and A, and within that "A" lies beta-carotene—vital for attacking free radicals. **Anything else?** There are currently more than 13 million bell pepper recipes on the internet—a testament to their world-wide popularity.

A certain number of people have problems digesting the skins.

☛ Friends **basil, olive oil, tomatoes, anchovies, garlic ...** Relations **chiles, tomatoes, paprika ...**
Recipes **Sicilian Grilled Vegetables p.166; Pinto, Black Bean & Chorizo Soup p.182; Sweet & Sour Pork with Cashews p.232; Jossy's Moorish Vegetable Tagine p.249; Egyptian Eggplant & Tamarind Stew p.252**

Pumpkin

Where do they grow? Originally in the New World, then brought back with Columbus on the *Santa Maria*. While still widely used in the US, the Caribbean, Central and South America, they are also popular in many different cuisines, including Italian, Iranian, and, more recently, Australian.

The smoother-skinned paler ones are better for eating, whereas the American darker more knobbly ones contain much more water and really are just bred to be Jack o' Lanterns.

The season generally lasts from October to February.

How do I use them? With their inherent sweetness you can go one of two ways with it: head for the American bakery for dishes like pumpkin bread, muffins, and, of course, pumpkin pie. Go East as in the heavily spiced stews and *khoresh* of the Middle East. Or, of course, there's the middle road trodden by the Italians, who think it sits well with risotto and pasta.

Their seeds are just as useful (see page 123), and the Mexicans do a great thing where they roast them with salt and ground chile as a snack.

What's in it for me? Let's hear it for the beta-carotene and also a pile of vitamins A, B_2, C, and E, all of which would make this a probable superfood if it wasn't so difficult to handle and was a little more user-friendly.

Anything else? Multiplying the number of segments around the outside by 16 will give you the number of seeds in the middle (give or take a few).

☛ Friends sugar, spice, sage, and butter ... Relations all the *cucurbitaceae* family...and please don't make me list them again ... Recipes Roasted Garlic & Pumpkin Hummus p.156; Chile Pumpkin & Wild Mushroom Soup p.181; Chicken, Pumpkin & Cranberry Beans p.231; (not very) Kashmiri Rogan Josh p.221; Susi's Pumpkin Pie p.269

Radishes

Where do they grow? Anywhere where there's light, rich soil, and a certain amount of sun; quickly and easily, which is why they are one of the easiest home-grown vegetables. The little ones we mainly eat here grow in about a month or less, but their big cousin the mooli, so loved by the Japanese, can take a full growing season.

Our name for them comes from the Latin for root, *radix*. They were first noted in Britain in 1548. The Egyptians, however, mention them as an aphrodisiac around 1,000 B.C.E.

How do I use them? Quickly! Because even overnight in the fridge they start to shrivel up. You can store them in iced water to keep them crunchy, but only as a temporary measure because it tends to dilute the fire.

Fred, another Leon food hero, says radish tops are delicious sautéed in butter with garlic.

Salads and crudités with celery salt, not forgetting as part of our favorite Persian predinner snack, *sabzi*.

And then there's the tradition of Thai flower-carving for plate decoration.

What's in it for me? Overall there's not that much to shout about, but raphinol, the thing that makes them hot, is a bit of a cholesterol-buster. Also folic acid for the promotion of new cell growth.

Anything else? The Sakurajima radish can grow to more than 26 pounds in weight.

The *Peanuts* cartoon strip is called Radish in Denmark.

Nobody loves a radish like the Japanese, and agrobiologists there are developing new strains using super-radish Dokonjo Daikon's DNA.

ii *iii*

i

☛ Friends salt ... Relations turnips, wasabi, horseradish ...

Radish (right) *i.* French Breakfast Radish; *ii.* Bunched Radish; *iii.* Mooli/Daikon

Celeriac

Celeriac is a specially cultivated European variation of the celery plant, and is not the root of the same.

Despite its unpromising look, when the flavor is allowed to open up it has something surprisingly interesting to say. Mellow, woody, with, of course, a back flavor of celery, this knobbly root is most versatile: you can grate it raw with crème fraîche, mustard, and lemon as the much-loved celeriac *rémoulade*, but it also loves a bit of liquid to soften up in, so it's ideal for soups or gratins; works as part of a vegetable *al forno* too, but does have a tendency to shrivel and dry out.

Lasts nearly all winter in a cool, dark place.

Is strongly attracted to fatty things and can often be found hanging around the back of the dairy, making eyes at the Friesians.

OUR ROOTS

This mighty collective of soil-dwellers are often less appreciated than their summery counterparts (such as peas in the pod or spears of asparagus). All we can say to their detractors is more fool you—these great roots have always supported us through eras cold and bleak: soups, gratins, casseroles, roasted, and even in salads. As a troop they are strong, and if the vegetables went to war, I know whose camp I'd be in, butching it up with the beets and pillaging with the parsnips.

Parsnips

Parsnips have been big in Britain for more than 500 years—at the time of Elizabeth I they were more popular than potatoes and were much used as a way of feeding the exploding population of London. British colonists took parsnips with them to the US in the early 1600s but by the middle of the nineteenth century the potato replaced the parsnip as the main source of starch. Since then parsnips have struggled to find popularity, even though roasted parsnips and maple syrup were made for each other.

Souped up or roasted are this extended root's fave destinations: when souping, they like the seed spices (caraway, cumin, fennel), whereas if they are heading for the oven the accent changes to a sweet-sharp thing, with all the natural sugar inside them being brought out and partnered with honey, orange, and mustard.

Also likes apples, chestnuts, and mushrooms. (We bought this amazing parsnip at a London Farmers' Market. As an urban cook I find the veg on offer is too often drably uniform so finding one that's really done its own thing always makes me smile. As nature intended.)

Rutabaga

Thought to be a cross between a cabbage and a turnip (which it resembles), the name comes from the Swedish *rotabagge*. They were first cultivated in Sweden before they were taken to Britain, so the Swedish connection also explains why the British call this vegetable a swede, while Americans opted for rutabaga.

There are two ways to bring out the most in it: either braise it in stews and casseroles, where it greedily absorbs the flavors in the cooking liquor without collapsing into a mush; or peel, cube, and boil it up with half a pat of butter, plenty of S & P, and a good grating of nutmeg.

Rutabaga forms the basis of my annual Christmas lunch root vegetable purée, which continues to please all, from babes in arms to our truly great aunt.

It *is* part of the brassica family, but really contains little or none of their renowned might. High GI (71—not so good) but low in carbs (1g per 100—better).

Carrots

Were originally purple, or yellow, but certainly not orange. Almost up there with the onions for all-round vegetable support, their feathery leaves were noted in the Hanging Gardens of Babylon.

Part of the French threesome that gets so many parties started (onions and celery being the other two), these fat sticks of beta-carotene are seriously good for you, and as always, raw is best (i.e. just like that, juiced, or in a salad) to get all that vitamin A out (see Allegra's Beautiful Juice page 286).

Jerusalem Artichokes

Distant member of the artichoke family (their Christian name comes from a mispronunciation of *girasol*, meaning sunflower in Italian), and also a cousin of theirs. In North America, where Native American people cultivated them well before the arrival of the Europeans, they're called sunchoke or sunroot.

These knobbly tubers have a gentle and interesting flavor. They make a lovely silky soup, which sadly, inexplicably and frequently is tarnished by clumsy chefs with a bottle of cheap truffle oil.

For a different approach give them a good scrub and roast them whole (see Roasted Arties & Newies, page 161).

Apparently a pinch of asafetida (an Indian spice and one of the most malodorous things in the kitchen) will reduce the potential for flatulence that is associated with this root.

Turnips

Officially part of the Brassica family, but are also related to mustard. The part under the earth is a lovely pure white, working up to a pleasantly purple crown. Lovely fruit of the earth sadly going through a bit of a decline in popularity at the moment. Crunchy and peppery with a slightly radishy zing, you can eat them raw, like a *rémoulade*, or braise in stock and a bit of duck fat until *à point*. Very French and very good.

Morocco still has strong French traditions from its old colonial days, and the love of turnips seems to have survived independence: you often see them featuring in tagines of different kinds—they do that braising thing so well, soaking up flavor without falling apart.

Beets

Thrives in four out of the five continents (not Africa) but is strongly associated with Polish and Russian food, so we can deduce that it likes it a bit nippy. The season for garden beets is pretty much year-round now. A fascinatingly colored variety, known as a chioggia or candy cane beet, has red and white concentric rings.

Use with enthusiasm: beets work well in soup (borscht), roasted, grated raw in salads (see page 206), gratins, and all kinds of bakes.

Contains plenty of potassium and something called betain, which is what gives it the superfood status it enjoys— it's said to have an anticancerous effect. There's also a fair amount of natural sugar in that there redness, making beets good for the energy levels.

Sprouts

First of all there are seeds then, given the right conditions (namely light and water), these hard little pellets split their skins and pop out a tentative shoot. Seeds are great and all that (see page 122) but eating them as much more than a sprinkling (albeit a hefty one) on top of something else a bit more interesting (i.e. salads, rice, oatmeal) can leave one feeling a little birdlike.

Sprouts, on the other hand, have all the same kind of wonderfood properties as seeds, that is to say impressive and intense amounts of vitamins, minerals, and generally essential parts to becoming a fully grown plant/tree/bush. But they taste good, really good, just as a snack in a little bowl with some sea salt, a bit of decent vinegar, and a splash of extra virgin olive oil.

As you may have gathered by now, these sprouts do not come from Brussels, and are not the babies of the Brassica family. They are, in the case of the Leon menu, most commonly alfalfa (or alfa-alfa, as John still insists on calling it), which we use with gay abandon on all our Superfood Salads. Their flavor is as intense as their goodness, and even a light sprinkling brings not only bonus nutritional points but also a distinct, earthy, fresh nuttiness to the party.

There's another group of sprouts out there that are neither alfalfa nor Brussels, and that also follow our mantra of "Tastes good, does you good," and they are the sprouting legumes. Lentils, chickpeas, azuki, and mung are some of the more common ones you might come across, usually in small cartons, and although they look a bit hippy woo-woo, they are delicious and not to be looked at with the same narrowing of eyes that the "peace and love" brigade usually are.

Also look for radish, onion, cumin, and the brightly colored beet sprouts—fun and yum.

POTATOES...

At Leon we shy slightly away from most kinds of potato. A lot of varieties, particularly the better-known British ones, tend to have a high GI, and also sit heavily on your stomach. While we would never underplay their importance in a well-balanced diet—and doubt any of us could live without mashed potatoes or fries—we figure that this is probably one vegetable the average Brit gets enough of. When we do have a potato dish on the menu we try to use super-waxy baby fingerling or new potatoes, which have a lower GI. For all your potato forays at home, here are some tips and an at-a-glance guide.

If Leon did potatoes:

King Edwards mash, roast, or bake

are a much-loved all-rounder in the UK. Floury, beige, with pinkish eyes. Fluff up well for mashed potatoes, too. As a substitute the yellow-fleshed Yukon Gold potato will rise to the challenge.

Roseval boil, roast, or sauté

potatoes are a small, oval, waxy, and red. They handle being cooked *al forno* very well, or boiled. Varieties include Chieftain, Dakota Rose, and Norland.

Round Reds mash, sauté, boil, roast, or bake

love being wedged and baked, which makes them caramelized and chewy. John's mom says these are best for roasting.

Fingerling boil, roast or sauté

are a finger-shaped waxy potato with a knobbly skin and a superior nutty taste. Look for Russian Blue, Red Thumb, or French Russian Banana.

Russets mash, sauté, boil, roast, or bake

are highly versatile and the most widely used American potato. Major varieties include Burbank, Ranger, Norkotah, and Shepody.

New Potatoes boil, roast, or sauté

are simply young potatoes of any variety that haven't been in the ground long enough to convert their sugar fully into starch, which means they have a waxy flesh and undeveloped, thin skins. The season for new potatoes is spring to early summer.

Anya boil, roast, or sauté

were developed in Scotland in the last century and are a cross between Desiree and Pink Fir Apple (which is actually another potato and not an apple at all). They splendidly straddle the divide between waxy and fluffy—like most of the littler varieties they are ideal in salads, while retaining a creaminess inside.

Sweet Potato

Sweet potatoes are a bit of a different deal. Technically they are not a potato at all but an unrelated starchy tuber with the stunning Morning Glory as a distant cousin. These are one of the varieties to come out of the Americas in the middle of the

last millennium, and 10,000-year-old traces of sweet potatoes were found in a Peruvian cave. We like them for their flavor, color, and low GI-ness. Slow-release sugars and whacking amounts of beta-carotene to up your immunities make this something of a blockbuster. (See our Sweet Potato Falafel, page 153.)

Corn

Where do they grow? Cobs of maize, the mama of the corn family, have been found to have grown in Mexico more than 6,000 years ago, making them one of the oldest known foods on the planet. Maize was grown all over the Americas by the indigenous people, from the Mayans and Aztecs to the Mohicans and Canadian Iroquois.

Most maize currently comes from the Southern States, and most of that is of the variety that's used to feed livestock. Even so, corn is still a largely American thing, with European crops being relatively minor.

As you'd expect from its color, corn really likes lots and lots of sun.

How do I use them? Really, on the cob, either steamed or grilled, is the only way to get the most out of them. More fun too, all that gnawing.

You can also cut the kernels off the raw cobs and stir them into soups like chowders or Asian broths at the last minute. Any more than a couple of minutes maximum cooking of the individual kernels is damaging to their taste, crunch, nutritional value, and sense of fair play.

A nice by-product of this method is the naked cob, which makes an excellent stock or soup-base-to-be.

What's in it for me? Medium GI (54), which isn't great, but on the other side there's plenty of fiber, vitamin A, natural sodium, and polyunsaturated fats.

As for corn on the cob, any vegetable that's eaten that close to raw can't be a bad thing.

Anything else? In Mitchell, South Dakota, a corn-growing epicenter, their motto is, "It's corn that fattens our hogs, sweetens our muffins, and puts the starch in our shirt collars," thus nicely illustrating some of corn's more varied uses.

☛ Friends **butter, chile, tuna mayo ...**
Relations **corn oil, corn syrup, cornstarch, popcorn, baby corn, polenta ...** Recipes **Roast Chicken & Corn Soup p.175**

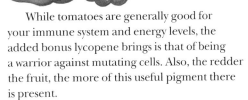

Tomatoes

Nowadays tomatoes grow just about everywhere that's warm enough, and quite a few places that aren't, hence all the poor-quality ones that are available out of season. Obviously the best ones come from a climate that suits them naturally (hot), as opposed to the millions of tons produced each year in polytunnels all over the world.

First choose your tomato wisely: skin color and scent are reasonable instant guides to the flavor inside. You want it to be red red red (but not all the way through ripe and out the other side).

Then from the biggest **beefsteak** to the tiniest **cherry** type, all tomatoes (and most fruit in general) taste better if they've been allowed to ripen on the vine.

At Leon, for raw we stick to a **vine-ripened plum** tomato all year round for consistency and flavor. On the other hand, our breakfast tomato we would never serve raw, because it has a less full flavor, but once roasted it's perfectly pitched for brekkie. For our ketchup we opt for what we know as the **Double M** tomato; again, not that pretty or fun raw,

but we will be reducing it considerably and so more wateriness is desirable to allow the spices and sweet-sour balance to develop before getting too thick. When the true season is upon us, our summer salads have often featured the sweet (in all senses of the word) cherry type. And what on earth would we all do without cans of **peeled plum tomatoes**?

So the long and the short of it is: pick your fruit wisely, because the tomato patch can also be a bit of a ketchup-splattered minefield.

As well as the endless joys tomatoes bring to our lives that we so take for granted, they also carry plenty of antioxidant properties, and a super-special-something in their skin called lycopene.

While tomatoes are generally good for your immune system and energy levels, the added bonus lycopene brings is that of being a warrior against mutating cells. Also, the redder the fruit, the more of this useful pigment there is present.

And then there's the ultimate pleasure a good slice of pizza can bring…

Originally from South America, the yellow variety was the common one when they were brought back to Europe by the conquistadors. Generally regarded with much suspicion, partly because they looked so similar to their cousin, deadly nightshade (they're also related to the tobacco plant and the potato), demand didn't get going in European continental cuisine until the 18th century, and we Brits didn't take this dear fruit to our hearts for about another 100 years after that.

When it did first arrive on our shores we simply translated what the French called it—*pomme d'amour*—and it wasn't for some decades yet that our "love apples" turned into tomatoes.

The origin of the French name seems to be a bastardization of *pomo d'oro* ("golden apple," now of course *pomodoro*), which is what the Italians named them because of the color of their yellow skins.

Finally, never put your tomatoes in the fridge. Taking them below 40°F destroys their cell structure and with it their flavor.

....

☞ **Friends** salt, and the rest you already know …
Relations peppers, chiles, deadly nightshade, eggplant, tobacco plant, potato …
Recipes understandably just too many to mention …

...some words about our BAMBI:
stubborn, sexy, fun and kind
FRENCH & FABULOUS ~ happy
serious and silly : perfect for us!

LOVE x LEON

PRETTY DESK

DAIRY

DAIRY

Milk is the beginning of the whole dairy story and it all starts with cow juice. It takes an average of 175 squirts from a cow's teat to make a pint of milk, and that's a whole load of teat-tweaking.

Milk is mostly water (between 85 and 90%), with less than 5% fat, and the rest being lactose, or milk sugars.

One 8-ounce glass of milk has one-quarter of the recommended daily intake of calcium, phosphorus, riboflavin, and vitamin D. Such a great gift from the cow to us.

At Leon we use an English organic milk. If you leave unpasteurized, unhomogenized milk to sit, what comes to the surface over time is Cream. Last year, of the 300 million or so liters of organic milk produced in Britain, half of it went on to become cream or butter.

In traditional cream-making, the stuff that came to the top over the first 12 hours was called single (light) cream, and the part that was thicker and took 24 hours to separate was called double (heavy) cream.

At Leon we don't use a lot of cream (unless you count what goes into our ice cream), but when the English strawberry season is upon us, what else can we do?

And so to Butter, one of life's absolute essentials. These bars of gold fall into that fabulous category of food that makes you feel good, which is as important really as food that's good for you. Few things can be more soothing to the soul on a cold, wet day than a really great piece of toast with the butter melting into it. We don't use it that much in our cooking, but at breakfast and teatime there is no substitute.

Butter is made from churning unpasteurized cream, and although it is 80% fat, well, it's not like you need a lot of it. The benefit with butter is at least you know what you're getting is natural, not like all that hydrogenated stuff or the blends of oils available on the market.

Enjoy butter responsibly.

The three above are the great dairy trinity, but there's something else we use more than any of these (except maybe milk in all those teas and coffees), and that's Yogurt. In the months before we opened our first restaurant we had lots and lots of tastings, anything from bacon to coffee to chicken to cakes. I have a distinct memory of standing in a damp parking lot in Hemel Hempstead outside a potential tea supplier and Henry opening the back of his van to reveal around 40 different yogurt samples. About an hour later we'd sipped and slurped across a white divide and nailed it; we opted for a Greek one that has most of the creaminess usually associated with them but without being quite so full-on. We found that the rich-to-sharp ratio, firm consistency, and overall flavor fitted the bill perfectly for all of our breakfast, smoothie, and sauce needs.

Most of our yogurt doesn't get sold at breakfast: we use it as an oil replacement in our version of aïoli (which is usually taken to mean garlic mayo) to make it lighter and healthier—see recipe on page 259.

Yogurt is made by introducing bacteria to milk ("Hey, Milk, this is Bacteria"). The bacteria then eat all the sugary lactose and make lactic acid. As with all acids, this sours the milk and causes the proteins to tangle up and solidify.

Yogurt is digested around three times quicker than milk into our systems, and is famously good for the friendly folk who live in our guts.

FRESH TODAY

Ingredient we love

And no dairy list would be complete without an offering from the French, a nation obsessed with *fromage*. We don't actually use any cheeses from France, not because they aren't excellent, but because their style doesn't really suit our menu. **Crème fraîche**, however, is a very welcome addition to this eclectic dairy shelf. Originally discovered by accident through unpasteurized heavy cream that had fermented, it is rich, thick, slightly sour, and pretty sexy. In fact, it is not dissimilar to sour cream. There are times and places where it wins over regular cream hands down, with that twinge of sharpness that elevates your dessert in the same way that a squeeze of lemon at the end can awaken so many sleepy savory dishes.

Surprisingly the low-fat version doesn't really taste like you're missing out too much (but it's not quite the same).

Crème fraîche is becoming more widely available in the US in gourmet delis and in the larger supermarkets, but it can also be ordered online from specialist suppliers.

Other territories with interests

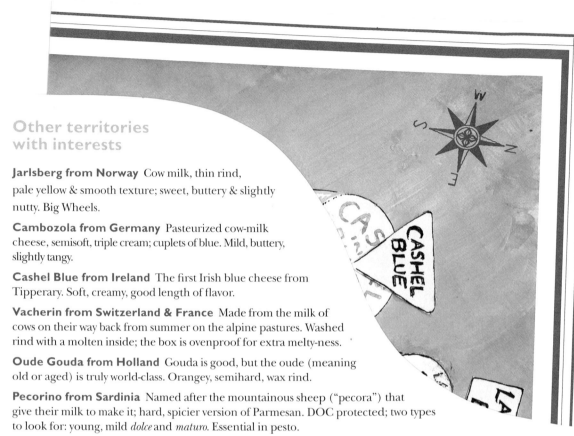

Jarlsberg from Norway Cow milk, thin rind, pale yellow & smooth texture; sweet, buttery & slightly nutty. Big Wheels.

Cambozola from Germany Pasteurized cow-milk cheese, semisoft, triple cream; cuplets of blue. Mild, buttery, slightly tangy.

Cashel Blue from Ireland The first Irish blue cheese from Tipperary. Soft, creamy, good length of flavor.

Vacherin from Switzerland & France Made from the milk of cows on their way back from summer on the alpine pastures. Washed rind with a molten inside; the box is ovenproof for extra melty-ness.

Oude Gouda from Holland Gouda is good, but the oude (meaning old or aged) is truly world-class. Orangey, semihard, wax rind.

Pecorino from Sardinia Named after the mountainous sheep ("pecora") that give their milk to make it; hard, spicier version of Parmesan. DOC protected; two types to look for: young, mild *dolce* and *maturo*. Essential in pesto.

Mozzarella originating from southern Italy near Napoli *Mozzarella di Bufala Campana* (DOC) is only made from the milk of water buffalo; produced by immersing curd in hot whey or water and then stretched repeatedly. Unlike anything else in the world.

Ricotta from Italy A fresh cheese, moist; cow and/or sheep and/or goat, and sometimes water buffalo. Creamy and fabulous.

Cheddar from Somerset Britain's finest addition to the world's cheese board. Cow's milk, semihard, and a good one is strong to the point of almost stinging.

Lancashire from Lancashire Creamy but with a proper taste of sour. Nobody does it better than Mrs. Kirkham.

Lanark Blue from Scotland Unpasteurized cheese made of ewe milk in the style of Roquefort.

Caerphilly from Wales Mild and flavorful; crumbly with a taste of the country. Cooks well.

Brie from France From Ile de France where it has been made from cow milk since C.E. 774. A real treat when ripe and oozing…a crowd pleaser.

Mont Enebro from Spain Goaty, ovoid from Avila; same mold as used in Roquefort. Creamy, sharp.

Gruyère from Switzerland The eponymous Swiss cheese—the one with the holes—fatty, semisoft, and great for cooking.

Camembert from France Inside the white rind are both crumbly and soft parts, thus distinguishing it from the similar-looking brie. Named after the Normandy village where it has been made for 200 years.

...and on to the wonderful world of

CHEESE

If ever there was a random (and short) list of cheeses, this is she.

Most proper cheesemakers (as opposed to mass-scale factories) really like it if you don't eat their cheese with anything other than more cheese, or maybe a bit of fruit or fruit juice—like wine. Leon is not really the kind of place for a five-course dinner, and we use cheese more as an ingredient in a dish, rather than on its own. So our little cheese moment is based purely on what we use in our restaurants; this is in no way a reflection on the great British cheesemaking tradition, but more a question of which cheeses sit well as part of the kind of food we make at Leon.

Having said that, we couldn't have a cheese page without mentioning some of the all-time greats and looking at our map, even our micro-cheese list gives an intriguing glance at the variety of cheese-making across Europe.

The text below was all transcribed by British code-breakers from scraps of radio interference picked up during the epic Second European Cheese War. Even though this was clearly some years ago, the factual information still holds true.

Victory for Italians in cheese war
GERMAN firms who make hard cheese for grating will no longer be able...

TELEGRAM

"The filing time shown in the date line is STANDARD TIME at place of origin. Time of receipt is STANDARD TIME at place of destination."

FETA SHEEP- AND GOAT-MILK CURDS ARE MIXED TOGETHER THEN SLICED (FETA MEANS SLICE IN GREEK)... KEPT IN BRINE...BIG ON FLAVOR FRONT... CREAMY-TANGY... MUCH NEEDED FOR OUR ORIGINAL SUPERFOOD SALAD...

MANCHEGO... SPANISH EWE MILK... LA MANCHA... FIRM TEXTURE DOTTED WITH TINY HOLES... CAN BE EATEN FRESH, OR AGED FOR ONE YEAR... LIGHT AND NUTTY TO FULL-ON SHARP... SPAIN'S SECRET WEAPON

SENDING STATION
PARIS, FRANCE

SYMBOLS: DL=Day Letter NL=Night Letter LC=Deferred Cable NLT=Cable Night Letter SR=Ship Radiogram

PARMESAN BIGGEST CHEESE IN THE WORLD... 55–77LB. ... EMILIA ROMAGNA (LIKE THE HAM AND VINEGAR)... USES YESTERDAY'S WHEY AS TODAY'S STARTER CULTURE... NOT VEGGIE, USES CALVES' RENNET (ENZYMES FOUND IN STOMACH), TO SPLIT THE MILK INTO CURDS AND WHEY... PEAKS AT 24 MONTHS BUT GOOD FOR 3 TO 4 YEARS... VITAL FOR SUCCESS OF OPERATION PASTA... DOES NOT BOUNCE...

THE COMPANY WILL APPRECIATE SUGGESTIONS FROM ITS PATRONS REGARDING ITS SERVICE

HALLOUMI CYPRUS... MIX OF COW, GOAT, AND SHEEP MILK... RUBBERY, FIBROUS TEXTURE... CURDS ARE DRAWN TOGETHER, KNEADED WITH SALT (AND SOMETIMES WITH MINT), FOLDED LIKE PUFF PASTRY, THEN CUT INTO BLOCKS... SALTY... GRILLS WELL... LOVES LEMON... DON'T EAT IT RAW...

FISH

FISH & SHELLFISH

Worms have long been a part of fishing, and now more than ever the metaphorical can that they wriggle out of is absolutely at the heart of our fishy choices. Eating fish regularly is an important part of a healthy diet, but we live in a time where pretty much every fish we are familiar with has been graded by those in the know (like the MSC* and MCS*) as being in trouble to some degree. The fish and seafood on our list are not necessarily there because they're in a terribly sustainable state at the moment, but because we like them, and globally they are local to our shores. In our oceans everything is changing both slowly (in terms of stock repletion) and quickly (in terms of guidelines) so to ensure you are choosing well for the planet as well as the plate, check on the Ocean Conservancy website (www.oceanconservancy.org). Ocean Conservancy has worked for more than 20 years to support sustainable U.S. fisheries.

If you think about it, buying small or very young fish is clearly not going to help breeding levels and rejuvenate stocks. Also, always make sure you buy line-caught fish. The alternatives are big nets that drag up anything and all in their path, and discard anything they've caught that wasn't what they were after, but only after it's died for nothing. Extremely damaging to the biodiversity of the sea.

*The Marine Stewardship Council (MSC), has a standard for environmental and well-managed fishing. In Britain, looking for the the MSC logo is the easiest way to make sure you are supporting fishermen who are catching responsibly. As the quantities of fish in our sea are a constantly changing state of affairs, checking regularly with the MSC website (www.msc.org) is the only way to be sure you're not damaging the stocks and being absolutely certain your choices are sustainable. The Marine Conservation Society (MCS) are kind of like the sea police who can comment on what we can and can't fish for—see www.fishonline.org.

THE OILY ONES
BEST FOR YOU

....

Anchovies *(1)*

Anchovies swim in massive shoals in any coastal, warmish (above 50°F) waters, with up to a million per school. This silver slip of a fish lives all over the world, shimmering its blue-green back as it energetically swims toward the lights hung from ships that fishermen use to attract them. They feed on phytoplankton and in turn are pretty much the bottom rung on the fishy food chain.

Fresh anchovies are pure pleasure—but not for those who squeal at bones—and are available almost all year round. Best ways forward are grilled or fried (deep-fried is good) with a sage leaf and a couple of slivers of garlic between the fillets.

The Spanish love their *boquerones* almost above all others and have learned to preserve their flavor in three ways: *escabeche* (lightly pickled in vinegar, which cures the flesh white); tightly packed whole in crystals of sea salt; or fillets packed in oil (or brine), which bring up the rear in terms of flavor.

High in niacin, selenium, iron, calcium, and phosphorus—all essential trace elements—and also in oils (some of which are good omegas) but some of the prepared ones can be very salty. On balance, still good for you as long as you don't eat them like popcorn.

Anchovy fillets can be melted in warm olive oil or butter as an excellent first step to sauces, etc., with onions and garlic; great unobtrusive background seasoning.

Asian countries salt and ferment them to make fish sauce (see page 126), and Britain uses them in Worcestershire sauce.

Right now anchovy fishing in the previously abundant area of the Bay of Biscay has been halted, and the state of the other Mediterranean stocks is uncertain, so proceed with caution.

Mackerel *(4)*

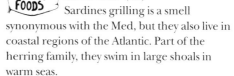

Mackerel is Leon's top fish: it's from British waters and good for you. Just about the most beautiful fish in the sea, with its blue-green iridescent skin and black zebroid squiggles, it is literally swimming in goodness: an ocean of amino acids and proteins, omega oils, and selenium.

As well as the smoker, this distant cousin of tuna also enjoys a good pickling, broiling, and searing, and all those oils lead to the desire for a bit of cut-through sharpness, hence the 17th-century recipe for mackers with gooseberries. We use it smoked in our Magic Mackerel Salad (see page 204), and line-caught is best.

A mackerel sky means tomorrow it might rain (not that that means much around here).

Salmon *(5)*

Salmon, in their natural habitat, prefer the cooler waters of the Northern Hemisphere, where they mature in the sea but return to coastal streams and rivers for spawning in December to August.

Truly multifaceted, the salmon can be handled in many ways: steamed, grilled, poached, baked, smoked, broiled, or eaten raw as sushi.

Wild (and wildly expensive) salmon, which has the most delicate taste and flesh color to match is best coming from the Pacific. Atlantic salmon is the pink pastel shade we usually see farmed. At present there is no regulatory agency in the US that sets organic standards for salmon. However, fish sold with a "Responsibly Farmed" logo at the Whole Foods Market® are raised following strict guidelines.

Four ounces of salmon provides a full day's supply of vitamin D, protein, and, of course, omega oils.

Sardines *(15)*

Sardines grilling is a smell synonymous with the Med, but they also live in coastal regions of the Atlantic. Part of the herring family, they swim in large shoals in warm seas.

Half and half protein and good fats, and stuffed with retinol as well, they are power-packed with goodness.

Along with tuna and anchovies, they handle canning/jarring exceptionally well, and sardines on toast on a cold winter evening is terribly comforting.

Beautiful to look at, beautifully easy to scale, and they eat beautifully too.

Tuna (9)

Tuna is stupidly big for such tiny cans. Both oily and lean in places, it's a great source of protein, and when it's eaten raw or seared (the best way) you get pretty much all the goodness and an abundance of omega 3, vitamin A, iron, and other essential minerals (but sadly not from the canned stuff).

Warm-blooded, they move fast to keep oxygenating their gills and have been known to hit 48 miles an hour, but that's not fast enough to beat the fishermen: blue-fin stocks are near collapse, and yellow-fin are also in trouble. Other kinds of tuna, like skipjack or albacore, are still fine conscience-wise to buy canned.

The Japanese tuna fishermen that catch the best tuna have a chute on their boats which they push the enormous fish into, and as they fall they freeze solid around 66 pounds of flesh in less than a minute. This method of extreme flash-freezing allows most of the goodness and flavor to stay captured within the flesh, rather than allowing any deterioration on the long journey home.

WHITE FLESHED
BEST MULTIPURPOSE

Cod (13)

Cod from the Atlantic is best left at the moment to get its stock levels up, and buying it only encourages less environmentally aware chefs, restaurateurs, suppliers, and fishermen.

Wild Pacific line-caught is fine and there is some sustainably fished stuff around. But most people don't bother asking, so they can end up with the unsustainable one. Not good.

Haddock (3)

One of the favorites of the fish'n'chip shops as well as upscale restaurants, haddock hang out on both top sides of the North Atlantic i.e. from the Bay of Maine right across to Iceland and Norway. The fish are recognizable by having a black lateral stripe across their whiter side, and the flesh inside cooks like a dream. Pure white, firm, and flakey, and with a skin that crisps up nicely in the pan. Scottish, off both the east and west coasts, are Leon's best local buy.

Pollock, Whiting & Coalfish

Pollock, whiting, and coalfish are the new whites. While it is indisputable that some of the old school (like cod and turbot) have superior flesh, it is also indisputable that we are running out of them, and in order to preserve the biodiversity of the planet we need to adjust our eating habits.

The three above all work absolutely fine in things like fish pies, cakes, stews, and soups. But, with the exception of pollock, we may choose to use mackerel and maybe even farmed fish for our perfect, portion-sized seared fillets.

Now a quick word on our new friends:
Pollock (6) is mostly from the coast of Portugal and hits all the health buttons, being high in protein and fishy oils but low in fat. Solid flavor and very easy to fillet. Not to be confused with Alaska pollock or Walleye pollock.
Whiting (12) are cousins of cod, but are geographically closer to us in the UK since they are available off the southern coast of England and the Irish and North Seas from around September. Grow to only about 2 pounds.
Coalfish (16), in terms of flavor, is the closest to cod. Historically she was thrown back into the water in favor of cod so as not to exceed the fishing quota landed, but now is being sought and fished in her own right. Not that cheap. Confusingly, it is called pollock in the US and coley or saithe in the UK. Good firm flakes.

Sea Bass (2)

Sea bass are most plentiful from January to May and again from September to October. Cousins of the groupers, who live in warmer tropical

waters, sea bass hang around the Med and Atlantic seas, particularly enjoying rocky coastlines, and most of the wild ones here are found off the south and east coasts.

Sea bass has done an amazing job on its brand lately, retaining the positive association with all things Med, and yet due to the farming side of production has become relatively mainstream.

Clearly the best is line-caught, but the farmed fish are also decent.

Back to bass: very simple to handle and versatile in the kitchen, this fish likes the grill, being baked whole in salt or foil, pan-fried, poached, and even sashimi'd. Rarely losing its moisture or flavor, *branzino*, as the Italians call it, provides nearly 50% of your daily protein needs per portion, as well as a bunch of minerals and good omegas.

SEAFOOD & CRUSTACEA
BEST PRESENT FROM NEPTUNE

Crabs © *(18)*

There are many species out there, from the tiny pea crab to the 10-foot-wide spider.

The most sustainable way to catch them is in pots, so ask specifically about their trapping.

This hand-size, decapod crustacean has lots of zinc, vitamin B_{12}, copper, and, above all, protein within its reddish-brown exoskeleton, and even though the pretty white meat is considered the higher prize, many believe the brown to have the better flavor.

You can tell if it's really fresh if it's still moving. The American Humane Society has undertaken studies and concludes that spiking (inserting a knife into the crab's head to destroy the main nerve centers) is the least traumatic way to kill a crab for cooking.

Hens (F) differ from cocks (M) by the shape of their abdominal flap: a male crab's is small and triangular, while a female's is broad and oval-shaped… common sense really.

©See Suppliers, page VI in Appendix.

Mollusks *(7, 10, 11)*

Mollusks, in terms of value and ease of cookery, have got to be the best seafood, with mussels leading the way. Also including everything from clams to cockles to oysters, this family of bivalves (meaning two shells) get their nutrition by filtering sea water for all its algae and phytoplankton. They live where the land meets the sea, with cockles and clams erring on the sand side, and mussels and oysters preferring to be submerged in the water. Mussels are harvested on ropes they cling to with their byssi or beards.

Very high in protein and low in fat, as well as the usual bank of minerals associated with the sea, mollusks tick all the boxes and when eaten raw (oysters or the enormous and rude Cherrystone clams) feel, taste, and look like sensuous brain food.

Octopus *(17)*

Octopus is really only included because we have a great recipe and picture of Fred (great friend of Leon) preparing his favorite dish. See Fred's Millennium Octopus, page 245.

Shrimp *(8)*

Shrimp is one of the world's best-loved seafoods. It exists in some form in nearly all the planet's seas, from the tiny brown shrimps we love to pot right through to the so-called colossal shrimp found in warmer waters that are best BBQed.

Quick environmental: wild-caught tropical shrimp account for more than one-quarter of the world's bycatch by trawl fisheries (very bad). Tiger shrimp are also savagely overfarmed in Asia, then flown all over the world, so double negative points there, and, to make things worse, wild fish are scooped up to feed farmed tiger shrimp, damaging biodiversity even more.

Whether it's a poach, broil, or a grill, these multilegged crustaceans always cook more quickly than you think they will. They love garlic, chile, and lemon.

BIG AND
STRONG

MEAT

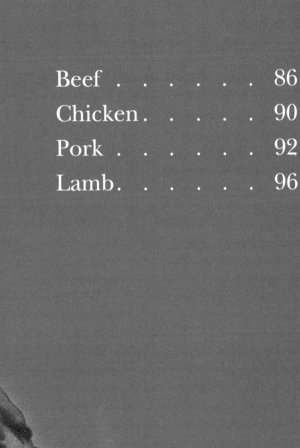

CUTS of BEEF

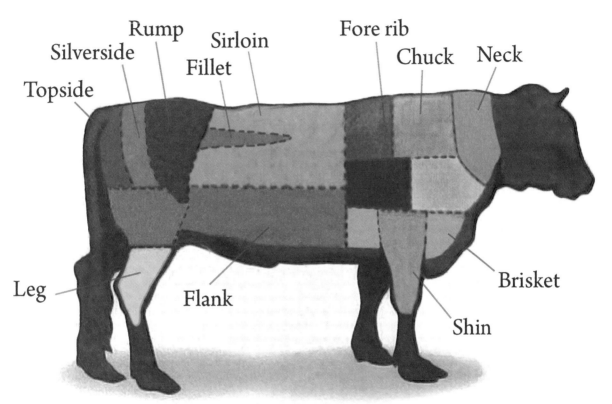

Topside
Silverside
Rump
Sirloin
Fillet
Fore rib
Chuck
Neck
Leg
Flank
Shin
Brisket

IT'S ALL ABOUT

FEED & REARING

They live in fields and eat grass...
but when it gets cold
they move inside.

BEEF

Meaningful Steak Steak is their most prized possession, so treat it with respect. Always let your steaks come up to room temperature before you start to cook them never cook fridge-cold steak. Every steak needs and deserves at least 5 minutes' rest in a warm place after cooking—the difference it makes to the texture is worth the wait.

Tenderloin is considered the crème de la crème, and that's a title you pay for. It's a long muscle inside the ribs, nestling next to the spine. Virtually no fat, so suits pan-frying better than grilling, and has very Gallic tendencies: *au poivre, tournedos Rossini, Chateaubriand*. A great tenderloin cooked properly should cut like butter.

Rib-eye steak is an American invention, so-called because of the little eye of fat that's supposed to be in the middle, which many rib eyes of today seem to be missing. Cut from the small end of the rib and can have the most fantastic marbling of fat. Gets a fab wobble on when cooked rare.

Rump steak is from the hindquarters of the animal, and is considered by those in the know to be the best tasting of all the steak cuts. Sometimes a little toughness comes with all that flavor, so it needs to be rare and have a good rest after cooking. Best to make friends with your butcher to ensure a good cut. Excellent chewing flavor.

Standing rib The king of roasts, absolutely majestic at any table, sitting proud. If you're going to spend this much money on a piece of meat, try to find the extra bucks to go the distance and get one from a good breed that's hung a minimum of three weeks. And when it's

Sirloin is a prime cut of beef that runs from the ribs to the rump with a special slab of fat running along one side. Perfect for grilling, but pan-fries well too. As a whole piece it makes for a terrific roast. If cooking for two or more, get one big thick piece and carve it into slices for a richer rareness and taste.

T-bone is an extremely imposing cut: imagine splitting the cow down the spine, then on a different axis slicing through the ribs to get to this monster steak. It is cooked on the bone for maximum flavor, and you get to gnaw on the big bone after. The stuff of American steak legends. In one restaurant in Amarillo, Texas, if you can get through one of their 72oz steaks you don't pay!

on the table, just for a moment you'll feel like a king, though more Henry VIII than Charles.

For ease of carving, get your butcher to take it off the chine bone (but leave it still attached to the ribs), then tie it back on for the cooking—the flesh cooks better if it still has protection on one side from the fierce heat. The string is a lot less likely to burn and burst if you soak it overnight in saturated salt water.

And don't let yourself or the cow down by serving with anything less than fresh horseradish (which you can keep in the freezer and cut a bit off as and when you need).

Shank And so to the legs. At this point the meat is taut with tendons, but the muscles need to be strong to support all that immense weight, and so have great flavor. "Foreshank" refers to the front legs and is usually used for stewing steak.

Oxtail Does what it says on the label but it's beef, not ox. Treat it like *osso buco* (see Veal, below) but expect a much darker, more gelatinous and richer finish. If you can bear to go one step further after you've already been cooking it for some 6 hours, pick the meat off the bones and do yourself proud with an oxtail soup with pearl barley, or an instant nap-inducing suet pudding.

Chuck The ultimate cut for braising or stewing steak, this is a serious hunk of meat with not a whole lot of fat or gristle. Goes through the most amazing transformation as it moves from being red raw to tense, tough little nuggets through to being all languid and relaxed; then its work is done.

Brown it first in a very hot oven with some seasoning and onions (this gets the flavors moving), then add stock or water and just let it to do its thing. Sometimes it takes a ridiculously long time, but somewhere down the line, as long as the quality is decent, it will soften up and stop being tough. It always does. Patience. The basis of every great slow-cooked beef dish from *Boeuf Bourguignonne* to Steak and Kidney Pie to our Beef and Guinness Stew.

Being another much used and needed muscle, the neck is also a cheap cut that is good for braising.

Brisket This is the cut of choice for salt beef and pastrami. A bit of breast with very little fat or fun in there naturally, so we've learned to brine it, then simmer it for ages and ages. Then it becomes something special. Hot salt beef sandwiches with mustard and dill pickles are quite rightly the stuff of legends. Those incredible textured strands of meat are unseen anywhere else on the animal.

Ribs These are for people who crave ribs but don't eat pork. As there are more Jewish folk in NYC than there are in Israel, and ribs being an American thing, they do a fine trade in beef ribs. For how to handle see Pork, page 95.

VEAL There are many, many different kinds of cow, and all of them are amazingly giving beasts; the beef you eat does not come from the same kind of cattle as the milk you drink, and when a dairy cow gives birth to a male calf, that calf is of little or no value to the farmer. Raising cows is an expensive business, one the farmer is loath to embark on unless there's a market for it. So, in Britain, people are encouraged to eat more veal to stop these little calves being born for nothing. Six months of fun and ending up making somebody happy has got to be better than being shot at two days of age. There can be no better example of this than *osso buco*, the Italian favorite where cross-sections straight through the leg are braised for hours and hours until the clumps of meat move away from the central bone and the molten marrow at its center.

Alternatively, veal escalopes flash-fry in seconds for an excellent light supper, finished with a squeeze of lemon. Roast whole loins for the exceptional summer special *Vitello Tonnato*, use ground veal for meatballs, or stew this beautiful blonde meat in chunks for a lighter slow-cook—*Blanquette de Veau*.

Shank And so to the legs. At this point the meat is taut with tendons, but the muscles need to be strong to support all that immense weight, and so have great flavor. "Foreshank" refers to the front legs and is usually used for stewing steak.

Oxtail Does what it says on the label but it's beef, not ox. Treat it like *osso buco* (see Veal, below) but expect a much darker, more gelatinous and richer finish. If you can bear to go one step further after you've already been cooking it for some 6 hours, pick the meat off the bones and do yourself proud with an oxtail soup with pearl barley, or an instant nap-inducing suet pudding.

Chuck The ultimate cut for braising or stewing steak, this is a serious hunk of meat with not a whole lot of fat or gristle. Goes through the most amazing transformation as it moves from being red raw to tense, tough little nuggets through to being all languid and relaxed; then its work is done.

Brown it first in a very hot oven with some seasoning and onions (this gets the flavors moving), then add stock or water and just let it to do its thing. Sometimes it takes a ridiculously long time, but somewhere down the line, as long as the quality is decent, it will soften up and stop being tough. It always does. Patience.

The basis of every great slow-cooked beef dish from *Boeuf Bourguignonne* to Steak and Kidney Pie to our Beef and Guinness Stew.

Being another much used and needed muscle, the neck is also a cheap cut that is good for braising.

Brisket This is the cut of choice for salt beef and pastrami. A bit of breast with very little fat or fun in there naturally, so we've learned to brine it, then simmer it for ages and ages. Then it becomes something special. Hot salt beef sandwiches with mustard and dill pickles are quite rightly the stuff of legends. Those incredible textured strands of meat are unseen anywhere else on the animal.

Ribs These are for people who crave ribs but don't eat pork. As there are more Jewish folk in NYC than there are in Israel, and ribs being an American thing, they do a fine trade in beef ribs. For how to handle see Pork, page 95.

VEAL There are many, many different kinds of cow, and all of them are amazingly giving beasts; the beef you eat does not come from the same kind of cattle as the milk you drink, and when a dairy cow gives birth to a male calf, that calf is of little or no value to the farmer. Raising cows is an expensive business, one the farmer is loath to embark on unless there's a market for it. So, in Britain, people are encouraged to eat more veal to stop these little calves being born for nothing. Six months of fun and ending up making somebody happy has got to be better than being shot at two days of age. There can be no better example of this than *osso buco*, the Italian favorite where cross-sections straight through the leg are braised for hours and hours until the clumps of meat move away from the central bone and the molten marrow at its center.

Alternatively, veal escalopes flash-fry in seconds for an excellent light supper, finished with a squeeze of lemon. Roast whole loins for the exceptional summer special *Vitello Tonnato*, use ground veal for meatballs, or stew this beautiful blonde meat in chunks for a lighter slow-cook—*Blanquette de Veau.*

Meat **89**

ThE Chicken

BREAKING DOWN YOUR BIRD

	Best Use
Whole Bird	The best way to get your money's worth out of a bird gently simmer whole with veg and aromatics (see stock in 'Carcass') until the legs fall off, then use the stock to make soup (famed for its healing properties), or a velouté (like a white sauce but using stock instead of milk) which then forms the binding for a pie Stage 2 is to pick the meat off the bones to make your pie filling, or sarnies, or salads or whatever. Two meals in one. And then there's roast chicken but once you've feasted on the meat remember you can still make a stock from the bones
Leg	At Leon we use only leg, as it keeps moister for longer and we think it tastes better. It also braises the best, especially when kept on the bone, so legs should be your choice for dishes like *coq au vin*.
Breast	The other main source of meat on the bird is the leaner cut. Loved by calorie-counters and those with cholesterol issues, breast does have its benefits, but generally it is inferior flavour-wise and is less juicy than the darker meat. Use it for fast cooking like grilling or pan-frying (including stir-fries), but try to give it a marinade first, as that makes a real difference.
Liver	Great source of iron and yummy in warm salads (flash-fry in a really hot pan and deglaze with balsamic) or the ubiquitous pâté/parfait/terrine. Good recipe for this in Larousse, but we leave out the parsley.
Parson's Nose	When your bird has been roasted, if you like fattiness, this is a great little cook's snack - it contains the oil glands that the birds use when preening. Legendary Roman chef Apicius wrote recipes for cooking specifically just the pygostyle (technically it only becomes a parson's nose once it's cooked).
Heart	Like the liver, the heart contains plenty of iron but it also has stacks of protein and vitamin B12. Tastes meatilicious and is very good kebabbed. Too good to throw away.
Gizzards &/or intestines	Sadly underused in the UK, but almost everywhere else they are not wasted. In South-east Asia they are sold grilled as street food, while in South America they are battered. Hungarians do it with paprika (unsurprisingly) and the Portuguese stew 'em up with beans.
Oyster	The crime of most roast chickens is that not everyone flips their bird to remove what are the jewels in the chicken's body. They are found in their own smooth, concave holder, towards the base of the spine on either side, just in and up a bit from the leg joint. Trust the French to revere them, as they should be, often making them the stars of their own dish. Simply exquisite, and seriously tender.
Feet	Popular Chinese cuisine – fried, marinated, boiled, then sucked dry. Two thousand years after they were first eaten in the Orient, they are still to catch on in the West.
Carcass	Stock. Onion, carrot, celery, bay, peppercorns, garlic, thyme, parsley. The single most useful thing to have in your fridge.

AIN'T NOBODY HERE BUT US CHICKENS

DECCA

LOUIS JORDAN

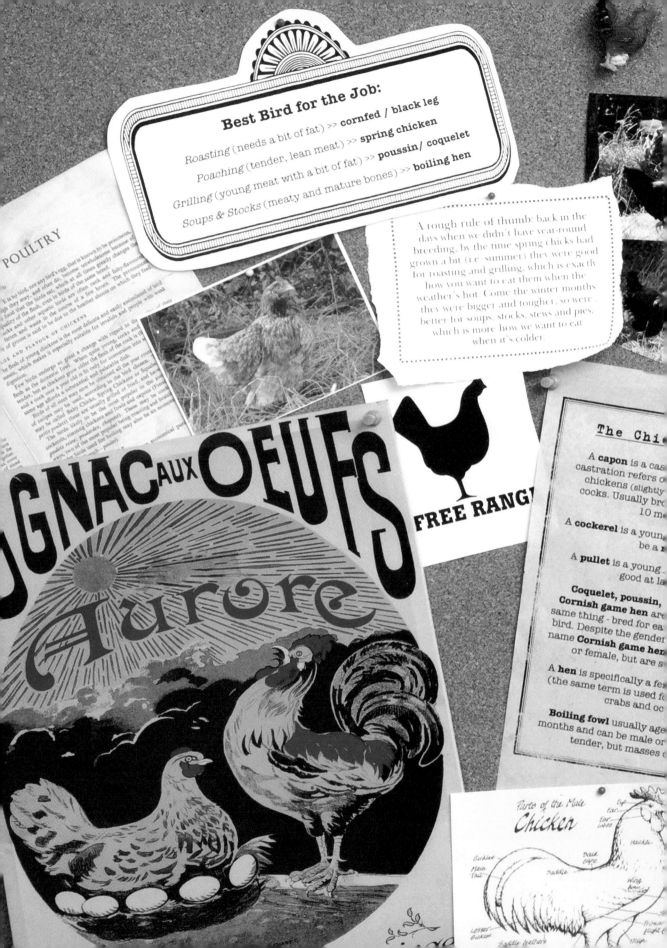

Best Bird for the Job:

Roasting (needs a bit of fat) >> **cornfed / black leg**

Poaching (tender, lean meat) >> **spring chicken**

Grilling (young meat with a bit of fat) >> **poussin / coquelet**

Soups & Stocks (meaty and mature bones) >> **boiling hen**

A rough rule of thumb: back in the days when we didn't have year-round breeding, by the time spring chicks had grown a bit (i.e. summer) they were good for roasting and grilling, which is exactly how you want to eat them when the weather's hot. Come the winter months they were bigger and tougher, so were better for soups, stocks, stews and pies, which is more how we want to eat when it's colder

POULTRY

FREE RANGE

GNAC AUX **OEUFS**

Aurore

The Chi...

A **capon** is a cas...
castration refers o...
chickens (slightly...
cocks. Usually bro...
10 me...

A **cockerel** is a youn...
be a r...

A **pullet** is a young...
good at la...

Coquelet, poussin,
Cornish game hen are...
same thing - bred for ea...
bird. Despite the gender...
name **Cornish game hen**...
or female, but are s...

A **hen** is specifically a fe...
(the same term is used fo...
crabs and oc...

Boiling fowl usually age...
months and can be male or...
tender, but masses o...

Parts of the Male
Chicken

leon
FOOD LEON LOCAL FRESH SEASONAL
FREE RANGE
CHICKEN
GT. MARLBOROUGH ST. LONDON

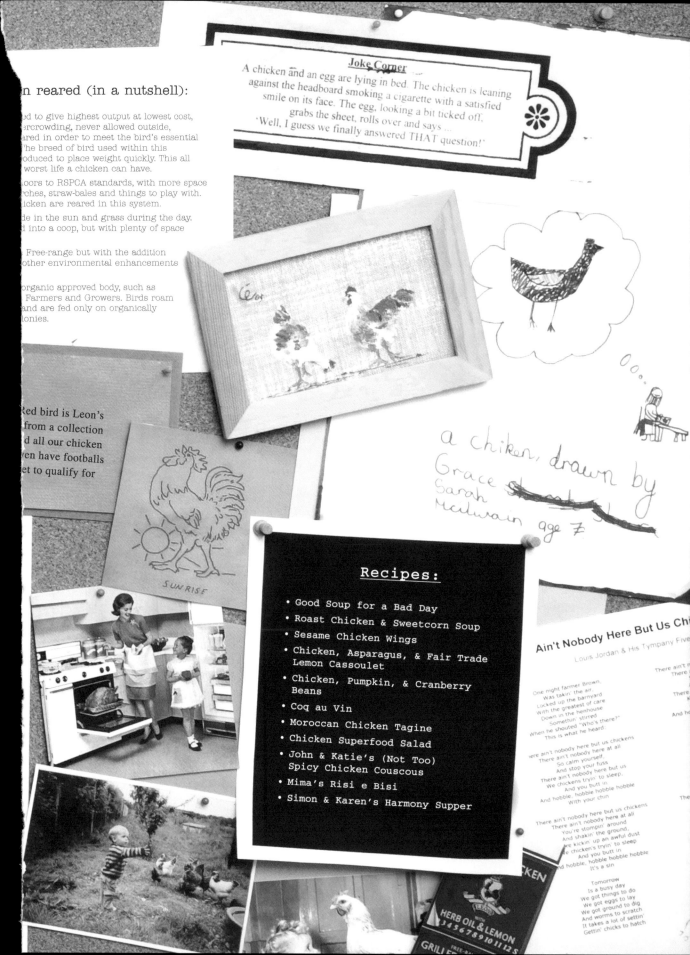

...n reared (in a nutshell):

...d to give highest output at lowest cost,
...ercrowding, never allowed outside,
...ared in order to meet the bird's essential
...he breed of bird used within this
...oduced to place weight quickly. This all
...worst life a chicken can have.

...oors to RSPCA standards, with more space
...ches, straw-bales and things to play with.
...icken are reared in this system.

...de in the sun and grass during the day.
...d into a coop, but with plenty of space

... Free-range but with the addition
...other environmental enhancements

...organic approved body, such as
... Farmers and Growers. Birds roam
...and are fed only on organically
...lonies.

...Red bird is Leon's
...from a collection
...d all our chicken
...en have footballs
...et to qualify for

SUNRISE

a chiken, drawn by Grace Sarah McIlwain age 7

Recipes:

- Good Soup for a Bad Day
- Roast Chicken & Sweetcorn Soup
- Sesame Chicken Wings
- Chicken, Asparagus, & Fair Trade Lemon Cassoulet
- Chicken, Pumpkin, & Cranberry Beans
- Coq au Vin
- Moroccan Chicken Tagine
- Chicken Superfood Salad
- John & Katie's (Not Too) Spicy Chicken Couscous
- Mima's Risi e Bisi
- Simon & Karen's Harmony Supper

Ain't Nobody Here But Us Chi...

Louis Jordan & His Tympany Five...

One night farmer Brown,
Was takin' the air.
Locked up the barnyard
With the greatest of care
Down in the henhouse
Somethin' stirred
When he shouted "Who's there?"
This is what he heard:

...here ain't nobody here but us chickens
There ain't nobody here at all
So calm yourself
And stop your fuss.
There ain't nobody here but us
We chickens tryin' to sleep.
And you butt in
And hobble, hobble hobble hobble
With your chin

There ain't nobody here but us chickens
There ain't nobody here at all
You're stompin' around
And shakin' the ground.
...re kickin' up an awful dust
...e chicken's tryin' to sleep
And you butt in
...and hobble, hobble hobble hobble
It's a sin

Tomorrow
Is a busy day
We got things to do
We got eggs to lay
We got ground to dig
And worms to scratch
It takes a lot of settin'
Gettin' chicks to hatch

There ain't m...
There...

There...

And he...

The...

HERB OIL & LEMON

GRILL...

What's Really Important:

When it all comes down to it there are really only two things that reflect the flavour of your bird.

The first is FEED, because chickens are just like us and you are what you eat. The value of a good diet is huge, as without it the birds will be tasteless. Chickens with a yellowish look to them have often been fed on corn, and are yummy.

The second is REARING CONDITIONS, because whether the bird has been allowed to run around and grow muscles directly affects the texture, make up and integrity of the meat.

How your chicken has bee[n]

- **Intensive:** Chicken hell. Design[ed] with no regard for the bird. Ov[er] dim light and feed that is prep[ared] dietary needs without variety. [The] system has been genetically p[ut] contributes to making this the[...]
- **Freedom Food Indoor:** Bred in[...] to roam and the addition of pe[...] Only slow-growing breeds of c[...]
- **Free-range:** Free to roam outs[ide] At night-time birds are ushere[d] and comfortable furnishings.
- **Freedom Food Free-range:** Lik[e] of the slow-growing breed and [...] such as straw-bales.
- **Organic:** Reared to spec by an[...] the Soil Association or Organi[c] freely by day in organic fields[...] certified feed. Bred in small c[...]

The Devonshire Red

7

Happy chickens make Happy eggs
— the same rules of flavour apply.

Leon's chicken

The slow growing Devonshire [...] chicken of choice. We buy only [...] of farms in the West Country, a[nd...] and eggs are free-range. They e[...] to play with, but at present are y[...] any major internationals.

Chicken Licken

WELL-LOVED TALES

Odd facts

- Catherine de' Medici liked fried artichoke hearts with cock's kidneys and combs (the bit on top of their head like an inflated rubber glove).

- Chickens are descendants of the Red Jungle Fowl (Gallus gallus), a bird found in the Malay jungle.

- No such thing as chickens' eggs — once they lay eggs they stop being chickens and start being hens.

- The first mention of the chicken crossing the road joke was in a New York mag called The Knickerbocker in 1847.

- It takes a hen between 24 and 26 hours to lay an egg.

- Chickens were domesticated a staggering 8,000 years ago.

- The longest chicken flight on record was the equivalent of 17.7 double-decker buses.

- Alektorophobia: fear of chickens.

- If a rooster is not present in a flock of hens, a hen will often take the role, stop laying, and begin to crow.

- Along with turkeys, chickens are the closest living relative of the T-rex.

PORK

Chilley Farm, E. Sussex, Jan 2008

No finer beast has ever waddled this world than the pig. They're revered the world over: Taiwan even holds an annual "Pig of God" festival, and everybody knows that getting your RDA of vitamin P is as important to your mental and physical health as the ones at the beginning of the alphabet.

We've said it before but we'll say it again: it all comes down to what they're fed on and how they live.

As well as being great to eat, pigs are also great eaters and will schnuffle down almost anything. Of course, at the intensive end of the scale (of the big four meats, chickens and pigs are the two that can be reared intensively) that eagerness to please is cruelly taken advantage of, and what little flavor there was is diluted even further by water injection. However, true pig-lovers—and there can be few more enamored than the Spanish—make sure their best beloveds are treated with respect. For example, the world-class *jamón ibérico de bellota* is fed on nothing but acorns for the last few months, for a sensational finish to its life and our ham-to-be.

As for rearing, the pigs we use are free to snarf around the fields in the day, and have little Nissen huts for the night-time. This allows them to live and grow as nature intended, apart from their sleeping quarters, which probably provide better shelter than rural woodland.

Pigs are providers, and are so generous with their bodies for both the fresh and the cured counters.

When it comes to the fresh meat, the main area of misunderstanding is the cooking time for cuts that need to be *à point*, like roasts, loin, or chops. Few things are more disappointing than pork that's gone all mealy, grainy, and gray. To be fair, the pig has already been killed once.

Pork cooks quickly, and although it's not a meat you eat pink, once the heat has penetrated the center* turn it off and by the time it's done what all pigs do best, i.e. a sit and a rest, it'll be perfect.

Beautiful, versatile, and scrumptious in all their multimanifold forms, there simply is no other animal to touch them.

*There are two ways to do this: first and easiest is a meat thermometer—stick it in the center of the thickest part and once the center reaches 143°F take it out. The second and more old-fashioned method is to insert a skewer and after 10 seconds take it out and touch it gingerly to your top lip. If it's cold keep cooking, if it's warm you're close, and if it's shockingly hot you're buggered. I cook all my meat like this and love the antigadgetry approach; once you've got the hang of it you'll never overcook or undercook a piece of meat again.

When I grow up I want to be...

Pork belly Simply an awesome cut, pork belly is a magical thing. It can, of course, be cured for bacon and pancetta and, as if that wasn't impressive enough, it also cooks like a dream. Layers of meat and fat that when braised for hours with something to work with (for example, take spices, vinegar, ginger, fennel, and soy sauce as a starting point of ideas, but not all together), and coaxed into crackling on top, produces simply one of the most satisfying plates of food on the planet.

Ham hocks These do a job that no other part of the pig performs: the role of stock maker. Cheap and too often discarded, there is a load of flavor in the pig's lower hind legs (the muscles must be strong to keep the weight above moving), and as a base for a soup, stock, or pie they just chuck out flavor. Simmer for hours with all the usual stock-ish ingredients, pick the meat off, break it up a little, then launch yourself, the flavorsome stock, and the hog bits in whichever direction you wish to travel.

Loin The supreme roasting joint—the loin on any animal tends to be the choicest cut. The Italians do a wonderful thing where they braise it with milk and sage, while here it is more often subjected to a scorchingly hot oven to become the Sunday roast. Cook it carefully (see previous notes), because with this prime piece of meat the window for perfection is not open that wide.

Sausages Apart from soccer, few subjects can give rise to such instant xenophobia as the sausage: everybody thinks theirs is the best. The truth, of course, is that they're all good—and not just good but great. There are occasions where life wouldn't be worth living without sausages, and the person who first shoved ground-up pork into a length of intestine wins all the ingenuity prizes.

Salami (Italy) / Salchichon © (Spain) The word for the ultimate picnic food comes from the Italian *salare*, to salt. Pork meat and fat, salt and seasonings are tightly packed into differing casings and the result is hung up to dry. Fermentation, humidity, and maturation now play their part… and you wait, because the last vital ingredient is time.

Crackling Listening to various opinions on how to make the best crackling is like listening to politicians: "Rub salt into it," "Don't rub salt into it," "Baste with fat," "Baste with water," "Never baste with fat or water"… and then there's always someone at the back shouting, "Brine it!" One thing everybody agrees on however, is a hot oven. Our money is on scoring the skin to penetrate the fat but not the meat, seasoning heftily with sea salt, a hot oven, and a bit of basting in its own juices. Any hecklers?

© *See Suppliers, page VI in Appendix.*

Ham To make ham you need one pig's leg, plenty of salt, lots of time, and a tried and tested recipe. From country to country all of the above vary, except for the one pig's leg. Originally a way of preserving the flesh, ham has gone on to be one of the world's most successful and accessible forms of pork (but the reconstituted stuff doesn't count). Gammon is from the same cut, but is made using the bacon-curing process. This one couldn't be more British, but for a very different kind of wonderful, try the Spanish *Pata Negra*©.

Bacon Strip bacon from the belly, Canadian bacon from the loin. Smoked or flavored? Any and all of it. Probably the pig's finest hour.

Ribs As is clear from the name of our Love Me Tender Ribs, this xylophone of meat and bone needs lots of time and TLC. Always bother to marinate them at least overnight, and in something punchy too. From there methods differ (ours is on page 226), but as with all cooking it's only *one* way, not *the* way.

Chorizo© Technically a sausage, but so magnificent it deserves its own airtime, Spain's most successful culinary export is made from pork that has been air-cured with salt, garlic, and paprika (either smoked or not), and sometimes sherry and/or oregano. Raw or cooked, salami-style or sausage-style, hot or sweet, there are many choices. But you'd have to go far, maybe even as far as Spain, to find one better than the Catalunyan type we use.

Black pudding© A sausage made of fat and blood. Not very Leon, but a good one will make you swoon… try Spanish *morcilla* for a life-altering experience.

A pork pie, and could you pass the English mustard, please?

© See Suppliers, page VI in Appendix, and the Pig Weekend, page 294.

LAMB

Spring lamb is actually a bit of a misnomer, because by the time it's really at its best to eat it's already early summer. True spring lamb is only weeks old and really hasn't had much time to develop good flavor, but it is much prized in some parts of Europe.

Once lamb gets to a year old, in the UK it is known as hogget; sometimes hogget has better flavor than lamb, and is much cheaper, too. Then at around 18 months to 2 years it moves into being mutton.

New Zealand now supplies the world and us with year-round lamb coming off enormous freezer ships.

Lamb varies a lot in both flavor and fat content, from the most buttery, tender, and attractive piece of meat to something tough, tasteless, and greasy.

In the best possible world you will befriend a farmer, not necessarily in person but over the phone or cyberly: that way you can see how your lamb is reared and find out about its feed; there can be no better assurance than this. Then place an order for a whole or half lamb (and see how dramatically the price drops from buying little cuts), and quickly go out and buy a bigger freezer before your meat arrives by courier tomorrow or the next day©. It really is as easy as that.

Shoulder is a great joint for braising whole, though others prefer to roast it and tug the meat away from the shoulder blade. A long cook of the whole shoulder has a Middle Eastern/Moroccan feel to it, so roll with that by using spices, saffron, preserved lemon, and argan oil in the roasting pan too. It's ready when the meat shrinks to reveal the rounded end of the scapula. Likes to be served with grains like bulgur.

You can also make shoulder steaks. These are cut straight through the bone and are therefore essentially ovoid with a slit of bone in the middle. These are good for grilling and braising.

Chump as it is called in the UK, is the equivalent to the rump on a cow, i.e. it's from the hind quarters above the ball and socket hip joints. As with its beefy counterpart, it's not famed for its tenderness, though it has got truly gorgeous flavor.

Leg is where most of the meat is at: roast it whole on the bone, studded with garlic, rosemary, and anchovies; or ask your butcher to bone it, then stuff with prunes, almonds, mint, and then roll it up and secure with string. Or get the meat ground or diced for the best quality you'll ever taste. Really, this is the big cut it's all about.

Stewing/braising cuts are a great way to get all the flavor out of the meat, from curries to stews. Likes a touch of fruity sweetness, like prunes or apricots, as well as members of the spice world, especially cumin. And just like any dice from the tougher cuts, it takes time to get to its flavor zenith. Primarily comes from the shoulder, breast, and leg, so there can be variations of cooking times, but they all come together at the end.

Above Shoulder steaks *(left)*, Whole shoulder *(right)*
© *See Suppliers, page VI in Appendix.*

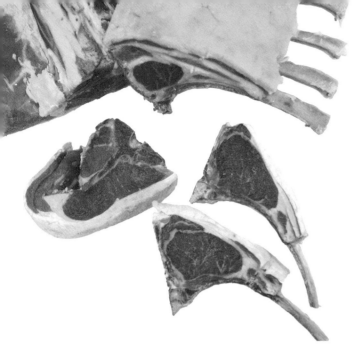

Lamb breasts are a seriously underused cut, so much so that they are often just thrown away by the meat industry. But the benefit of that (if you have a good butcher) is that they're very very cheap. Slender in shape, with ribs in between the defined layers of muscle and fat, which is what gives this slightly unpromising-looking cut such great rewards. Simmer for a few hours in a pot with some basic vegetables, star anise, thyme, cinnamon, juice of an orange, and 2 pints of liquid—half white wine, half chicken stock. Once the meat is easily releasing the rib bones, tug them out and press the meat under weights between layers of waxed paper overnight. Next day throw away the fat that has solidified on the top of the cooking liquor and reduce to a sticky sauce; meanwhile cut the meat into little pieces and fry for a couple of minutes each side for a an amazing appetizer with a little carrot purée.

Racks, cutlets, and chops are among the most superior and prized small cuts on a lamb. Racks and cutlets are both cuts off the rib, with the eye of meat coming from the fillet; chops are a loin cut. Running in the same place as a beef fillet, i.e. along the side where the ribs meet the spine, the loin is a tender, snakelike piece of meat. Each lamb has two racks, and the "best end" is a cut consisting usually of seven ribs, and comes from the end nearest the head. Cutlets are cut through the ribs to make individual rib + meat cuts. Loin chops are cut straight through the backbone very much like a T-bone in steak vernacular.

Seal and roast racks whole, and slice once cooked to show the inner pinkness. Chops and cutlets are best quickly grilled or broiled in order to yield great textures inside and out. Serve with mint sauce.

MUTTON, like hogget, suffers from a bad name. Having been out of fashion for some decades, in recent years it has become more popular. Very good flavor when slow-slow-cooked with other ingredients that need a bit of time, like whole spices and root vegetables. Extremely good value for money. Or take a leaf out of the Victorians' cookbook: mutton chops were the breakfast that built an Empire.

Shanks are from the legs of the animal and should be a bargain. They are taut with intra-muscular tendons—one of those cuts where you benefit price-wise from the fact that they take a while to cook, in the eternal pay-off between time and money. Brown them, then stick them in a pot with lots of wine, stock, onions, and aromatics—a bit of balsamic works well too. Cover and place in a medium oven, for around 1+ hours. Fave of the Moroccans for their tagines. The original "meat falling off the bone" cut.

DON PEVERELLI

BENNY

Where does he grow?
Leon's godfather of good food was initially spawned in sunny Nottingham, where he lived happily with his mom, dad, and two brothers until as a young, eager, bright-eyed chef the winds of change blew him down to London. We found him in the fish section of a West End restaurant and now he spends his time batting between the London Leons, making sure the food is as good as good can be. At night-time he hunkers down in East London with his wife Joey, she of Rhubarb Crisp fame (see page 268), and Cooper the big pup.

Why do we love him?
Benny has a natural, respectful understanding of food, along with a quiet pedantry for perfection and the patience of a saint. Along with only a handful, he was part of the starting lineup at Leon—several seasons before we even had a restaurant—and it has been a proud-making pleasure to watch him flourish, blossom, and continue to bloom. For Leon, Benny has been a truly essential ingredient (and he's well tasty).

What's in it for me?
The best food to the most people.

Anything else?
He can be a right trashbag at Leon parties.

LEON'S STORES

SPICES

Ingredient we love

Allspice

Aka pimento, the unripe berry of *Pimenta dioica*, grows almost exclusively in Jamaica. So-called because the English thought it tasted like all the spices (not to be confused with mixed spice, which is a blend of spices). Most commonly used in cakes (especially Christmas cakes), pickles, Arabic rice dishes (including our pilaf), and Jamaica's bombastic Jerk chicken. In the 18th century Russian soldiers put allspice in their boots to kill the stink. **If you don't have any…**try a blend of nutmeg and cloves.

Caraway*

Indigenous to Europe and Asia Minor, this seed has been long used in Arabic cooking. The plant looks a little like carrot leaves (same family), with its hollow stalks, and the preseed flowers are pinkish. Became popular in Elizabethan England mainly as a sweet snack, sugared and called comfits. The flavor can be most easily discerned in rye bread. Caraway is also big in Jewish food, harissa, apple dishes, sauerkraut, and a delicious after-dinner liqueur called kümmel (these little seeds are excellent for digestion—just chewing on a few can really take your gas away). One of the oldest cultivated spice plants in Europe, going back to the 13th century. **If you don't have any…**go and get yourself some. It's worth the trip and this spice walks alone.

Cardamom

Part of the ginger family, cardamom is native to southern India and Sri Lanka, which are still two of the top three producers. The nonedible pod, or pericarp, is the dried fruit, and is a three-sided ovoid; within each of the three internal chambers there are tiny seeds containing the essential oil, i.e. flavor. Aside from the obvious curries and rice, the taste is particularly suited to sweet

things like cakes, as well as drinks, such as Arabic coffee, Indian chai, or the Swedish gløgg (mulled wine), where the whole pods are infused, thus saving the pernickety task of trying to get the seeds out. **If you don't have any…** although nothing like it, cinnamon often works in its place, especially in sweet things.

Cayenne pepper

This is made from dried and ground whole chile peppers of the cayenne variety, including the seeds, which, as any chile lover knows, is where the fire inside lies. Clearly, then, it should be used with deference and attention… it's as hot as it looks. Cayenne is the capital of French Guiana, squeezed in between Suriname and the top of Brazil on the Atlantic coast. The name "cayenne pepper" is now a bit of a misnomer, because not all of it is made from cayenne chiles or comes from Cayenne. Particularly used with shellfish. See also Chiles, page 51. **If you don't have any…** you can use dried chili powder or paprika.

Celery salt

Made from grinding celery seeds (thus releasing their natural oil, apiol) with salt, this is a kitchen essential for three reasons. The first is ju-ju—the all-important art of making yourself feel at home, happy, and confident in your kitchen: for reasons that have sailed off into the mists of time, celery salt has more ju-ju points attached to it than any other spice, thus proving once and for all that ju-ju and usefulness have absolutely no correlation. The second is for dipping quail eggs in, and the third is Bloody Marys. **If you don't have any…** you'll just have to have your Bloody Mary without it.

©See Suppliers, page VI in Appendix.

Dried chiles *(whole, flakes, and powder)*

This all depends on the chile pepper it's made from: some chiles grow more potent as they dehydrate, but if they were ground long ago they may have lost their fizz. Whole is good to float in soups, slow-cooks, and stocks, especially if you go for some of the interesting thick-skinned, mahogany-colored sort—think mole or chili con carne. Flakes tend to be from the hot bird's-eye variety and are great for pizza. For much more on chiles, turn to page 51. **If you don't have any…** reach for any other kind of fire you can get your hands on, dried, fresh, or in a sauce like Tabasco.

Chinese five-spice

A blend of cinnamon, Szechuan pepper, fennel seed, star anise, and cloves. Nobody uses it in China, but it's useful as an easy way to get loads of flavor at a pinch. Likes duck and pork, however, the same negative principles of authenticity and freshness apply to it as to curry powder (see page 105). **If you don't have any…** use any combination of the components.

Cinnamon

The dried bark of the tree *Cinnamomum zeylanicum*, indigenous to Sri Lanka, this was one of the highest prizes for explorers in the 15th and 16th centuries. Once the outer bark has been discarded, layers of the inner bark are stacked, compressed, and left to curl up and dry, forming long quills. These are then cut into short lengths for sale. Letting the sticks infuse is a far superior way of getting their true flavor than using ground cinnamon, which is often mixed with the ground bark of its lesser cousin, cassia. Very at home with many kinds of cuisines, i.e. Indian curries, Moroccan tagines, Persian khoresht, and Mexican slow-cooks, with North Americans winning the prize for extremely generous use in their muffins, pastries, French toast, and coffee. Good with cooked fruit, too. **If you don't have any…** there isn't really an alternative but you could try a bit of clove, allspice, and cardamom.

Cloves

Tiny, tiny cloves are the unopened flower buds on evergreen trees that grow as tall as skyscrapers. One of the oldest spices recorded in the world, control of the clove trade was the cause of many wars based around the Moluccas, in what is now Indonesia. In the great age of discovery their production was monopolized in turn by the Portuguese, Dutch, and British, which was all very unfair for the locals.

Cloves have been used as a panacea for centuries for all sorts of maladies, from the plague to impotence to toothaches, for which oil of cloves is still the most recognized homeopathic treatment.

Synonymous with Christmas, mulled wine, pickles, pastries, and all things Renaissance.

A big white onion studded with a couple of cloves infusing in the milk is the only way to start your white sauce. **If you don't have any…** try a little cinnamon or allspice.

Coriander seeds*

An important spice for adding layers of flavor, these hard little buggers are vaguely reminiscent of sage, orange, and caraway, and taste nothing like the leaf at all. They are thought to have been introduced to Britain by the Romans as a meat preserver, but its origins are centuries older.

Important in Indian curries and widely used in Arabic countries for dishes like spinach, chickpeas, and meatballs. Meanwhile back in Europe, from northern to central, it features in pickles (including herrings), black rye bread, Belgian wheat beers, and German sausages. Its taste combines especially well with green chile. **If you don't have any…** in Asian dishes cumin seeds just about work, and put dill seeds in your pickles.

* The seedy ones all like to be dry-toasted and ground fresh for maximum effect.

Cumin seeds*

Cumin's origins are thought to be in Eastern Europe and North Africa, where it was much loved in the cooking of antiquity, but it now grows rampantly all over Asia. As part of the intercontinental ingredient trade instigated by Columbus, the Spanish took it to the Mexicans, who loved it as one of their own. Cumin is of the parsley family, recognizable by its feathery leafery and umbels of whitish flowers—but it is definitely the bolder cousin with its easily overpowering flavor. That strong, warm aroma sits extremely well with legumes, fish, roasted eggplant, grilled lamb, grains, and generally crosses borders and cuisines very easily.

1g of cumin has 5.31g of your iron RDA. **If you don't have any...** go heavy on the coriander seed and muscle it up with a few mustard seeds as well.

Curry powder

This is a European invention. Just like chicken tikka masala, it simply does not exist in India, where individual spices would be chosen to go with the flavors in each specific curry.

Ingredients and ratios vary enormously, but the one thing they all have in common is that they need to be cooked thoroughly and gently to re-arouse the cacophony inside. Usually based around coriander and cumin seeds, with curry leaves, mustard seeds, fenugreek, and turmeric also likely to make an appearance. **If you don't have any...** go buy some.

Fennel seeds*

Synonymous in flavor and smell with the ancient Mediterranean. The seeds are even more powerful than the bulb (see page 53), and when used judiciously add much to sausages, fish dishes, salami, and pickles. Later on in the meal you may find them in biscotti or infused into an herbal tea, because they are very good for digestion, shown too by their presence in *supari pan*, the Indian palate cleanser and breath freshener. Also used in hippy toothpastes. **If you don't have any...** fresh or dried dill in some cases and star anise for a more Eastern inflection.

Fenugreek*

This unusual word is a contraction of *foenum graecum*, which literally translates as Greek hay— the clue is in the name as to how abundantly it grows. Bitter in flavor, but with a slight sweetness to it, fenugreek is often one of the bases of curry powder, and is used widely in Middle Eastern cooking.

Its aromatic leaves are known as *methi* in the Middle East and are all-round pot flavorers, while the seeds can be sprouted and taste a little like cress. Part of the pea, soybean, and lentil family. As big in iron as it is in flavor.

Great way to freak up a chicken. **If you don't have any...** mustard seeds are not far off.

Garam masala

A varying blend from northern India, including some or all of the following: black pepper, cardamom, bay, coriander seed, cumin, nutmeg, mace, cloves, and cinnamon. All the seeds are roasted before grinding, which is why it is generally added toward the end or even after the cooking has finished.

It is the life-blood of a lot of Indian savory food, both dry and braised dishes. As with all blends, making your own is infinitely better. **If you don't have any...** make up your own with whichever of the ingredients you can lay your hands on.

Mace

Fresh mace is simply one of the most beautiful and astounding sights in nature: you break open an apricot-like fruit to reveal a fuchsia casing (the aril) that looks like it has been drip-glazed on, so tightly is it clutching its kernel (otherwise known as nutmeg).

Mildly flavored and mildly hallucinogenic, mace is the gentle partner to its more robust inner half, the nutmeg. Used subtly in potted shrimp, cream infusions destined for fish, corned beef, curries, and pickles.

Same family as magnolia, and mostly grown in the Spice Islands.

Mace has nothing to do with mace sprays. **If you don't have any...** use nutmeg please.

* The seedy ones all like to be dry-toasted and ground fresh for maximum effect.

Mustard seeds*

Their name comes from the Latin *mustum ardens*, meaning burning grape. As you'd expect, mustard is native to Europe and the Near East, and is a part of the great and diverse cabbage family. Although there are three different kinds of mustard (black, brown, and yellow/white), all of them have the same easily recognizable bright yellow four-petaled flowers. It was the Romans who promoted and spread mustard's use as a kitchen ingredient, as opposed to the medicinal purposes with which it had long been associated.

Most of the world's seeds go into making prepared mustard, but the baby balls themselves are invaluable in pickles, piccalilli, chutneys, and curries. Heat them dry in a skillet for a very interesting song and dance.

As you'd expect, they clear congestion. Mustard cress is no longer made from sprouting mustard seeds, but from a form of rape seed, which is also a cousin of mustard—same bright yellow flowers.

If you don't have any... mustard is the sensible choice.

Nutmeg

is the recipient of the tight mace-clutch, the kernel around which the mace is woven. Always buy it whole and grate it fresh. This seed grows into an evergreen tree, native to the Spice Islands, and now grows wherever it's light, humid, and hot.

One of the earliest and most successful spices to be traded by the Arabs.

Blatantly its primary use is grated on eggnog and custard tarts, and just try to cook spinach or cheese sauces without it. Often cited in the context of fish, bakery, and creamy pasta sauces.

The first English mention of its hallucinogenic properties was in 1576, when a woman consumed twelve nutmegs and became "deliriously inebriated." Cheap date.

If you don't have any... use mace, silly.

Paprika

This is a ground powder of dried sweet red peppers (seeds out first), which were said to have been taken to their spiritual home (Hungary) by the Turks, though as with all peppers they came originally from the New World. True Hungarian paprika is divided into different echelons of quality: noble sweet, semisweet, rose, strong, and commercial. The Spanish make a wood-smoked paprika (*pimentón*) that you can buy either sweet or hot. Indispensable in goulash, chorizo, deviling, and fish dishes.

If you don't have any... sniff out any chili powder lurking at the back of the cupboard, but use less.

Pepper

Black pepper is the still-green, unripe dried berries of a climbing vine, which is then fermented and sun-dried. White pepper is the seed of the ripened berry, with the fruit casing removed.

The word pepper comes from the Sanskrit *pippali*, meaning long pepper, and its fierceness comes from its volatile oil, piperine, and resin.

White pepper is weaker in flavor, and generally only used in pretentious French dishes where it is thought black flecks would spoil the look.

Much loved by the Romans, even though it was hideously expensive—Gibbon tells us that Alaric the Goth demanded 3,000 pounds of pepper as part of his ransom for Rome in the 5th century.

Pepper is ubiquitous worldwide now, and if there is a downside to its mass popularity, it is that people forget its true spice status and tend to overlook making it a star player in its own right. Singapore is now the center of the world pepper trade.

Pink peppercorns come from a tree, not a vine, and are therefore a completely different species.

If you don't have any... you must be the only person in the country who doesn't.

Ras-el-hanout

A romantic blend of supposedly 27 spices from North Africa, with variations from country to country as you move across the Maghreb. Of the 27, cumin, coriander seeds, turmeric, ginger, and cardamom are the only surefire staples, with cinnamon, oregano, cayenne, and damask rose nearly always being present too. Some versions in Morocco used to contain the notorious Spanish fly (which is actually a green beetle), but that was more for a desired aphrodisiac effect than for flavor.

A must in tagines and the Moroccan classic *bstilla* or *pastilla*, it's also particularly well paired with lamb, game, and birds.

If you don't have any… use whichever of the solo ingredients.

Saffron

The stigmas of the crocus plant, saffron is the most expensive spice in the world: 4,320 crocuses are needed to yield just under 1 ounce of saffron, and it is dried in sealed containers to prevent it from bleaching.

Originally from the Middle East but then spreading to India and Spain, all before the 10th century, it has been traded for centuries for medicinal reasons, for dye, and for food.

Its name comes from *za'faran*, meaning yellow in Arabic, and the Persian *safra*, which translates the same way.

It is generally thought now that the best stigmas come from southeastern Spain (the world's No.1 producer), but some still swear by the Iranian ones.

Some dishes that simply couldn't be made without saffron: *risotto milanese*, paella, rouille, biriyani, and, of course, Cornish saffron cake.

Zeus slept on a bed of saffron.

If you don't have any… use turmeric very, very sparingly and save up for some of the good stuff.

Star Anise

is so-called because of its beautiful appearance, with carpels off a central column and a seed in each one. Thought to be indigenous to Asia, and used mostly in their cuisine (it's one of the ingredients in Chinese five-spice), especially for pork and poultry. On the western side of the world, star anise is used for poaching fruits and in the making of Galliano (essential in Harvey Wallbangers), but its weirdest use has to be because of the shikimic acid in it. This was snapped up worldwide by pharmaceutical companies during the bird flu epidemic of 2005–6, since it is a principal part of the vaccine Tamiflu. Not related to anise, but is thought to taste a bit like it. **If you don't have any…** use fennel seeds and a pinch of Chinese five-spice.

Sumac

Made of ground-up hairy, berrylike things (not true berries) from a shrub of the *Rhus* genus, sumac was the original kind of sour, before lemons were on the Roman scene. Mainly used in the food of the Middle East and Africa, sumac brings a special kind of fruity tartness to any dish it's added to. Tends to be used at the end as a seasoning rather than for slow cooking.

Principal uses: sprinkled on the kebabs of Iraq, Turkey, and Iran, on fattoush salad, and on rice dishes. Part of the mighty trio that makes up *za'atar*, along with dried wild thyme and sesame seeds. This great blend is delicious baked onto flatbread or sprinkled on eggs. Sour and special.

If you don't have any… a little squeeze of lemon takes care of the sour thing, but the berry part is irreplaceable.

Turmeric

Turmeric is a rhizome—the horizontal stem of a plant that grows underground, just like ginger, its cousin. Noted much more for its color than for its flavor, turmeric is the oldest natural food dye in the world, and is now seen in ingredients lists as E100. When you cut into the fresh root it is practically orange, but once dried and ground that changes to a duller yellow.

Turmeric is indispensable all over Asia, but particularly in India, its principal producer. It features in most curry powders, and during the time of the Raj, the British took it back home with them and used it for piccalilli. **If you don't have any…** use a very small amount of ginger mixed with an equal part of dust.

---

* The seedy ones all like to be dry-toasted and ground fresh for maximum effect.

GRAINS, FLOURS & CEREALS

GRAINS

Quinoa

is mostly grown in Peru, with Bolivia being the next biggest producer, and has been for some 5,000 years (Leon's comes over on a slow boat).

The big news is that quinoa is being hailed as the food of the future for its massive protein count—just about double other grains, such as rice and barley. It also contains calcium, phosphorus, iron, vitamin E, and several of the B vitamins. Its oils are good and it's also a useful source of fat for vegans.

Pronounced keen-wa, it formed the staple diet of the Incas and their descendants, until the Spanish arrived and told them to grow something more European instead. Quinoa is only produced in developing countries that could do with a hand up, so there's global economic points free with every pack you buy.

Rinse it well first (or else it can taste bitter when cooked), then treat it like rice. Sprinkle it on salads, but to really motor through it try using it in place of couscous or rice. As with all grains, it's not all that interesting on its own, so sharpen it up with some herbs, lemon juice, and olive oil.

Pearl Barley

meaning barley without the skin, is up to 80% starch and can be used by us at a steady rate of energy for up to 10 hours. Barley is a seriously ancient grain (spotted in Japan 7,500 years ago), and malted barley (i.e. barley that's been allowed to germinate and then quickly dried to stop the process) has long been the basis for making beer.

It takes about an hour to cook and is the ideal grain for warming broths and winter stews; pearl barley seems to have a particular love for inexpensive cuts of meat that need long, slow cooking, like simmering with ham hocks and braises using mutton.

You can also handle it in the same way as risotto for a creamier finish. Or, by pour boiling water onto it and letting it steep, you can then strain it off to make barley water, which is delicious when flavored and good for your skin.

Bulgur

is generally made from the same wheat as pasta, durum, and has been steamed, hulled, and cracked, which goes to explain why it's sometimes known as cracked wheat. Another very good grain, with all the minerals and slow-release sugar and starch. Generally these granules of grain are just large enough to need little cooking (though Leon's great friend Claudia Roden does hers just with an extended sit in hot water in a warm place), but nothing more serious than a bit of a simmer. Loves olive oil, lemon juice, tomatoes, and herbs, as shown by being the grain of choice in tabbouleh.

Also likes stock, meat (rather than fish), and spices and can be used to make a very nutty-flavored pilaf.

Think of it as couscous's butch sibling.

Couscous

is widely liked because it tastes great and cooks faster than you can say "cup-a-soup." Synonymous with the food of Morocco, couscous is made from rubbed semolina, which in turn is bits of milled durum wheat, which makes it basically the same as pasta.

Apart from the less often seen use of adding it to soups and stews (right at the end), the tried and tested way to handle it is:

1. Tip the couscous into a bowl and pour on a glug of olive oil.
2. Rub the granules between your hands for a minute so they are all coated with oil.
3. Cover with seasoned boiling water or stock to just above the level of the grains.
4. Cover the dish with plastic wrap for a couple of minutes, then break up any clumps either by hand or with a fork.
5. If you're serving at room temperature, only add herbs once the couscous has totally cooled so they stay nice and green.

FLOURS & CEREALS

Flour, being essentially anything that's milled to a fine powder, is clearly a highly varied group, counting such extremes as rice flour, chestnut flour, and, the Romans' favorite, acorn flour in their number. This is the bunch of flours we use at Leon:

Whole-wheat

Though sometimes known as wholemeal, technically with flours it's whole wheat, and that comes under the umbrella of wholemeal. All "wholemeal" means is that the entire grain is milled, rather than the husks being removed. The reason why whole-wheat flours are better is that they are less refined, therefore they have more fiber and are a complex carb. This means it takes longer to absorb into your body and keeps your energy levels flowing and constant.

Besan

Also known as gram flour, this flour is made from chickpeas, and is a celiac's best friend when it comes to binding. We use it in our Sweet Potato Falafel because it soaks up the excessive wetness of the potatoes once they're roasted and also brings a pleasantly Asian little flavor to the mixture. Better known across the world as what usually holds onion bhajis together.

There are two main types of chickpeas: *desi*, generally coming from Iran and Ethiopia, are darker with a rougher skin, and *kabuli*, which are lighter and are the ones we use.

The main ingredient of *farinata*, a northern Italian baked bread, *socca*, the Niçoise equivalent, and endless delicious Indian pancakes, this is the gluten-free flour of the future to play with in our allergy-increasing times.

All-purpose

We use all-purpose flour for baking because whole-wheat pastry just isn't much fun. At six o'clock we switch to a grilled Greek flatbread that's made with white flour because the people who eat with us say they prefer something a bit less challenging of an evening. Fair enough.

If you are having the kind of day where you want/need something sweet, go the whole way and enjoy that sweet something, rather than denying yourself some of the pleasure by giving a cursory nod toward health. Pecan pie with whole-wheat pastry? I don't think so.

All-purpose flour isn't the worst thing in the world by any means, but to get to be that white it has clearly been refined and processed, which means it's lost most of its nutritional value. All of this leads to it being high GI, so eating lots of food with white flour tends to result in peaks and troughs of energy.

However, there are some things that just don't work with whole-wheat: pastry and pasta being prime examples. And arguably, delicate summer cucumber sandwiches.

"00" Flour

made from durum wheat—see Pasta, page 114.

Wheat Germ

is located at one end of the wheat kernel and is the nutritionally rich, as opposed to starchy, part of it. Particularly loaded with vitamin E (otherwise known as "the fertility vitamin") and folic acid, so specially useful and recommended for those trying to make babies, or indeed with one already under construction. Good protein and helpful oils too.

Millet Flakes

Millet is a grassy-looking plant, and although it is relatively unused over here in Britain it is central to the diet of vast amounts of the planet. It prefers hotter climates where wheat doesn't grow very well, such as Africa, and is high in fiber, protein, vitamins, and beneficial minerals. As far back as Neolithic times, long before rice was omnipresent, it was the staple of the Chinese and, even though the taste is nutty and mildly interesting, it's really for the nutritional value that it is an international blockbuster.

SALT°

Salt is one of the simplest, most important, and purest ingredients on the planet. In the hands of some mass-production food companies, salt has become a danger to our health, but equally it is as necessary as water to keep our organs working.

Those simple white crystals have been the cause of countless wars, alliances, and betrayals. Legions have been paid in it and revolutions have been started by it. Salt has been the basis of taxation and tyranny, settlements and symbolism, for as long as man has walked upright. It is mighty in so many ways, and the current hidden uses of it as a cheap flavor enhancer have socially battered this king of the kitchen into a cowering corner.

Salt is not, and never should be, a dirty word. The trouble is that it's our very genetic make-up that has allowed this sorry state of affairs to come about. The average adult's body needs about 6g of salt a day to keep functioning well, and over the last hundreds of thousands of years it's been hard for us (as in mankind) to meet our ideal RDA. Our bodies are evolutionarily preprogramed to get it where we can, but now that's all changed: the speed of the developing food industry has overtaken the speed of evolution and we can, and do, get salt (in staggering quantities) in almost all the prepared foods that are currently dominating our diet. So we have the interesting predicament of our brain trying to override our ancient-but-tried-and-tested survival instinct, which isn't really working. The result, as we know all too well, is a state of play where high blood pressure, heart attacks, and kidney damage are at an all-time high* but in the history of salt, our time, our season, is just a tiny granule.

Salt has always been won from the earth in one of two methods: you can either evaporate seawater in some way, or you can just dig it out.

The first way is the older, initially just letting the sun slowly do its thing, as in Maldon, in Essex, where man has been making salt for more than 2,000 years.

Other sources are provided by the salt mines of Poland and Austria (Salzburg means "salt mountain"). And the many vast salt lakes and deposits sitting there on the surface of our planet in such diverse places as the US, China, and the Sahara. Salt has and always will be a truly worldwide commodity.

And all this because man really needs it, and not just to pacify our pasta: at present the world is producing about 187 million tons a year, and a lowly 6% of it goes into the food business. The chemical industry takes the lion's share, for everything from PVC to bleach to water softeners.

But salt has been multitasking for years: long before fridges it was essential for making your food last. Thanks to the wonderful world of electricity, we take food preservation for granted, but you can't go around slaughtering a whole pig every time you need a sausage; the curing process has been vital to man's nutritional intake for centuries. Now, of course, we do it just for flavor, but many great dishes wouldn't exist without these ancient survival techniques—bacalau, duck confit, anchovies, preserved lemons, Parma ham… and who could imagine a world without pickles?

As with any ingredient, quality is a big factor: plain table salt does the job in the same way that a late-night kebab does. Nothing more. Maybe just for pasta or blanching water. Proper sea salt enhances and lifts the whole experience with its beauty and absolute purity of flavor.

Salt never spoils or goes bad—though sometimes it can suffer from a little damp, as well as the current bad press. Classically it is associated with both good and evil: in Leonardo da Vinci's *The Last Supper* Judas has a spilt cellar by his elbow, signifying something sinister, yet Jesus called his disciples the salt of the earth.

And he was right: not only as old as the hills, it is the hills, and the seas, and a significant part of all of us—blood, sweat, and tears.

Interestingly, a lot of this thought process can also be applied to the sugar-fest that is currently being laced through our foods, leading in turn to the globesity epidemic that is seizing the developed world.

PASTA

There is a romantic misconception that the recipe for rudimentary pasta was brought back by Marco Polo from his 13th-century Far East explorations. If we were just taking the Italians' word for it, we might be dubious of *their* claim of originality (in China, noodle-making is as old as parts of the Great Wall), but there are frescoes of activites similar to pasta-making on the walls at Pompeii (a city that stopped abruptly on August 24, A.D. 79, way before the great Venetian adventurer set sail) that support their claim.

What you need to know about pasta is...
There are two ways of making pasta: both use durum wheat ground into "00" flour (the double zero indicates the superfine grind needed for a smooth dough), and the simpler pasta uses only water to bring it together, while the other is enriched with egg. The Italians, who love making rules almost as much as they like breaking them, say that fishy pastas should never be made with the eggy dough because land and sea should not mix.

The best pasta is formed through a bronze die, not a modern Teflon or plastic one, which gives the pasta a much rougher texture. This is a good thing because it gives your sauce of choice, be it a traditional *ragù*, a meaty one, or a simple infused oil, more to adhere to and it doesn't all collect in the bottom of the bowl.

Salt the water liberally; Leon food heroine Elizabeth David says a drop or two of olive oil raises the boiling point and therefore it's less likely to boil over, but others we also respect believe it's the impurities in the salt that stop the overflow. Any which way, if you do both and keep an eye on the heat you won't make a mess of your stove.

The best pasta is made by people who grow, mill, and make their own flour—a lot of pasta packages that say "Made in Italy" has in fact been made using flour from other countries.

If your pasta is cooked but you need a few minutes before serving, leave it sitting in the water off the heat, rather than draining it and letting it get all claggy, sticky, and squashed in a colander.

In all our thorough and yet slightly idiosyncratic research we found an A–Z of pastas, from the tiny stuffed *agnolini* to the long, tubular *ziti*, with the exceptions of H, I, J, X, and Y.* Some are named after parts of the body, and in doing so nod toward the Italians' love of life and art—*linguine* are little tongues, *tortellini* your belly button, *orecchiette* means small ear, and *riccio* look like curly hair. There are some that are testament to their tumultuous past and religious fervor, like *strozzapreti* (strangle the priest) and *campanelle* (so called for their resemblance to church bells). Some pay homage to their romanticism—*gemelli*, being two twists of pasta intertwined, means twins. And then there's the inspiration of nature: *gigli* are lily-shaped, *penne* means feathers or quills, while *conchiglie* refers to conchlike shells. The language of pasta is like a stroll through everything that really matters to this greatest of countries: history, culture, beauty, and love.

Shape	Examples	What it's used for
Long & Thin	*Capellini, Linguine, Spaghetti, Spaghettini*	Smooth sauces with little bits—bolognese, pesto, extra virgin olive oil-based (chile, parsley, garlic), seafood.
Ribbon/nests	*Pappardelle, Tagliatelle, Fettuccini*	Primarily meat, veal, rabbit, bacon (carbonara) intense sauces—autumnal and wintry things.
Short, dry fun shapes	*Orecchiette, Penne, Farfalle, Fusilli, Macaroni*	Chunky sauces, handfuls of fresh leaves (arugula), and finishing with cheesy chunks (ricotta, mozzarella). Standard tomato sauce *al forno*—baked in the oven.

Unless you count a can of alphabetti spaghetti, but we think that's probably cheating.

GREAT RICES
OF THE WORLD

Red Rice

is a longish-grain variety that grows mainly in the areas either around the Himalayas or in the US. There is also a French version—named after the Camargue district in the Languedoc region—that is shorter and starchier. This beautiful rice is nutty, like brown basmati, and has a powerhouse of protein inside it. As with all kinds of rice, however, we are unable to digest all the protein in them because they don't provide us with the necessary amino acids needed to break them down. This is why rice is often eaten with beans and/or meat that do contain protein-digesting enzymes, so we can get out of it all that it has on offer. This is particularly true in poor countries where they can't afford to be wasteful with nutrients.

Risotto Rice

is a fat, short-grained rice that just reeks of all things Italian. It is loaded with starch, which we can then translate into units of energy. The most important region for growing risotto rice is in the north of Italy, in the Po Valley, where 500 years ago the Venetian Doges ordered the first rice cultivation. There are lots of different kinds of risotto rice, but really only two that people remember: arborio and carnaroli. The former is your all-purpose risotto grain, with a high starch content to get that lovely creamy finish. The latter is considered a bit more refined and is used as a back-drop for risottos featuring ingredients with a divalike status, like white truffle or lobster. Risotto rice grains are fairly similar in shape to both sushi rice (which is just a bit whiter) and pudding rice (which is just a bit shorter and fatter, as anything to do with puddings logically should be), and although you can't make sushi with risotto rice you can use it in puddings.

Whole books have been written on how to make the perfect risotto and, because the purpose of this book is to show you a snapshot of ingredients we love, we will leave the lengthy explanations to others. However, Leon's top risotto tips are: You need a great stock, not just a good one. Feed and starve baby, all the way. Once all the work is done, give her a good five-minute rest in private (i.e. lid on) with a big lump of butter slowly melting on top. Parmesan lastest, and don't forget a final look at the seasoning. Smaller portions are much more elegant and somehow yummier.

Brown Basmati

At Leon we use an organic brown basmati rice from India (Fairtrade when our supply allows) for our pilaf. Back in the day, we opened in Carnaby Street with white basmati as our resident carb, but after only a couple of months we ditched the white for two reasons close to our heart: taste and health. Brown basmati is low GI, which means that the natural sugars inside it are absorbed and released slowly into your body, making for sustained energy levels throughout the day. For those of you who think this is claptrap nonsense, we dare you to try a bowl of each for lunch on two consecutive days and see how your afternoon feels. Eye-opening stuff. Brown basmati is quite a long grain and still has the dark husk on, which the white does not, and in that casing there are things that are useful to our body, like fiber and B vitamins. You don't have to be a nutritionist to work out that the browner stuff, be it bread, flour, sugar, etc., is generally better for you, and rice is no exception to this. But health without flavor is no good in our book, and what swung it for us was the much more interesting texture and flavor that brown basmati brought to the party; nutty, chewy, and just a load more interesting than its anemic cousin—it even looks more varied and appetizing. You can use brown basmati wherever you might have used white; it takes about twice the length of time to cook, but that's a direct reflection of the fiber factor. Brown basmati rice particularly suits spicy dishes from the Middle East.

Wild Rice

isn't a rice but an aquatic grass seed. It's been called "The Caviar of All Grains," but clearly by people who've never had caviar. It is mostly cultivated in Canada and the US, past and present, and was a staple in the diet of the Native American peoples. True wild rice is harvested largely by canoe and therefore it's both deeply environmental and pretty expensive, so it makes sense financially to mix it with other kinds of rice, or scatter it through salads. It takes a while to cook—keep simmering until you see it just split and reveal a whitish inside—and, given its name, the flavor is suitably woody and natural-tasting. Nutritionally, wild rice is fibrous and loaded with protein, minerals (potassium and phosphorus) and B vitamins. In the last few decades a farmed version has appeared that is a lesser version of the proper stuff.

LEGUMES

Beans, being a kind of seed, are a warehouse of nutritional storage. They are a complex carb (i.e. low GI), while also high in protein, essential minerals, vitamin B, and fiber. It's not just Jack who thinks that beans are magical—beans are always close to Leon's heart.

Some kind of bean can be found pretty much all over the Earth, from the New World to the Old, Asia to the Antipodes. Each culture has its own native legume(s) that are much loved and take pride of place in the kitchen.

Although they may end up in a plethora of different dishes, the beginnings of dried legume treatment are all roughly the same (except for the first four on the table which don't need soaking).

Soak overnight in plenty of cold water—the bigger the bean the longer the soaking time needed. This softens their skins and stops them from splitting in the pan, as well as reducing cooking time.

Change the water and bring them up to a very gentle simmer with some flavorsome friends: onion, bay, half a head of garlic, thyme/rosemary, and a floating tomato or chile always feels about right. No salt at this stage, please, because it toughens the skins.

Once cooked (anything between about 45 minutes and a couple of hours, depending on size),

	Native to...	Kitchen usage	Culinary friends	Bit of chat
Split Peas *Yellow & Green*	Western Asia, Northern Europe, 17th-century England.	Dhal, tarka (with garlic) or chana (with chickpeas). Pea and ham soup if you don't have field-matured (known as marrowfat) peas.	Spices, stocks, pig bits. Very nice with crispy fried shallots on top.	When cooked they turn the most beautiful muted color with a sublime creamy texture.
Lentils *Red*	Another Indian favorite, as well as the whole of North Africa.	It's really all about the quick soup—half an hour from start to finish. And lovely soft dhals.	Coconut milk, spices, greens (like spinach or chard), onions, and butter.	Can be treated like rice and cooked like risotto, but beware because nothing happens ... and then they're mush.
Lentils *Brown/Green*	World over, but particularly the lentil of choice around India and Italy.	Curries, hippy bakes, *zuppa di lenticchie*, drizzled over warm salads and super with *bollito misto*.	These love a heavy oil like strong extra virgin or pumpkin. Strong herby things too, like salsa verde.	The cooking water is very nutritious. Think twice before discarding it because it makes a great veg stock/soup base.
Lentils *Puy*	France mainly, but since the '90s all over the Western world.	Anywhere you want your lentil to hold its shape. With cod and salsa verde—a classic.	Particularly good with fish and organ meants (not together). Dijon. Porky bits. All the herbs.	The most beautiful of the lentil family, with their green speckled skin... but don't they know it.
Haricot	Ubiquitous in the Western world.	Predominantly cassoulet and baked beans.	Meat (pork, duck), tomatoes, vinegars.	Haricot is a general term that includes navy beans, great Northern beans, and cannellini beans.
Flageolet	France, and increasingly in the US.	Classically with lamb, and to meet your other springier bean needs.	Cream, mint, and cider too, if in Normandy. Pigs, as well.	These are a bit more discreet and elegant, like French women.
Cannellini	Italy, specifically Tuscany.	Makes the best soups, since the texture goes all creamy when par-blitzed. Nice puréed and bakes well too.	Garlic, particularly when toasted to golden. Flat-leaf parsley, chicken stock. Extra virgin olive oil.	They take 80 days to grow. The bean of early summer.

drain them if you need to, like for salads, but for any other dishes like soups, bakes, etc., ideally any cooking water left will become a part of the dish because it's heavy with nutrients and flavor.

If you're heading for a salad or having the beans as a side just like that, dress them well now. You can be generous with your best extra virgin because it won't be going near the heat again. Some acid (lemon juice or a choice vinegar). A bit of minced garlic and herbage sits well. By now the beans will be craving salt, so satisfy them with a light flurry of flakes of sea salt. They are never better than when eaten still warm.

If your beans are to be cooked again, whether headed for the oven or the pot, then all that dressing isn't necessary yet. However, the list of their affinities above still holds true: beans like herbs, salt, garlic, spices, chile, oil, and vinegar. When you bake them again—whether for a stunning French cassoulet, a mighty Brazilian feijoada or a hippy lentil bake—always keep their friends in mind.

Ancient Egyptians believed that when the spirit passed on, it went to a place called the "Bean Field."

Leapfrog your legume...
If you can't get hold of your bean of choice then try the ones either side of it in the table below for something we think is a bit similar (except the jump from puy lentils to haricot, which admittedly is a bit of a stretch). Obviously cooking times will change depending on the size and density of the stand-in legume.

	Native to…	Kitchen usage	Culinary friends	Bit of chat
Cranberry Beans	Italy, especially early fall when you get the beautiful fresh ones.	Sits very well in soups, whether brothy *brodo* or thick *pasta e fagioli*.	Extra virgin, garlic, lemon, flat-leaf parsley—all the usual Italian faves and flavors.	When fresh, the most beautiful bean on the planet: off-white with pink paint splatters. Very special chalky texture.
Pinto	Central and South America.	Refried beans. Day-long, one-pot braises.	All the chiles and spices associated with their region.	Special chalky texture, like their cousins the cranberry bean. They are thought to have originated in the Andes.
Red Kidney	Central and South America, West Indies.	*Chili con carne*, or *chili sin carne* for that matter. Rice an' peas.	A meatiness to stand up to the beans. Latin and Caribbean spices. Chiles and tomatoes.	Kidney beans have a toxin in them, so change their cooking water once it has come to a boil and don't try to sprout them.
Black Beans	All about the Spanish and the Latins.	Headed for all the slow-cooks (like *feijoada*, with its multiple pork presence). Soup.	Cumin, lard, tomatoes, pig.	Aka black turtle beans; still big in Portugal (but not so much in Spain), as well as ex-colonies like Brazil.
Black-eyed Beans	China, Africa. Deep South—think soul food.	Asian stir-fries. With Cajun grills and gumbos. *Moi moi*—delicious Nigerian dumplings.	Things with zing: chile, fresh ginger, scallions; crisp greens. Rice and spice.	Nigeria is the biggest producer; also known as black-eyed peas. Go inky-pinky-purple when cooked.
Chickpeas	*Tous le Med* since time eternal.	Hummus by the truckload. In brothy/brodo type dishes. Falafel.	Olive oil, lemon, chorizo, shellfish, especially mussels. Herbs, peppers, tomatoes, and garlic.	Aka *garbanzo*—so much fun to say.
Lima Beans	They really like big beans in Greece and all around the Med.	Because they're so rich and fat they hold up very well on their own, i.e. meat-free.	Braised (with tomatoes), smoked or spiced pork, like chorizo. Tripe too if you're Spanish.	In the South, fresh Lima beans are served with collard greens. Yum.

Ingredient we love

SEEDS

Seeds, lentils, and sandals have all been loved by hippies (or New Agers, as they prefer to be called now) for decades beacuse of their natural, earthy flavor. We use a mix of the four below on many of our dishes, from pilaf to porridge to Superfood Salads because it rings the bell on our two biggest food principles, flavor and health.

They just taste delicious; little bites that crunch and burst into a nuttiness in your mouth. And then there's what's inside them: lots of protein, masses of minerals (especially zinc, iron, and calcium), B vitamins, and polyunsaturated oils.* Surely it's just rude not to take advantage. Little seeds make big things, which works for us both nutritionally and philosophically.

They are even better for you if you don't toast them, which we do, but it's a pay-off with flavor (we like what happens to them as they gently roast), and they do retain plenty of their goodness through a little heat.

Flax seeds

Flax seeds are rich in Omegas 3 and 6, which are essential to our bodies. In my youth their oil was also essential to my artful lacrosse stick because it is used for enriching wood to stop it from becoming dry and brittle.

They are exceptionally good for our intestines, and to absolutely get the most of them—as anyone who's done a detox program knows—we should soak them overnight and eat them by the teaspoon in the morning (soaking them releases a mucus which makes them more cooperative with our guts).

They work for farmers, too, because they are one of the fastest-growing cultivated crops, and also need notably little human intervention in the form of fertilizers or chemical sprays: naturally clean and healthy.

The plant these tiny teardrops grow into has been known since time immemorial for the fabric that comes from flattening its stems, linen, and some varieties make a very pretty true blue flower, as rarely seen in nature.

Sesame

A sesame plant grows to about 5 to 6 feet tall, with large purple or white bell-shaped flowers that look a bit like foxgloves. The plant has hairy leaves and the seedpods, which are just over an inch long, hang down below the flowers. When they are ripe these pods dramatically ping open, which led to the phrase "Open Sesame" in the *Arabian Book of 1,001 Nights*.

Sesame seeds are 50% oil, 25% protein, and the rest is made up of vitamins, minerals, fiber, and the like.

They are the main component in tahini—vital for hummus—and in a sweeter sense in halva.

Probably the single most useful of the seeds, and one of the earliest crops to be cultivated for its oils and flavor—there are pictures in an Egyptian tomb of a baker sprinkling them on bread 4,000 years ago—while the Chinese were burning them to make soot for ink a couple of millennia B.C.E.

Sunflower

Nothing quite sings of sunshine like the sunflower, and internally they bring sunshine to your body too. Along with all the usual protein, and powering vitamins and minerals, there's lots of vitamin E in them as well, which careers though our system neutralizing the free radicals that rust our cells.

All of these four seeds are also associated with oils, but none on such a mass scale as the sunflower, or *girasol* as the Spanish call it (see Oils, page 132).

Be sure to get the right kind, because the striped ones fed to birds are much lower in oils than the grayish ones.

Pumpkin

It's obvious that pumpkin seeds are stupendous things—such tiny greenness grows into such massive orangeness (not to mention twisting vinelike tendrils up to 16 feet long) with the addition of nothing except sun and rain. The mother fruit, *Cucurbita maxima*, is pretty much wall-to-wall goodness anyway (see Pumpkins, page 59), and it puts everything it needs back into its seeds for proliferation.

Particularly good for men's prostates.

Buy in small amounts and keep in the fridge for maximum effectiveness.

DRIED FRUIT

Apricot See page 17.

Currants

These little babes are the result of drying black Zante grapes, and the first ones came from Corinth in Greece. Mostly used in baking (think Eccles cakes, spotted Dick, and squashed fly cookies) or in ethnic rice dishes—at Leon they currently (haha) go into our pilaf for a proper Middle Eastern flavor.

They have nothing to do with fresh, summer currants, and it is thought they were named after their Greek birthplace (by someone with a serious speech impediment). Originally they would have been sun-dried for winter sustenance, which is largely how we still use our dried fruit stores.

They now come from most of the places you associate with New World wines, like Australia, California, and South Africa.

See also Grapes, page 20.

Dates

Indigenous to Arabia, then spread with the caravan trails all around the Med, these are nature's perfect gift to the desert traveler: lots of natural sugar, protein, vitamins, minerals, and fiber, all encased in a small thing that's easy to transport, hence the Arabs' name for the date palm, the Tree of Life.

All palm trees make a datelike fruit, but it is only *Phoenix dactylifera* (cool name) that makes the dates we adore. They grow in massed bunches, a little like bananas, on drooping arms known as bracts, each laden down with an average of 45 pounds of fruit.

Cooking with them in savory dishes brings a multileveled, sweet, fruity richness, particularly good in slow braises with duck or pork.

The basis of Britain's much-loved sticky toffee pudding (along with lots of baking soda). Medjool dates are like natural toffee.

Figs See page 18.

Goji berries

This new kid on us Westerners' superfood scene has only been allowed to be sold in the EU since 1997 but has been adored by Tibetan monks for thousands of years. Chinese medicine believes the color on their outside matches the parts inside you they are good for i.e. liver, kidneys, and lungs, as well as being general immune-boosters. A scant cup of goji berries, or wolfberries as they are also known, provides you with one-quarter of your total mineral RDA, and all of your iron, zinc, selenium, and riboflavin; having a handful in your pocket to munch on through the day is not such a bad idea.

Closely related to tomatoes, and if you squint at both of them in their dried and shriveled state they even look a bit similar.

Dates, Eastern Med, 2007

Anchovies See page 81.

Chipotle in adobo © Chipotles are jalapeño chiles that have been dry-smoked, which gives them the most exceptional flavor. The "adobo" part means they've been cooked in a vinegary tomato sauce, but you can also buy them dried. If you chuck one into a sauce it adds a sweet, earthy, and BBQ-like taste; we use them in our Smokin' Chili Sauce.

Capers and their berries Capers come from a straggly plant with juicy round leaves that grows wild out of tiny cracks all over the Med. Their flowers are spectacular and recognizable by their four white pink-tinged petals, a firework starburst of purple stamen in the middle, and a golden heart. Capers are the tight triangular buds and they are graded from *surfines* (tiny) to *capucines*, and the berries are the fertilized fruit. Fresh, they are very bitter, but when stored in salt or vinegar they mellow out and take on the taste we couldn't live without. In salsa verde, *beurre noisette*, and with fish or veal, these tiny buds are literally bursting with flavor. The berries make for excellent tapas.

Chocolate Our chocolate of choice is Valrhona's Guanaja; as everybody knows, chocolate is one of the goodies Columbus brought back from a small island off Honduras, which happens to be called Guanaja.

Micro-moment on making chocolate: slimy seeds in white goo are pulled out of the fruit, which are then fermented and dried. Then they are roasted, ground, and a liquor comes out that can be broken down into cocoa solids and cocoa fat. The 70% referred to in Valrhona chocolate is the amount of cocoa solids, which means that only 30% is made up of cocoa butter, sugar, and anything else. This is excellent, high-quality chocolate (just to give you an idea, Hershey's Special Dark has 45% cocoa solids). We use Valrhona 70% to make our hot chocolate.

Coconut The brown nut is actually the seed once surrounded by a fruit with a green husk. Poke a skewer into the three little eyes and out comes a clearish liquid that has exactly the same isotonic electrolyte balance found in isotonic sports drinks. Neat. The white flesh is delicious eaten right there and then, or can be grated and dried for desiccated coconut. Creamed coconut and coconut milk are made in a way surprisingly akin to their dairy counterparts: hot water is poured onto desiccated or freshly ground coconut and, as it cools, what floats to the top is coconut cream and what stays below is coconut milk. The clear water naturally inside the "nut" is not involved at all.

Adding coconut milk to your curry makes it wonderfully creamy, and in a dairy-free kind of way. Much more nutritious too.

Fish sauce *Nam pla*, as it's known in Thailand, is a violent condiment that is made from the water that runs off rotten salted fish, commonly anchovies, and always of a small variety. Tastes a lot nicer than it sounds. Never used on its own, but added to sauces, dips, curries, soups, and stir-fries, it brings layers of flavor. Widely used in all southeastern Asian cooking and the Romans were rather fond of it, too.

Ingredient we love

Fructose is a simple sugar naturally occurring in fruits, plants, and honey, and root vegetables, such as beets or sweet potatoes. It is sweeter than sucrose (common sugar) and, as a rough guide, you use two-thirds the amount of fructose that you would sugar. This is a good thing because using less of anything that has been extracted is better for you and the planet.

The big reason why we like it so much is that of all the common sugars, it has the lowest GI by far, meaning that it is absorbed more slowly into the bloodstream and therefore makes for a longer energy release. All sugars are carbohydrates, which simply means they are made of hydrogen, oxygen, and carbon molecules in some arrangement or other. It is the structural layout of the molecules that defines whether we absorb them easily or not.

For most of us the slow-release option is favorable, on the fairly basic level of avoiding the notorious highs and lows of a sugar rush, but for people with diabetes or hypoglycemia it is an important and useful way to maintain sugar in the bloodstream.

So, essentially, we h better kind of sugar; it flavor from the granul cane that we're all use baking it is impossible taste the difference.

Not sure it's quite

Gherkins Clearly cucumber family, from cornichons (which inc are mainly produced i Caribbean) to the big in the pickle barrel, th a must-have for any kit cupboard. Made easily bathing the cucumber couple of days. The on Netherlands (we trust really know how to pic they chicken or falafel without them.

In some of our res gherkin cans enjoying funky lampshades, tha bonkers Fr (see page 6

**Guaran booster, gu native to th seeds inside the berry- more caffeine in them sell it as a booster to g smoothies for those da get going, but as with a want to go overboard.

Used for longer th indigenous tribes of S

Miso Soy beans live (edamame), and miso lactic bacilli and yeast ferment and finally sm Highly concentrated s minerals, a bowl of mi you feel better, someth soup in its emotional p

The Japanese have nearly all their meals,

lieve fructose to be a
as a slightly different
refined from sugar
to, but in situations like
as near as dammit, to

ght in tea, though.

embers of the
he tiny French
lentally
the
amas
se are
hen
y salting and then
in pickling liquor for a
s we use are from the
ose lowland folk to
e) and our wraps, be
would be much the less

urants you can see our
second life as rather
ks to our brilliant-but-
nch style guru, Bambi
).

Famed as an energy
rana comes from a plant
Amazon basin, and the
ke fruit have three times
han coffee beans. We
n our juices and
s when it's a little hard to
stimulants, you don't

we'll ever know by the
h America.

4 in a pod
he result of adding
hem, allowing them to
ing them into a paste.
ce of vitamins and
oup really does make
like Jewish chicken
erties.
owl of miso soup at
n breakfast, but always

ee Suppliers, page 299.

Ingredient we love

Prunes

Becoming a prune
is the greatest thing
that can happen to a plum, and it's the ones
from Agen that win the prize.

Arguably the best dried fruit for snacking,
the prune has been used since ancient times
to enrich all manner of vegetable and meat
dishes; its virtues are infinite, its actions regular.
Essential to tagines and *khoresh* (Iranian stews),
and loves a good long soak in a bath of
Armagnac for a boozy dessert.

California now produces two-thirds of the
world's prunes, and we all know how they like
to be healthy inside and out on the West Coast.
See also Plums, page 16.

Raisins

Another kind of dried grape,
this one from a different
variety, bigger than a
currant, and darker and
drier than a golden
raisin. Of the three dried
grapes (currants, golden raisins,
and raisins) mentioned here, raisins are by far
the most popular—might have something to
do with that cute Sunmaid.

Golden raisins have been dried away from
the sun, because, like us, fruit goes darker in the
direct rays. Also, as with apricots, they have quite
often been treated with sulfur to adjust the
color, so buy organic.

Raisins were requested as taxes in Ancient
Egypt.

See also Grapes, page 20.

Golden Raisins

Our last variety of dried grape, this
time of the green type that darkens
as it desiccates. Plumper and juicier
than a raisin, with a lighter, less
intense flavor.

Although their roots are firmly
in the Middle East, in Victorian times an
Englishman called William Thompson arrived
in the US and brought a seedless grape cutting
with him; Thompson's grapes are now the most
commonly used for drying into golden raisins in
the Western world.

It takes $4^{1}/_{2}$ pounds of grapes to make 1 pound
of golden raisins. See also Grapes, page 20.

Sour cherries

These are a variety of
cherry that hasn't had the tartness bred out
of it. Sweet cherries are the result of cross-
breeding, whereas their sour cousins are
closer to the original wild cherry trees.

Particularly used in Middle Eastern
cookery, these gems (which is what they
look like) are becoming increasingly popular
elsewhere. Braising them with fatty meats, like
pork or duck, works well to cut through the
grease, and they impart the delicious sour
fruitiness that you expect to all sorts of food.
Great snack food. See Cherries, page 18.

Tamarind

The fruit held inside a seed casing that looks a
little like a large, hard, reddish-brown fava bean
pod with a bit more of a curve to it. The pods are
picked and dried, and then the fruit is
scraped out, seeds and all, and
compressed into a pulp.

The name comes from the
Arabic for Indian date, *tamar hindi*.
This fruit is extremely sour, but when
added to curries the sourness becomes muted
and a fresh, tart, fruity flavor is left
lingering. An important
ingredient in sweet and sour dishes
(not the scary MSG-saturated
orange Chinese kind), like our
Benny's Sweet & Sour (see page 261).

Big in Africa, India, and Central and
South America.

s are made in pretty
e seeds are cracked or
eased, which when it
sible for all the
re. Left to its own
on is spent after
t it was discovered
e vinegar) at the
ower could be
rmation in mind,
re dried Colman's
strength of the fiery

cereal crop *Avena*
n and high in fiber.
als (iron, selenium,
e the only whole grain
olesterol. They're also
ou from hitting the
naking them just
he day.
make our porridge,
ver Smoothie.

an kitchen cupboard
ncient fruit, and
ten on their life-
s start off green and
re bitter as hell, but
can move on to a
nes are ripe and
eing Greek Kalamata.
eral volumes' worth—
s and their oils, turn

e world's soy crop has
it is the most widely
d massive rainforests
uth America to make
hat, there has been
Brazil over the past
stainably.
first to make it, then
beyond. It is
g, highly nutritious.
at, which is

Stringy-bark honey

Like the Aborigines, who have been eating this mighty honey for thousands of years, we like to make a bit of a song and dance about it (they also do tree paintings of it, and have their own honey spirit, Mewal, though as yet we haven't gone that far).

The essence of this honey is that the bees live in the stringy-bark trees of New South Wales (Ned Kelly territory), where they feast on the flowers of the eucalyptus trees. Then they buzzzzz all the way back into their homes inside the trees, and go to work making their exceptional honey.

The Australian air is particularly clean, giving the bees the right environment to make this very pure honey, but what we particularly like about it —and why we bother to bring it over every three months on a slow boat—is the fact it is low GI, which is good news for all of us, but especially diabetics. Most mass-produced honeys are made by leaving a vat of sucrose (i.e. common sugar) outside the hives, which the bees devour and then excrete to make honey. But there is not much natural about this process, other than that the bees have physically filtered the sugar, so it comes out with pretty much the same GI as before, i.e. high. With stringy-bark honey, the bees are gathering natural fruit sugar (see Fructose, page 126) in eucalyptus trees, thus producing a honey that can be slowly absorbed and released into our bodies.

So that's why we bring over what we think is the best honey in the world from the other side of it.

Sugar

Apart from fruit sugar (fructose), Leon uses surprisingly little sugar of any other kind. By far the lion's share of what we buy in is for all those thousands of cappuccinos, lattes, Earl Grey teas, and mint steepers that we make each week.

The sugar industry is a vast one, historically synonymous with cruelty and exploitation, and only now are the people whose countries make the sugar becoming the ones who benefit from it. It's good to use Fair Trade.

The rough rule of thumb is that anything that's brown is better for you: bread, rice, and sugar being three mainstream examples. It's

to do with the fact that they have been processed less, so that the natural goodness that is present (whether it be in the outer husks/casings, as with rice and grains, or from inside the plant, as with sugar) has not been bleached and refined out of existence. It's good to go brown.

And lastly, sugar generally comes from poorer, developing countries, so the farmers are quite rightly going to do whatever they can to protect their valuable crop. Sadly this can lead to sprays and pesticides that we now know are less than brilliant for the body, so as a final word, we think it's worth paying extra for organic.

We also keep unrefined golden granulated sugar in our restaurants. Some people think it tastes nicer than fructose in tea and coffee.

Sun-dried tomatoes

Those who live in the sun know how to use it to full effect, and by drying out the fruits of the summer they allow their flavor to roll on into the winter. Split them, salt lightly (to keep the flies off), then lay them out and let the sun do its work.

Much better when they are replumped than just chucked raw into salads and pastas, where their flavor can be unpleasantly overpowering.

Italy makes more than 6 million tons of them a year, with 60% coming from Puglia and Campagnia in the south, where the sun is hottest.

Tahini

An essential part of hummus, this is a smooth paste of hulled sesame seeds that have been soaked, roasted, and blended with olive oil. Also good for sauces and meze dips, and goes well with grilled eggplant, mint, and yogurt. (See also Sesame Seeds, page 122.)

Vanilla beans and extract

These amazing sticky black bean pods are the only spice native to the New World, and look how greedily we all took to them. One of the world's most intensive and therefore expensive crops (they have to be pollinated by hand and need close inspection and maintenance), they should be kept either in sugar or in an airtight jar because they dry out and harden very quickly.

Extract is made from the beans, alcohol, and a stabilizer, whereas essence is nothing to do with vanilla, and is sometimes produced from pine trees.

Mustards All mustar
much the same way. As th
ground a volatile oil is rel
reacts with water is respo
pungency we know and lo
devices, this furious react
some 10 or so minutes, b
that by adding an acid (li
height of it, some of the
suspended. With this info
we should all be using mo
powder to witness the full
potential in all its glory.

Oats These seeds of th
sativa are very low in glute
They are masters of miner
zinc, phosphorus), and ar
recognized as reducing ch
pretty filling, so they stop
snacks midmorning, thus
about the best way to start
 We use organic oats to
granola, and Breakfast Po

Olives No Mediterran
is complete without these
many a word has been wri
loving properties. All olive
unripe; at this stage they a
given a good soak in brine
most special flavor. Black
squishy, the most famous
So much more to say—sev
but for a bit more on olive
to page 132.

Soy sauce Most of th
been genetically modified
used bean on the planet a
are being hewn down in S
way for more. Having said
progressive movement in
few years to cultivate soy s
 The Japanese were the
it spread west to China an
indispensable as a seasoni
 Soy sauce contains wh
fermented with the beans.

NUTS

Almonds are the most important culinary and nutritional nuts in the business; number one in the world in terms of commercial importance, they are enjoyed for their oils, their flavor, their incredible texture-giving properties, and their health benefits. Almond trees first get a mention right at the beginning of the world, in Genesis, when Jacob stripped their bark in Asia Minor (where they had descended from wild indigenous trees).

What everybody gets excited about with almonds are their high protein levels, power-pack of minerals and vitamins (especially beneficial to the skin), cholesterol-lowering skills, and their monounsaturated fats, which are the second-best kind—see Oils, page 132.

Whole, roasted, and salted is still one of the best snacks, and coupled with a good olive (like the Spanish do with their flat *almendras*), something special happens. Sliced work well as cake decoration, part of a trail mix, toasted on banana splits, or sprinkled on broccoli. Ground are a celiac baker's best friend, and are also useful for giving curries a dreamy creamy texture. Their milk and oil are extracted for both cooking and beauty products.

California is the world's biggest producer.

"Strength, flavor, and energy" is the motto on the Almond family crest.

Brazil nut trees are one of the largest in the Amazonian forest and can be up to 1,000 years old. The nuts are encased in a giant fruit pod— and each tree makes only around 300 of these a year—which hits the ground at up to a skull-shattering 50 miles an hour. Anything this big (and Brazils are the biggest nut around) takes time to grow, and these footballs of flavor need a full 15 months to develop. They grow wild in the South American rainforest, as well as being cultivated, but interestingly the plantations do not produce as much fruit—and therefore as many nuts—as the wild ones.

Brazil nuts are exceptionally oily: only 20% protein, and a whopping 60–65% of them are fats; three-quarters are either mono- or polyunsaturated— and that's a really good thing. But like all good things, you can have too much of it, and the fat side (that's 872 calories in 1 cup), along with the fact that they take so long to grow should tend us toward making these a special-occasion nut, like at Christmas.

One nut holds all your RDA of selenium, which is the trace mineral that's good for hormonal growth, especially of skin and hair.

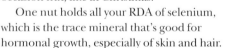

Cashews ℗ are held in a casing that hangs off the bottom of the cashew apple, one per fruit, which makes them extremely inefficient to cultivate in terms of time and space. Taken by the Portuguese from the New World, they landed in Goa in the 16th century and immediately found a home in the native cuisine, in both sweets and savories. It is ironic that it is now India that is supplying the United States (the biggest importers) with their own native fruit.

℗See Suppliers, page VI in Appendix.

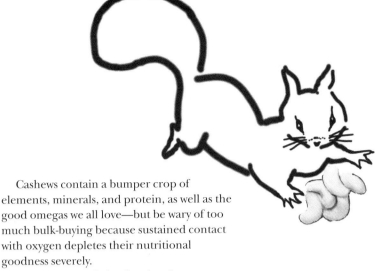

Cashews contain a bumper crop of elements, minerals, and protein, as well as the good omegas we all love—but be wary of too much bulk-buying because sustained contact with oxygen depletes their nutritional goodness severely.

The cashew apple is related to the mango and the fruit itself has five times more vitamin C than an orange.

Chestnuts

Chestnuts are unique in the nut galaxy because of their starchy nature, to the extent that they can be milled into flour. They are also more innately sweet than most nuts, and so as a result they have been very useful to many civilizations all around the Mediterranean for thousands of years. Famously paired with game, puddings, and Nat King Cole, these are Christmas in a shell.

Nowadays chestnuts can be bought cooked and vacuum-packed, sweetened, and puréed in a can, or raw to roast yourself (make a little slit in the domed side and put them into a hot oven for 15 minutes, until the shells start to open. Let them cool a little, but always peel when still warm for ease). And if you do ever see the flour, which is most likely to be in Italy in the cooler mountainous north, buy some and play with it in breads (as the Romans did), pastry, and pasta. Pretty special.

Plenty of zinc and iron in there too for blood-strengthening.

Hazelnuts are close cousins of the British cobnuts that hit UK markets in early fall. In Britain, cobnut trees, which are native to our fields, play an important part in the hedgerow ecosystem, and have long been used for their incredibly durable wood—they were the trunks of choice for waterwheels. In the US, filberts are the name for cultivated hazelnuts. In France, filberts are known as *noisettes*, and worldwide they are known as one of the two magical ingredients in Nutella. It would be foolish to think Nutella has much nutritional goodness, but it does do a fantastic job as a comfort food.

However, once you take a close look at the hazelnut on its own, this is what you find: the vitamins B_1, B_2, B_3, B_5, B_6, B_7, the minerals Cal, P, K, Cu, Fe, Zn, and, when you line them up like that, it looks like a six-a-side game of soccer brought to you by Omega.

One of Leon's favorite nuts to cook with.

Super Foods

Peanuts ©grow underground (which is why they are also called groundnuts) and belong to the same legume family as lentils, fava beans, and peas. Once the plant has flowered, the stalks of the flower grow down toward the ground and the embryonic peanuts dig themselves into the soil so that they can absorb all the nutrients. They are the easiest nut to grow, and whereas historically most were traded from Africa, they are now produced in dizzying amounts in Asia and the US; China takes care of a staggering 47% of the world's production, but recently Fair Trade smallholder farmers in Malawi have put themselves back on the global export scene with their excellent and ethical nuts.

Despite the growing number of peanut allergies, production has been steadily rising at the rate of 10% per annum, with the oil becoming increasingly popular because of the good fats in it.

Pecans are largely an American affair, in terms of both production and usage, and are grown from coast to coast in a belt extending across the warmer bottom half of the United States. The pecan tree is enormous and grows up to 55 yards high. Pecans are related to the hickory family, famous for their hard wood (traditionally, baseball bats are made out of hickory), as well as being America's wood of choice for smoking foods.

At 70% oils, and HDL happy oils at that, it's not surprising that a diet of pecans has been shown to reduce your cholesterol levels by around 10%, by really going at the clots that clog up your arteries. High in protein, and ⅛ cup of pecan halves contains one-tenth of your recommended daily intake of fiber.

Long before the Europeans landed in North America, the Algonquin people used to make a pecan butter that was essential nutritional support to get them through the winter.

Pine Nuts *Pinus pinea*—the pine tree that makes the cones that house the nuts—grows on a huge scale in one of two places in the world: Spain or China. Of course, in fact, they grow all around the Med, from North Africa right around to Turkey, and are deeply popular with the Italians, for example, in pesto. However, if you look on the side of the package these are the two places that are most often listed. The Spanish ones are considered superior and look squatter and less pale than the Asian variety, which are cheaper and have a weaker flavor.

Somehow pine nuts, with their delicate resinous flavor, seem to have come out on top as the nut with cachet, while also remaining nonexclusive. Everybody loves them, and you will find pine nuts right at the heart of the cuisine in any one of the five continents.

Often overpriced, overused, and overrated, they have become ubiquitous in a

©See Suppliers, page VI in Appendix.

nonmeaningful way, but if you want to fall back in love with pine nuts, take a stroll in the Middle East and see what wonders they bring to sweet baking.

In my slight tiff with pine nuts I might have forgotten to mention they are very good for you.

Last tip: buy them often and as fresh as possible to get a whiff of evergreen forest.

Pistachios are generally headed in one of two directions—bar or baklava (and other sweets of that ilk). In their spiritual home, Iran—the biggest producer in the world—they are more widely used in savory dishes like rice and chicken. And then there's the ice cream…

They grow in clusters a little like bunches of grapes on deciduous trees, and as they ripen to red over the long hot summer a tiny sliver of a split opens in their outer casing to reveal a magenta inner membrane. Inside that, of course, is the brilliant green nutmeat. They are harvested in September almost all over the world, except in Australia, where it all happens in February, and are then left to dry out and split open even further.

Regular pistachio-eating is shown to be beneficial to the blood, skin, liver, and hair.

Other relations are the cashew, mango, and mastic trees.

Pistachios in storage have been known to spontaneously combust, due to the volatile nature of that incredible green oil.

Walnuts are considered one of the most English of nuts, but they actually only arrived in the UK in the 15th century. Before that they'd been hiding out somewhere around the Caspian Sea, and were much loved by the Romans and Ancient Greeks, who thought they were good for brain-ache because they looked like mini versions of our lobes. In fact, their Afghan name *charmarghz* means four brains.

Walnuts contain as much protein pound for pound as eggs, and eating them after a super-fatty meal (like fried bacon and eggs) has been shown to lessen the absorption of cholesterol into the blood. Some research has shown walnut oil to be better even than olive oil; it's delicious on salads—never cook with it—but goes bad annoyingly quickly and is plenty expensive.

The green fruit of the walnut tree is called a drupe, and at its heart lies the nut containing the edible kernel. Wet or green walnuts are picked in early fall at the stage where the nut casing has not properly formed or hardened, and these are the ones used for pickling, an ancient and special pastime.

OILS
THE BIGGER PICTURE

Without launching into a chemistry degree, there are some basic principles about fats and oils that are worth getting your head around.

Some fats and oils are essential to our body (like the famous Omega triplets, 3, 6, and 9), because they help with cell growth, organ function, nerve nourishment, cardio health, and basically making sure our bodies run like well oiled machines. Other fats we can make ourselves and are therefore surplus to requirements, and these are the ones that clog up our arteries and make us overweight.

All fats are essentially chains of atoms, and this is where the saturation aspect comes in: atoms have a varying number of potential bonds that want to be attached to other atoms. If all the bonds are filled up, the chain just sits there feeling satisfied and stable, but essentially not doing anything. These are **saturated fats** and are a bad thing because it's better for things to keep moving and doing something in your body.

Monounsaturated fats have one free bond, and therefore allow for a bit of interreaction with other molecules. **Polyunsaturated fats** have many bonds free, making them unstable, which although not such a great thing in life, is what you want from the fats inside you.

Trans fats do not exist in nature at all so our bodies cannot process them. They were once vegetable oils with free bonds, but then got blasted with hydrogen atoms to take up the empty bonds, thus making them stable and solid at room temperature. This was largely a rationing thing when butter was scant, and people wanted something to put on their toast, but now it's considered an absolute no-no in terms of health, and in 2013 the FDA said they are no longer "Generally Recognized as Safe (GRAS)."

You can also have **hydrogenated oils** that are liquid at room temperature, and these are the ones that are mostly used for deep-frying because they are stable and don't burn at the high temperatures needed to crisp things up. There is also a small rule about anything that's solid at room temperature not being so good for you (think of it as being solid in your arteries and clogging them up), whereas anything pourable just cruises around your body.

Ingredient we love

EVOO

Generally speaking we use extra virgin olive oil for almost everything we do, the exception being when the strong flavor of the oil would be overwhelming or we need to heat it high, in which case we use Spanish sunflower oil or a mixture of the two. Olive oils are produced in many different countries, each one with its own natural characteristics, and even oils produced in the same country can have huge flavor variables. As a little tip, oil from the place your dish is from will suit it best. Olives for eating and olives for oiling are usually from different varieties, but there are a few clever cross-overs like Arbequina.

Sesame Oil

The best ones are organic when the seeds have been toasted, then cold-pressed and filtered through paper. Clearly the cheaper and more mass-produced brands go for a higher extraction level, which generally means ground, and treated with heat and chemicals. Indispensable in Asian cooking, and as with all oil, the better the quality the lower the burning point.

The oils we use at Leon are all poly- or monounsaturated (with the exception of a little butter at breakfast), which allows them to still be useful to our bodies. We never deep-fry. First it involves a truckload of grease being absorbed into the food, and second it is mostly done with hydrogenated oils, which we don't use. There are plenty of places out there to get the deep-fried fix we all need sometimes.

A note on the extraction of oils from fruits, nuts, and seeds:
The best oils are **cold-pressed**, or cold extracted, which means that a little bit of heat can be used—up to 80°F with olive oil. (The importance of keeping the temperature right down is to preserve the natural taste and aromas.) Oil that is produced like this has an acidity of less than 3% and is called **extra virgin.** It's worth differentiating between blended extra virgin olive oils, which most of the supermarket ones are, and **estate bottled extra virgin** ©, which are like chateau-bottled wines and sometimes cost as much, too. The difference in flavor though, justifies the price—use the everyday, standard stuff to cook with generally but it's worth finishing a great salad with the good stuff.

Storage
Olive oils have natural antioxidants and do not degenerate too quickly if you keep them cool (but not in the fridge) and away from bright light.

Nut oils do not have these natural preservatives, so buy them in small quantities and keep them in the fridge.

Seed oils can be treated like olive oils.

Peanut Oil

This is the way to get your stir-fries going authentically because it has a higher smoking point than most oils. Not used as widely by Asian cooks in the West due to our startling rise in peanut allergies, and the anaphylactic reaction is worse once the nuts have been heated than when raw. Less strong taste than sesame oil but brings a beautifully subtle and authentic flavor to the dish. Cold-pressed ones are very good for finishing Thai-type salads.

Sunflower Oil

When we need to get some proper heat into our oil, we use *aceite de girasol*, which is Spanish sunflower oil, mostly a combination of monounsaturated and polyunsaturated fats with a low level of saturated ones, which is what stops it from burning. We often use it in conjunction with extra virgin—a splash of each—because one brings flavor and the other stability. Although it has been treated with heat it comes from sunflower seeds so it can't be that bad.

VINEGARS

Vinegar has been used for thousands of years—much, much longer than lemon juice—to give that special tang in cooking. Making vinegar is an organic process where any fermenting liquid reacts with the right kind of bacteria, known as the mother, making acetic acid.

There are two usual starting points for vinegar: the first, and by far the most popular, is fruit juice, be it grape (heading for wine, sherry, or balsamic vinegars), apple (destined for cider vinegar), or anything else you feel like vinegarizing. The second is starchy beasts, such as rice.

Both of these have to be fermented, which means using yeast to turn the sugars, either natural or added, into alcohol and oxygen. The mother culture is then introduced, and she uses the oxygen to turn the alcohol into more of herself (i.e. acetic acid), which is why she's called a mother.

As the mother grows, she forms a velvety grey island on top of the intended liquid and then sinks into it, whereupon she looks a bit like a slimy web. This is perfectly harmless to ingest, but just looks a bit gross. If you are embarking on a vinegar-making career, you can transfer your mother from bottle to bottle by careful straining.

Wine left uncorked will turn sour, hence the derivation of the name from the French: *vin aigre*, literally meaning sour wine.

You can only make vinegars out of alcohols below 18% volume, otherwise the mother just gets drunk and falls over.

Tarragon vinegar, the popular French *vinaigre de framboise* (raspberry), and others of that ilk are all made by infusion.

The oldest doctor known to us, Hippocrates—he of the oath—used vinegar as a common healing remedy, and in Britain, Mrs. Beeton prescribed a sweetened berry-vinegar base drink with brandy added at the end for fevers and colds.

Vinegars are an amazing kitchen ingredient: loaded with masses of built-in natural flavor and with an endless shelf life, they have somehow come to play second fiddle to oil. (Extra virgin is undoubtedly a top ingredient, but its press profile is on overload and if it becomes any more fashionable it'll just have to go into rehab.)

In Leon's kitchen, vinegar is considered a major player and the most natural taste enhancer in the world. Using the right vinegar can kick your salad to stratospheric levels, whereas, given a choice without thought, it would have only just touched the clouds.

Add a healthy splash to slow-cooks and braises with the stock at the beginning, and watch as the layers of flavor develop. Think of vinegar as an ingredient where somebody has already done lots of work to get the taste just right and, in the case of the better end of the market, that taste is a knockout. Clever cooks know that deglazing your roasting trays or pans with 2 tablespoons of vinegar gives your sauces a massive flavor kickoff. Dare to spend as much on your vinegars as you do on your oils (and we're not just talking about paying for the fancy bottle) and feel the effect on your palate.

Here are a few of our favorites:

Wine vinegars—*red, white, and sherry*

There are two things that define the quality of your wine vinegar: grapes and process. The grapes can be any resulting in an evenly balanced flavored wine, and once the mother has been introduced the wine can be matured for years in small wooden barrels. The purpose of the casks is just the same as in wine- or some spirit-making: to allow an exchange of enzymes through the semiporous wooden walls. The longer the process is allowed to continue, the better the end result, and with proper wine vinegars, barrels are continuously on the go, with vinegar siphoned off once it is developed to the right strength and flavor, and the barrel topped off with wine again.

As with anything, the mass-producers out there have found a way around this age-old and quality-approved system: the Germans developed a way to make red wine vinegar by pouring wine onto beechwood shavings and it's ready in twenty-four hours—can't speak for the flavor though…

The very best wine vinegars are made from specific grapes (like Merlot, Cabernet Sauvignon, Chardonnay, etc.), and the names of some of the producers are synonymous with wine production.
Red wine vinegar is an essential in braised red cabbage, vinaigrettes, and for deglazing roasting pans.
White wine vinegar forms the basis for vinegar infusions. It gets simmered down at the start of a lot of French sauces (like hollandaise and *beurre blanc*), and light fish dishes.
Sherry vinegar—*Vinagre de Jerez*—comes from the south of Spain near Cádiz and is made from a blend of wines, just like its parent alcohol. The flavor is much deeper than standard wine vinegars because it is generally aged for a longer time, hence the deep color. When buying cheapish vinegar, sherry is a better deal than red or white.

Exceptionally tasty stuff, and particularly loves all foods Spanish and autumnal—beans, root vegetables, pork, nuts, dried fruit, and bitter leaves.

Cider vinegar has long been popular in England, Normandy, and the US, not only for its flavor but also for its supposed health-giving properties. Attractively light in flavor and color, this apple-based vinegar suits all manners of things fruity and, of course, porky. Also makes a great vinaigrette for fall/winter salads, and sits well with anything that natively neighbors on an orchard, like nuts and wild fruit.

Balsamic vinegar is not made from wine but from grape must, which is a mixture of crushed

grapes and juice, to which the mother is added. It is then left to age for years, decades, and even centuries in barrels, and it is the barrels and the aging that hold the key to the flavor. Big commercial producers age theirs in steel, but the proper ones are done in a combination of barrels whose make-up is a closely guarded secret: mulberry, juniper, cherry, and oak are some of the types of wood used. The longer it ages, the darker and more viscous it becomes because the enzymes keep eating away at the original fruit.

Balsamic vinegar has been given a DOC status, so it must come from Modena or Reggio in northern Italy, and the price of a bottle from an exceptional vintage and producer will make your eyes water.

Uti, non abuti—"Use, don't abuse," as they say in Rome.

Malt vinegar, made from unhopped beer, is good for pickling. And fish and chips.

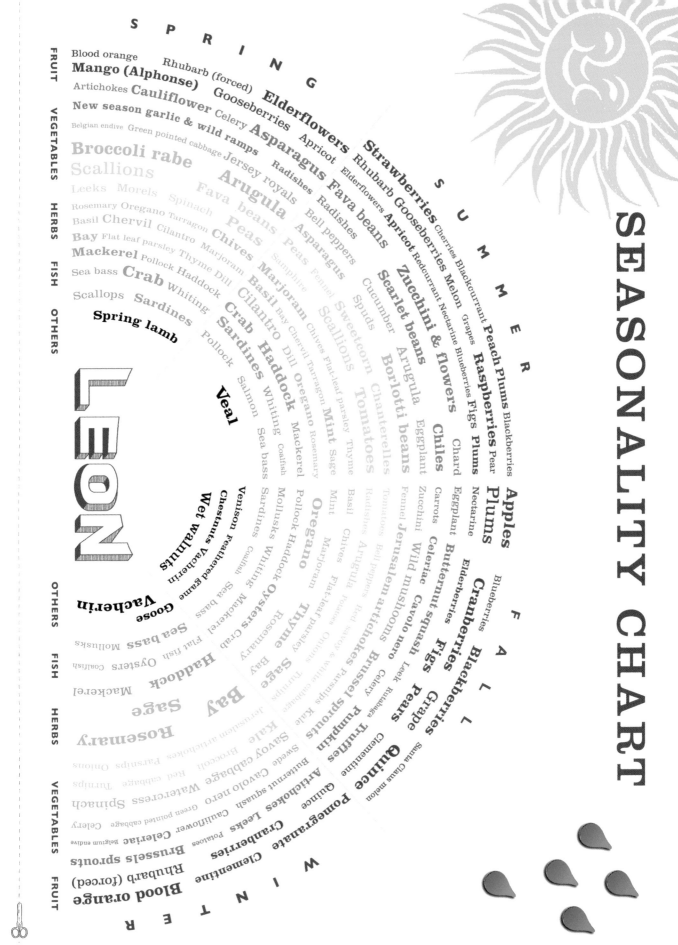

SEASONALITY CHART

LEON

THE RECIPE BOOK

If the Ingredients Book was your six o'clock cocktail, then what follows is the meat and two vegetables. All the knowledge you've gleaned so far isn't very useful unless you get excited about doing something with it.

Over Leon's young life we've had a real mix of dishes on the menu, born out of many tastings when Benny (see page 99) and I have put heart and soul into making a spark of an idea taste as good on the plate as it does in our minds. The recipes are made up of our past, present, and even future ideas for menus, a bit like *A Christmas Carol*, but without all the chain-rattling and generally a lot cheerier.

For Leon regulars, some dishes will be familiar—classics from Moroccan Meatballs to our Original Superfood Salad. Others we hope you might remember and be pleased to see again, like Leon Biyaldi or Rainbow Superfoods. To us food is a little like the old family photos you see on the walls of our restaurants: flavors are logged in our memories and revisiting them can bring a real rush of happiness.

This is why we've also included a bunch of recipes from the people who have helped Leon live and grow, from the founders to the fantastic people who run our restaurants, to all those behind the scenes who make it happen. I asked them to give me a recipe for a dish that really means something to them. For food can be so much more than fuel to keep your body going, and taste memories are just as evocative, and somehow more surprising, than visuals in their vividness.

✓—good carbs/good sugars ❤—no or low animal fat V—vegetarian
WF—wheat free DF—dairy/lactose free GF—gluten free

BREAKFAST

LEON CLASSIC

BREAKFAST POWER SMOOTHIE

✓ ❤ V WF

This is one of only a handful of things that have been on the menu since day one at our first restaurant on Carnaby Street, and with good reason. It's a classic Leon recipe because it tastes good and does you good. Everything in there has a job: the oats provide a slow-release carb to keep you powering through untill lunch, the bananas are loaded with potassium and other goodies to keep you strong, the honey gives it a touch of sweetness, and the dairy pulls the whole thing together. We now do seasonal variations, adding strawberries in summer and blackberries in fall. When we first put it on the menu, one of our regulars described the Strawberry Power Smoothie as "another small step forward for mankind."

MAKES ENOUGH FOR 4

3 big handfuls of oats, preferably organic
1 really big or two small bananas, preferably Fair Trade
2 tablespoons liquid honey (we use stringy-bark honey©, see page 127)
1 cup Greek yogurt
generous $1^1/_4$ cups whole milk

Everything goes into the blender with a few cubes of ice. Process until smooth but not a total purée. That's it.

© See Suppliers, page VI in Appendix.

Leon Granola ✓❤ v *DF*

Granola is essentially like roasted muesli, which gives it a whole lot more textural crunch and chew, as well as a baked nuttiness. We mostly serve ours with yogurt and seasonal fruity compote, but a whole bowlful with some fresh fruit and milk is also a great start to the day. Or you can just have it as a stand-by in-between nibble at your desk, thus avoiding the perils of other less brilliant snacks.

Once you've made your own granola/muesli, as anyone who's done so will tell you, there's no going back to store-bought—no matter how fancy the packaging.

MAKES ENOUGH FOR LOTS OF BREAKFASTS—2¼ LB

scant ¹/₂ cup honey
¹/₄ cup sunflower or peanut oil
3 cups rolled oats
1³/₄ cups bran
1 cup sunflower seeds

³/₄ cup hazelnuts
5 to 6 pitted dates, the fresher the better
³/₄ cup dried apricots
scant ³/₄ cup golden raisins
1 cup less 2 tablespoons wheatgerm

Preheat the oven to 350°F.

Pour the honey and oil into a pan and heat gently until the honey has melted.

In a bowl mix the rolled oats, bran, and sunflower seeds, then add the liquid from the pan and mix well. Spread out on a large baking pan.

Roast for 20 to 25 minutes, turning everything three or four times, then let cool.

Meanwhile, roast the hazelnuts to golden brown (takes about 10 minutes), then roughly chop, along with the dates and apricots.

When cool, mix everything together with the wheatgerm and store in an airtight container; lasts for about a month.

There are a couple of other things we do in the morning at Leon...

… not so much recipes as ideas that you might like to try for something a little different:

Our Bircher ✓❤ v

GOOD TO GET 1 PERSON GOING
IN THE MORNING

*¹/₂ an apple, cored and cut into rough chunks
   (you need a crunchy apple with a bit of bite)*
2 tablespoons seasonal fruit compote (see page 149)
*2 heaping tablespoons granola—obviously we use
   our own (see above), but any would do*
3 heaping tablespoons Greek yogurt
good splash of apple juice

Put everything in a bowl, give it a good stir, and, if you can, let it sit for 5 minutes before tucking in.

Fruit Combos ✓❤ v *DF* *WF* **GF**

Some fruit combos to get you thinking…

Melon, Mint & Pomegranate:
Nice way to get your vital vitamins all year round.
Pineapple & Basil:
Sounds freaky McDeaky but is a winner on the old taste buds.
Strawberries & Black Pepper:
Now officially a club classic. Only to be eaten in summer.

Left: Melon, Mint & Pomegranate
Right: Our Granola with yogurt & Blackberry Compote

Leon Ketchup ✓ ♥ V *DF* *WF* **GF**

This is a different kind of ketchup, and much better for you too: it's finished with real tomatoes for a bit of freshness, and uses fructose so it's not loaded with refined sugar. If you can be bothered to make your own ketchup, this recipe will make you very happy: it's been making the bacon on our breakfast menu happy for years. Lasts for ages in the fridge in sterilized jars, so you only need make it once a season.

MAKES 3 PINTS – DO A BATCH AND FREEZE HALF

3 large onions, chopped
2 cloves of garlic, smashed
1 teaspoon Spanish paprika
3 cloves
1 blade of mace
1 teaspoon celery salt
1/3 cup sunflower oil
3 x 14-oz cans of chopped tomatoes
1/4 cup fructose
1 cup apple juice
2/3 cup red wine vinegar
3 very ripe tomatoes, cut into eighths
salt and pepper

Gently cook the onions, garlic, and all the spices with the oil in a big deep skillet, until the onions are translucent but still have some bite and the spices are aromatized—about 15 minutes.
Add the canned tomatoes, fructose, apple juice, and all but 1 tablespoon of the vinegar.
Season and turn the heat right down.
Allow to simmer very slowly for 2 hours to reduce. Then add the fresh tomatoes and continue cooking for a further 30 minutes.
Process to a purée in a blender or food processor and season heavily with salt and pepper.
Once cooled, stir in the remainder of the vinegar adding a splash more if it's a little sweet for your taste.
Have one last taste, season if necessary, and then divide between sterilized bottles (as explained in Blackberry Compote, page 149). Once opened, keep sealed in the fridge for up to 3 months, or finish it off within 3 weeks once opened.

Brown Sauce ✓ ♥ V *DF* *WF* **GF**

I'm unfeasibly fond of this recipe—to me it signifies all that is right with our approach to food. We don't buy anything in unless we're 100% sure about all the ingredients in it. We couldn't find one on the market we felt truly comfortable with, so we decided to make our own.

MAKES 3 X 9-OZ JARS/BOTTLES

1/4 cup olive oil
3 cups diced onions
1 1/2 cups diced celery
a blade of mace
1/2 teaspoon ground cinnamon
1/2 teaspoon ground cloves or 2 whole
1/2 teaspoon cayenne pepper
1 teaspoon coriander seeds
1/2 teaspoon celery salt
1 x 14-oz can of tomatoes
3/4 cup roughly chopped pitted dates
2 bay leaves
scant 1/2 cup fructose
3 tablespoons tamarind paste
3/4 cup malt vinegar
2 tablespoons peanut oil, or something
*   suitably light*
salt and pepper

Gently heat the olive oil in a large skillet. Add the onions and celery and sauté them on a high-ish heat for 20 minutes, until nicely browned. Stir in the spices and cook for a further 5 minutes. Add the tomatoes, dates, bay leaves, fructose, half the tamarind, two-thirds of the vinegar, and 1 scant cup of water; let it all simmer and bubble slowly for about half an hour, or until it reaches a saucelike consistency.
Season well and purée until smooth in a food processor (not a blender, which turns it a shade of orangey-beige), adding the peanut oil and the last of the tamarind and vinegar.
Depending on how you're feeling about your consistency, if you like it pourable (like ketchup), as opposed to knifeable (like mustard) you may want to loosen it down with a little water.
Keep in the fridge in sterilized bottles (explained in Blackberry Compote, page 149).

James's Rhubarb & Ginger Jam ♥ V *DF* **WF** **GF**

Our James is an ideal mix of foodie and techie. His surname is Backhouse, but we (very amusingly) call him James "Back-of House" because he's the one who keeps it all running behind the scenes. We also, and maybe more flatteringly, refer to him as "The Prof," because he's very, very clever.

We didn't have any cheesecloth when it came to making this stunning jam so we used two new cleaning cloths, doubled up, to no ill effect.

MAKES 5 SMALL OR 3 LARGER JARS

Leon's Family Recipes

Jam-making at home seemed a sporadic thing to me, but there was a certain rhythm to the big, bubbling pots of fruit. Marmalade was always the first of the year, as soon as the Seville oranges came in, with the rhubarb and ginger not far behind. Still, it was anyone's guess how old any jar of neatly labeled jam was— dust it down, peel off the wax paper, and off you go. I was never quite sure which was my favorite, the rhubarb and ginger or the plum jelly, but I think this one just wins out.

James

Rhubarb & Ginger Jam

2½ lb (it a good kdc) rhubarb + same of sugar
Juice of 2 lemons
1oz (25g) root ginger, bruised & tied in muslin bag
4oz (100g) preserved ginger (can use crystallised but ...

James, aged 1½ outside the house in Wing

about 2¼ lb rhubarb, cut into 2-inch pieces
same weight of sugar (or about 3¼ cups fructose)
juice of 2 lemons
1oz fresh ginger, bruised and tied in a
    cheesecloth bag
3½ oz stem ginger in syrup (you can use candied
    but perhaps better with stem because the syrup
    can be used too)

Layer the chopped rhubarb with the sugar and lemon juice in a large bowl or stainless steel canning pan and let stand overnight.
The next day put the mixture into a pan of necessary size, slot in the bag of fresh ginger, and slowly bring to a boil, stirring to make sure all the sugar dissolves.
Boil strongly for 15 minutes.
Remove the bag, add the finely chopped stem ginger (and any spare syrup) and boil again for 15 minutes, or until the setting point is reached.
Pour into jars and seal in the usual way.

Baby George Dimbleby Born 4 December

Recipes

This crumbly, nutty, whole-wheat bread is so simple anyone can get it right, and it takes minutes of your time to make. I added the spelt flour and the four milk-producing spices recommended by our midwife, Odette—aniseed, caraway, fennel, and fenugreek—which give it a lovely mild aniseed taste. Mima had two slices of toast every morning for breakfast when our son George was born, and her milk gushed forth to such an extent that Odette suggested she go down to one slice in the first week. If you would like a breakfast bread without the milk-inducing qualities, simply replace the aniseed, fenugreek, and fennel with equal quantities of sesame or other seeds.

Henry

George's Breast-feeding Bread ✓ ❤ v DF

George is Henry and Mima's newly born son (and if you want to
know who they are, Henry's recipe is on page 244 and Mima's is
on page 222). He truly is a Leon baby, because without Henry and me getting
together to do Leon, I never would have asked my good friend Mima to the opening party of our first
restaurant and they never would have got married and they certainly wouldn't have made George.
Although he is young, his bread is delicious… and slightly addictive. We recommend doubling the
batch and freezing a loaf for later.

MAKES A 2¼-LB LOAF

soft butter
2³/4 cups strong whole-wheat spelt flour*
scant 1¹/2 cups bread flour*
heaping 1 teaspoon rapid-rising active dry yeast
2 teaspoons crushed sea salt
1 teaspoon aniseeds
1 teaspoon caraway seeds
1 teaspoon fennel seeds

1 teaspoon fenugreek (ground in a mortar and
    pestle or coffee grinder)
⅓ cup pumpkin seeds
⅓ cup sunflower seeds
2¹/2 tablespoons extra virgin olive oil
generous 1¹/4 cups warm water
2 tablespoons extra sunflower and pumpkin seeds,
    for the top
¹/3 cup pine nuts

Smear a 2¹/4-lb loaf pan with butter. Mix all the dry ingredients (except the pine nuts and seeds for the
top) together in a bowl large enough to knead the dough in. Add the oil, then the water, stirring until
the mixture sticks together. Knead in the bowl for just a few minutes until smooth. You can add a little
flour if it is too sticky, but remember the maxim—wetter is better. It doesn't matter if a little sticks to
your hands.
Shape, then put into the pan. Cut a pattern in deep gashes on the top and sprinkle the extra seeds
into the gashes; slightly push the pine nuts into the surface and dust with a little extra spelt flour (or
bran if you have some handy) all over.
Put the pan into a large plastic bag that can be tucked under the pan to enclose the loaf but leaving
room for plenty of air to circulate around the dough. Let stand until the dough has doubled in size.
This will take about 2 to 2¹/2 hours in a warm kitchen.
Bake in a preheated oven at 450°F for 20 minutes, then turn down to 400°F for a further 20 minutes.
Invert onto a wire rack to cool.

*If you can't get hold of spelt, you can use normal whole-wheat flour. You can also
replace the white bread flour with whole-wheat (the loaf will just be a little heavier).

SEASONAL COMPOTES

If jam-making seems a bit daunting, compotes are their simpler sister.
The theory is always the same: fresh, seasonal fruit, some sugar to help consistency and flavor,
then a gentle simmer to bring it all together. Good for yogurt, toast, oatmeal… and a good dollop
on the side of a pudding is enhancing. A really good way to deal with fruit that's past its best.

Blackberry Compote

✓ ❤ V *DF* **WF GF**

MAKES ABOUT 7OZ OR A SMALL JAM JAR FULL

$2^3/_4$ cups blackberries
$^1/_4$ cup fructose*
a squeeze of lemon juice
a splash of water

Put all the ingredients into a heavy saucepan.
Cover and place over very low heat for
10 minutes. Uncover and, if necessary, simmer
for a few minutes more for a firmer consistency.
If you're planning on keeping your compote for
a while, sterilize your jar first by filling it with
boiling water (and separately immersing the
lid). Tip the water out, pour the hot compote
in, and seal it up all hot like that. Once opened,
keep in the fridge.

Summer Berry Compote

✓ ❤ V *DF* **WF GF**

MAKES A SMALL JAM JAR FULL

1 cup raspberries
2 cups strawberries, halved and hulled
$2^1/_2$ tablespoons fructose*
2 tablespoons water

Put the berries, fructose, and water into a
heavy saucepan. Cover and place over very low
heat for 15 minutes. Then uncover and simmer
very gently for another 45 minutes to a jammy
consistency.
If you plan to keep your compote for a while,
then sterilize your jar by filling it with boiling
water (and separately immersing the lid). Tip it
out, pour the hot jam in, and seal it up all hot
like that. Once opened, keep in the fridge.

Rhubarb Compote

✓ ❤ V *DF* **WF GF**

MAKES ABOUT 1LB—ONE BIG JAM JAR

2 lb rhubarb
$^3/_4$ cup fructose
$1^1/_2$ vanilla beans
a squeeze of lemon juice

Top and tail the rhubarb. Wash it and cut it into
2-inch batons.
Put the rhubarb into a saucepan with the
fructose, $^1/_4$ cup of water, and the vanilla beans,
split down the middle with the seeds scraped
out (chuck the bean pods in, too).
Cover and set on low heat for about
10 to 15 minutes, stirring occasionally.
Uncover and let it slowly bubble away on the
lowest heat until the rhubarb has completely
broken down and doesn't look too wet, about
45 minutes to 1 hour, and then stir in the lemon
juice. Let cool (unless keeping for a rainy day, in
which case sterilize a jar as described for
Blackberry Compote).
Note: this compote should be quite liquid and
have the appearance of
runny jam.

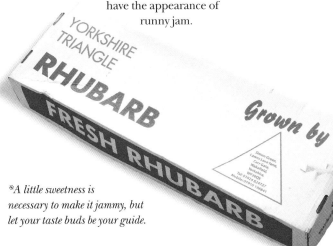

*A little sweetness is
necessary to make it jammy, but
let your taste buds be your guide.

Good Morning Muffin! (Banana, Bran, Maple & Pecan)

❤ V *DF*

Becca is a friend of Henry's who makes lovely muffins and used to make them for our restaurants before she decided to make a baby instead. This is a case of a recipe that spans the divide in people's minds between tastes good and does you good. A great way to get going without all the white flour and sugar normally associated with morning bakery. Adding a bit of apple sauce is a good trick to keep the muffins moist, and you can do the same thing with cakes too.

ABOUT 8 IN A PROPER DEEP MUFFIN PAN

2 eggs
1/3 cup + 1 tablespoon sunflower oil
3 heaping tablespoons apple sauce or stewed apple
1/2 teaspoon vanilla extract
1 ripe banana, mashed with a fork
1/4 cup maple syrup
1 1/2 cups whole-wheat flour
1/3 cup + 1 tablespoon soft brown sugar
1 teaspoon baking soda
1 teaspoon baking powder
1/2 teaspoon ground cinnamon
1/4 cup bran
a big handful of chopped pecans
scattering of oats, pumpkin, or sunflower seeds for the tops

Becca at her sister's birthday party, Hampshire, 1995

Preheat the oven to 350°F.

Whisk the eggs in a large bowl. Beat in the sunflower oil, followed by the apple sauce, vanilla, banana, and maple syrup.

In a separate bowl, mix together the dry ingredients: flour, sugar, baking soda, baking powder, cinnamon, and bran.

Tip the dry ingredients into the wet ones and mix thoroughly until you have a batter. Stir in the pecans. Spoon into paper muffin cups and bake in muffin pans, scattering the top of each one with a little of the oats and/or seeds.

Cook for around 30 minutes on the top rack of the preheated oven; they will probably start spilling out over the edge of the cases, but don't be alarmed—this is one occasion where a good muffin top is desirable.

Also delicious to serve with afternoon tea, and for a proper bit of tea-time naughtiness try them broken open with some extra maple syrup poured in.

JUST MADE

HOME COOKING

LEU
POR
& Y

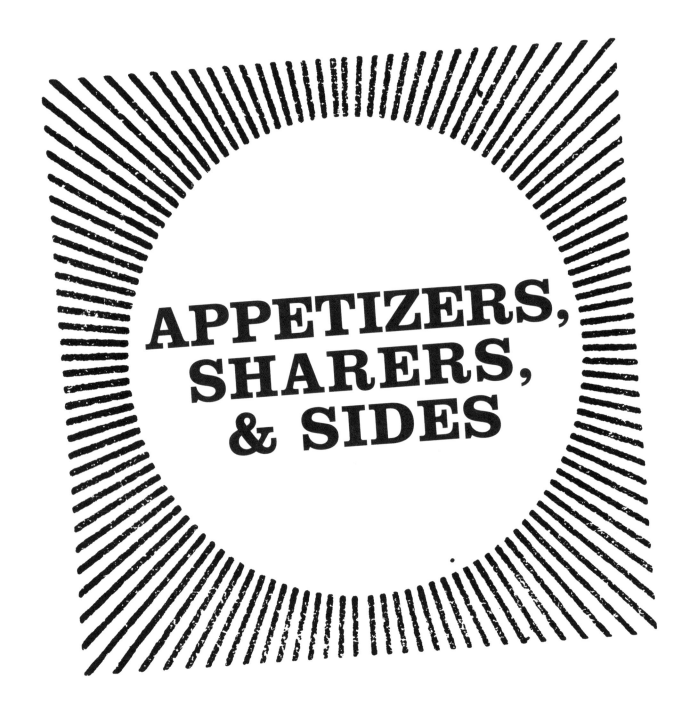

APPETIZERS, SHARERS, & SIDES

Sweet Potato Falafel ✓ ❤ V *DF* **WF** **GF**

These firm favorites came about because we all wanted falafel on the menu, but try as we might we couldn't make the normal ones because way back in the beginning we chose not to have any deep-fat fryers and baking them just made them crumbly and dry. So back we went to the drawing board (or kitchen), where Benny had a stroke of genius about basing them on roasted sweet potatoes, then binding the mix with besan (chickpea flour), thus still giving them their falafely credentials. Back flavors of spices, punched up with fresh herbage, make these a year-round winner and our most popular vegetarian dish to date. As a meze, we serve these with chopped tomatoes and pickles (for zip and freshness), and aïoli (see page 259) to cut through the sweetness. Also good inside a flatbread with chilli sauce.

MAKES AROUND 18 FALAFEL—ENOUGH FOR 4 FOLKS

2 medium sweet potatoes (orange inside, please)
weighing around 1¹/₂ lb in total
1¹/₂ teaspoons ground cumin
2 small cloves of garlic, chopped
1¹/₂ teaspoons ground coriander
2 big handfuls of cilantro, chopped
(about 1oz)

juice of ¹/₂ a lemon
1¹/₃ cups gram flour
a splash of olive oil
a sprinkling of sesame seeds
salt and pepper

Preheat the oven to 425°F and roast the sweet potatoes whole until just tender (about 45 minutes to 1 hour). Turn off the oven, let the potatoes cool, then peel them. Put the sweet potatoes, cumin, garlic, ground coriander, fresh cilantro, lemon juice, and gram flour into a large bowl. Season well, and mash with your hands (or a potato masher if feeling particularly weak) until you have a smooth mixture with no large chunks. Chill in the fridge to firm up for an hour, or in the freezer for 20 to 30 minutes. When you take it out your mixture should be sticky rather than really wet. You can add a tablespoon or so more gram flour if necessary (sweet potatoes vary in water content enormously). Heat the oven back up to 400°F.

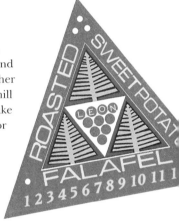

Using a couple of soup spoons (put a heaping spoonful of mixture in one spoon and use the concave side of the other to shape the sides) or a falafel scoop if you have one, make the mixture into falafely-looking things, and put them on an oiled baking pan. Scatter the tops with sesame seeds and bake in the oven for about 15 minutes, or until the falafel are golden brown on the bottom.

MEZE

Spring Greens ✓ ❤ V *DF* **WF** **GF**

A more robust and slightly anglicized version of the classic summer dish *petit pois à la française*, we liked this on our spring menu because it heralded the beginning of a lighter time with greens. Away with kale and on to a brassica cousin that takes a whole lot less cooking. Very fast and full of flavor.

MAKES SHARER OR SIDE FOR 6-ISH

2/3 of a green pointed cabbage, shredded
1 medium leek, sliced into 1/2-inch diagonals
1/2 teaspoon caraway seeds
scant 1 cup fresh or frozen peas (if fresh, use
    1 lb 2 oz unshelled pods)
3 scallions, thinly sliced

1 1/2 tablespoons cider vinegar
2 tablespoons extra virgin olive oil
a big handful of mint, chopped
a small handful of flat-leaf parsley, chopped
salt and pepper

In a large wide-bottomed saucepan heat 1 cup of water to boiling and drop in the cabbage, leeks, and caraway seeds.
Cover and simmer for 4 minutes.
Uncover and add the peas and scallions.
Stir and simmer fast for no more than 5 minutes, or until all the vegetables are cooked and the water has largely evaporated. Turn the heat off and finish with the vinegar, olive oil, herbs, and some seasoning.

Sesame Chicken Wings ✓ ❤ *DF*

The key is in the marinade, full of fiery ginger and other strong flavors synonymous with Asia. Give the bird bits plenty of time to absorb all this greatness, then cook 'em till crisp for a whole lot of suck and a little bit of chew. Great snack.

MAKES ABOUT 14+ PIECES, DEPENDING ON THE SIZE OF YOUR CHICKENS, AND WHETHER YOU GO FOR WINGS WITH ONE JOINT OR TWO (BETTER)

10 cloves of garlic, smashed
5 1/2 oz fresh ginger, washed but not peeled,
    roughly chopped
scant 2 tablespoons fish sauce (see page 126)

2 1/2 tablespoons dark soy sauce
2 1/4 lb chicken wings, preferably with 2 joints
generous 1 tablespoon sesame oil
1 1/2 tablespoons sesame seeds

Process the garlic, ginger, fish sauce, and soy sauce in a food processor to make a coarse purée.
Pour onto the chicken wings and mix thoroughly with the sesame oil and seeds.
Let marinate in the fridge overnight.
Next day preheat the oven to 350°F. Set one of the oven racks near the top of the oven.
Spread the wings out on a baking pan and place them in the oven on the top rack for 45 minutes, or until golden brown.

Hummus ✓ ❤ V *DF* **WF** **GF**

A long-term committed member of the menu, we must have turned the annual chickpea export of several small countries into hummus over the last few years. This is one of those dishes that we never had total success with while we were using dried chickpeas and cooking them ourselves; as soon as we switched to canned we didn't have a problem. Strange but true. Lots and lots of people do it, but once we'd got over the issue of the cooking we never looked back with this recipe. It just works, and once you know the recipe, it can be assembled in five minutes.

PART OF A MEZE FOR 4, OR NIBBLES FOR 6

1 x 14-oz can of chickpeas
2¹/₂ tablespoons lemon juice
1 clove of garlic, minced
1 tablespoon tahini

generous ¹/₄ cup extra virgin olive oil
1 teaspoon cayenne pepper
salt and pepper

In a bowl mix all the ingredients together except the seasoning, then add to a food processor and purée. Pour the mixture back into the bowl, stir well, and season. Spoon into a suitable hummus receptacle and serve with a good shot of extra virgin, an extra sprinkling of cayenne, and floppy, warm flatbread (see recipe opposite).

Roasted Garlic & Pumpkin Hummus ✓ ❤ V *DF* **WF** **GF**

This was a lovely idea (mine) that never got onto a fall menu due to some wrangling about trying to simplify things in our kitchens. There's a constant and healthy tussle between the folk who want to change lots with each seasonal menu, and the sensible people who know that too much new stuff would lead to system breakdown; it's hard to introduce lots of new dishes, recipes, training, and tasting notes across lots of restaurants all at once in the same week. But sometimes the creatives forget that and get bossy. Ho hum.

MAKES ENOUGH FOR A PICNIC FOR 4, MEZE FOR 6, OR NIBBLES FOR 8

1 lb 14 oz pumpkin (or butternut squash), peeled
*   and cut into 2-inch chunks*
2 tablespoons olive oil
¹/₄ teaspoon cumin seeds
¹/₄ teaspoon ground allspice
6 cloves of garlic, peeled

¹/₂ a red chile, thinly sliced
a few pumpkin seeds
1 x recipe hummus (see above), minus the
*   extra sprinking of cayenne and the garlic*
feta cheese (optional)
salt and pepper

Preheat the oven to 350°F, and put your roasting pan in to get hot too.
Put the pumpkin chunks into a bowl with the oil, cumin, allspice, whole garlic cloves, chile, and seasoning. Mix it all around so that everything gets coated.
Get the hot roasting pan out of the oven and pour everything into it.
Roast for 45 minutes to 1 hour, turning the contents over and generally giving it all a good stir. Take special care with the garlic to make sure that it doesn't burn but just gets nicely caramelized, taking it out early if need be.
Meanwhile, make the hummus base.
Blend the pumpkin and garlic to a purée and fold into the hummus with some extra seasoning. Finish with the pumpkin seeds on top.
Would be nice with a crumbling of feta on there too.

Kew gardens, October

Flatbread ✓ ❤ V *DF*

This isn't the recipe for the flatbread we use in the restaurants (which our Syrian baker makes for us), but because a lot of the food in this book leans over to the far side of the Med, it seemed churlish not to include one in case you felt like making your own. I've been using this recipe for years and years—it was first handed to me on a scrap of paper in San Francisco, of all unlikely places, but it works like a dream and, as I discovered when I got back to London, is the default flatbread recipe for many great cooks I know. This is the basic recipe, but if you want something with a bit more fun—and if you're going to the trouble of making your own then why not—try sprinkling it with dried thyme, sesame seeds, sumac, or all three to make the Lebanese classic *za'atar*. Just run the rolling pin over it again once you've done your sprinkling.

1/2 teaspoon dry active yeast
1 cup warm water
4 cups all-purpose or whole-wheat flour,
*   or a mixture of both*

1/4 cup extra virgin olive oil
sea salt, for sprinkling

Dissolve the yeast in the warm water, or if the package says it's OK just add it straight to the flour. Put the flour into a big bowl and make a wide well in the middle.
Pour in the extra virgin olive oil and the water/yeast mixture and stir slowly with your hand until it all comes together.
Using the heel of your hand, incorporate all the flour until your dough is elastic, bouncy, and pleasing. (Depending on the flour used you could either have a few straggly bits at the bottom of the bowl, in which case throw them away, or a slightly sticky dough, in which case knead in a little more flour.)
Cover with plastic wrap and let rest for an hour or two in a warm place.
Either heat up a ridged grill pan or get your oven fired up to 425°F. If you're using the oven, slip in two sturdy baking pans to get them nice and hot.
Divide the dough into 6 and roll out to ¼ inch thick. Sprinkle evenly with sea salt and any other spices you like and either bake in the oven on your preheated pans (drizzle the pans with a little extra virgin olive oil first) for 6 to 8 minutes, or arrange them carefully on a hot grill pan for

3 minutes, at which point they should have lifted a tiny bit at the edges and you can turn them. Cook for the same amount of time on the other side. Considering they come from the same dough, the breads taste quite different whether they have been grilled or baked, so the first time you make the recipe try both ways to see which you prefer. Serve immediately.

Leon Biyaldi ✓ ♥ V *DF* **WF** **GF**

This, in truth, is what happens when a biyaldi meets a babaganoush: the story behind the Turkish classic Imam Biyaldi is that the Imam, or prayer leader, for whom the dish was specially made, was so overcome by the delicious richness of it (due largely to the generous amounts of olive oil) that he fainted, or biyaldi'd, as they say. In the traditional recipe the cooked eggplant flesh is packed back into the skin and rebaked: service-wise this was a bit of a nightmare for us, so ours has the appearance of a babaganoush and the flavor of a biyaldi.

MAKES MEZE FOR 4 TO 6

2 medium eggplant
generous $^{1}/_{4}$ cup extra virgin olive oil
1 medium onion, diced
4 cloves of garlic, sliced
1 tablespoon tomato purée
$^{1}/_{2}$ a 14-oz can of tomatoes

2 bay leaves
1 tablespoon fructose
3 small handfuls of flat-leaf parsley, roughly
*   chopped*
just a squeeze of lemon
salt and pepper

Put your whole eggplant either directly on a gas stove or under the broiler until thoroughly blackened on all sides. This should take about 15 minutes. Set aside to cool.
In your now favorite heavy saucepan, heat the olive oil and fry the onion and garlic. Stir in the tomato purée, then crush the canned tomatoes and add them and their juice to the pot too.
Turn the heat down and while it is slowly reducing drop in the bay leaves, fructose, and some seasoning.
Cut the tops off the cooled eggplant, peel completely, and roughly chop the flesh.
Stir the eggplant flesh into the tomato base with the parsley and continue to simmer slowly for about another 5 or 10 minutes—you'll be able to see when it's all come together.
Taste again and give it a last hand with the extra virgin. Best served with warm flatbread (see page 157).

Brazilian Beans ✓ *DF* **WF** **GF**

We have Juliana and family to thank for these beans, which we're thinking of putting on the menu soon.

SERVES 4 AS A SIDE

$1^{1}/_{4}$ cups pinto beans (aka red Mexican beans),
*   soaked for 2 hours in 3 pints water—you*
*   could use 2 cans of drained pinto or cranberry*
*   beans, but you miss the magic in the original*
*   cooking liquor)*
1 big bay leaf
$^{1}/_{2}$ teaspoon of dried oregano

2 tablespoons extra virgin olive oil
1 onion, minced
2 cloves of garlic, minced
$3^{1}/_{2}$ oz sliced bacon, rind removed, cut into little
* $^{1}/_{2}$-inch squarelets*
salt and pepper

After the beans have had a good soaking, put them into a pot with their soaking liquid, add the bay leaf, bring to a boil, and simmer gently for 2 hours. When they are well and truly cooked (or smooth as the Brazilians say), remove from the heat and season with salt, oregano, and a good grinding of black pepper. Set aside while you do the next part.
Heat the oil in a pan and gently fry the onion and garlic. When they are "gilded" (a fine turn of phrase from Juliana), after about 5 minutes, add the bacon and sizzle on down for 15.
Tip some of the cooked beans into the bacony-garlicky-oniony thing and swoosh around. Pour everything back into the bean pan and return to low heat for 15 more minutes. Season and devour.

Claire's Brazilian Cheese Balls ✓ V **WF**

Claire is one hard-working, hard-living chick. She got thrown in the deep end as the manager of the big bad Bankside restaurant, of which she survived the hairy opening weeks on sparkly green eye-shadow alone. Claire cooked these for us at one of our First Tuesday suppers when we all get together to eat, drink, and be merry. They went down extremely well with a lot of cold beer, and made us all want to run naked along the beach, which isn't very surprising given their country of origin.

MAKES ABOUT 30 BALLS

³/4 cup vegetable oil
³/4 cup water
³/4 cup milk
1 tablespoon salt
4 cups manioc starch* (tapioca starch, must be from cassava; choose one labeled "dulce," because this is the "sweet'"variety, rather than "bitter" cassava—there is an enzyme that is produced in cassava that makes the cassava produce cyanide naturally and sweet cassava has less of this, although it has obviously been removed in production from both types)
2 eggs
10 oz cheese—2 varieties (usually made with Alvao special selection cheese, made from cow and goat milk, and Casteloes original semisoft cheese; ideally should be cheese locally made in Minas Gerais, but any hard cheese is OK) †

Pour the vegetable oil, water, and milk into a large saucepan with some salt and bring to a boil, stirring from time to time.

Place the manioc starch, or flour and cornstarch combo, in a large bowl.

Add the hot liquid gradually to the starch and mix in with a spoon until all the liquid is used and a soft sticky mixture is formed (it should look a bit like mashed potatoes).

Knead the eggs into the mixture, using your hands. It will be very sticky but not liquid; knead vigorously.

Grate all the cheese as finely as possible and also mix in with your hands.

Preheat the oven to 400°F.

Oil your hands well and form the mixture into walnut-sized balls—they'll puff up a little in the oven.

Put the balls on to 2 well-oiled baking pans (remember their expansion plan) and place on the top and middle racks of a hot oven. After about 20 minutes the top ones should be ready (golden brown), so take them out, then move the other pan up, and give them another 5 minutes.

* We did a blind taste test using 2³/4 cups cornstarch mixed with 1¹/4 cups all-purpose flour (sifted) and couldn't tell the difference between that and the manioc (or maniac as we call it) starch.
† We used half pecorino and half Parmesan and they came out great.

Ernani (his recipe), Claire, and Junior

Leon's Family Recipes

The Restaurant at Bankside has a real party vibe and therefore this recipe feels darkly appropriate. The Brazilian family that taught me this recipe would desperately suit the place, the team and the people who eat with us. Every time I've enjoyed these cheese balls it has been among friends, which is just as well, as the recipe itself produces party amounts of Pao de Queijo, as they call them. It is quite simply intended to be a shared experience, I think, which is how all of us at Bankside feel about this restaurant too. It is a lot too special not to be shared with as many people as possible!

Fabrice's Ratatouille

✓ ❤ V *DF* **WF** **GF**

Fabrice is the charming Frenchman who has been running our Carnaby Street restaurant since the day we opened. To know him, as they say, is to love him, which is pretty amazing considering his idiosyncrasies. This is not a loud and shouty ratatouille as we have come to expect, but a much more muted, gentle, and subtle affair. When most of the people with Family and Friends recipes in this book got together at my house for a massive tasteoff, as everyone else was reaching over, shouting comments, and generally having a boisterous time, I found Fabrice eating his ratatouille quietly in the corner. I asked why he wasn't trying everybody else's food and he said in a very touching way with those big dark eyes looking at me, "It's my mom's. I love it." That was all he wanted; to him it was perfection. How very French.

Fabrice with his mom Nicole, daughter Isabella, and nephew Maxim

Leon's Family Recipes

It's now eleven years that I live in London and try to go Aix-en-Provence every summer. My parents are living in a house with a very big terrace and that is where we spend most of the time during the summer. The ratatouille reminds me of the days where the heat was waking me up and my mom was already cooking for lunch. Smelling the food that my mother was preparing was telling me that I should have a light breakfast to keep some room in my belly for this ratatouille. Lunch is coming, I help my mom to put the plates on the table and we are now all together. We eat, talk, drink, smile, and laugh. We love being together and we love the ratatouille ...

xxx Fabrice

SERVES 4 TO 6

2 to 3 zucchini, sliced
1 large eggplant, cut into 1¼-inch chunks
2 red bell peppers, cut into 1¼-inch chunks
1 big onion, chopped into ½-inch dice
2 cloves of garlic, chopped
4 ripe plum tomatoes, cut into wedges

1 teaspoon dried Provençal herbs (or oregano)
a couple of sprigs of thyme
2 bay leaves
a couple of tablespoons of olive oil
a few leaves of basil, if you like
salt and pepper

Put all the vegetables, herbs (except the basil), and oil with some salt and pepper into a large wide-bottomed pan with a tight-fitting lid on low heat for 30 minutes.
Then stir, put the lid back on, and let cook another 30 minutes.
When all the vegetables are soft, season again, dress with a touch more olive oil, and stir in the basil. Enjoy it cold or hot.

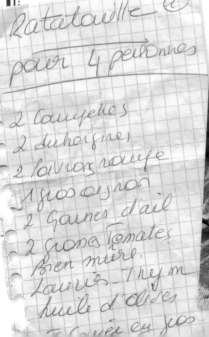

Magic Beans ✓ ♥ V *DF* **WF** **GF**

These are not the kind of magic beans that make beanstalks; their name came about as a mark of respect for the amazing things that can happen when the right ingredients are put together in the simplest of ways.

These humble beans surprised us all by turning into such a winner, and have truly earned their place in the Leon hall of fame.

PART OF A MEZE OR SIDE FOR 2

2 tablespoons olive oil
2 cloves of garlic, chopped
1/2 a red chile, roughly chopped, seeds left in
1 tablespoon rosemary, finely chopped

7 oz green beans, topped but not tailed
2 tablespoons lemon juice
3 scallions, cut into 3 1/4-inch batons
salt and pepper

Heat the olive oil in a skillet and stir in the garlic, chile, and rosemary quickly to release their flavors—just a minute or two.
Add the beans before the aromatics start to turn golden; shuffle well to coat the beans, then add the lemon juice and a couple of tablespoons of water.
Cover and cook on low heat until the beans are tender—that's through *al dente* and out the other side—about 15 minutes.
Stir in the scallions, toss well, season, put the lid back on, and leave on the heat for a couple of minutes just to wilt the scallions.
Turn the heat off and let rest for 5 minutes to let the magic happen. (They're good snack food straight from the fridge too.)

Roasted Arties & Newies ✓ ♥ V *DF* **WF** **GF**

This is almost a nonrecipe it's so straightforward, but if there is a useful trick about Jerusalem artichokes, it's that you don't need to peel these knobbly buggers if you roast them—the skin goes a wonderful kind of nutty while the inside turns almost creamy. Good with the regular potatoes in there too for contrast. Jerusalem phartichokes are a very special tuber.

A SIDE FOR 4 TO 6

*1 lb 5 oz small, waxy potatoes**
14 oz Jerusalem artichokes
1 tablespoon rosemary, chopped

3 tablespoons extra virgin olive oil
Maldon sea salt© and pepper

Preheat the oven to 375°F.
Scrub the potatoes and artichokes very well—no peeling.
Mix all the ingredients together in a roasting pan, giving them a good roll around in the oil and plenty of seasoning.
Bake in the oven for 35 to 45 minutes, moving them around halfway through. The timing depends on the size of your potatoes and tubers, but be sure to cook them until the arties are really squishy when you squeeze them.

*See page 65 for varieties.
©See Suppliers, page VI in Appendix.

Lima Bean & Chorizo Tapa ✓ ❤ *DF* **WF GF**

This involves Brother Benny's favorite cooking method for legumes, letting the beans slowly bubble for ages under waxed paper in the oven, which gives them a succulence not reached by stovetop cooking. Clearly Spanish in feel, it works great as a tapa, but equally if you go for a more generous bowlful it shuffles very comfortably over the border into a cassoulet-type main course. Rich, filling, and hard to stop eating.

This dish will only be as good as the chorizo you buy.

SHARER FOR 4 TO 6

6 oz dried Lima beans
3 tablespoons extra virgin olive oil
9 oz good-quality raw chorizo sausage◎*, sliced
$^{3}/_{4}$ inch thick
3 cloves of garlic, roughly chopped
1 medium onion, cut into medium dice
1 large carrot, cut into small dice

1 stick of celery, thickly sliced
$^{1}/_{2}$ a 14-oz can of chopped tomatoes
2 bay leaves
zest of 1 large orange
2 cups chicken stock
a small bunch of thyme, tied with string
salt and pepper

Soak the beans in water overnight.
The following day drain them and put them into a saucepan with twice the volume of water to beans, along with some cooking friends—garlic, red chile, bay, onion.
Simmer until softened but not totally cooked through—about 45 minutes.
Take a deep heavy ovenproof saucepan (like a Dutch oven) and heat up the oil. Over medium heat fry the chorizo until the oil has gone that gorgeous color and the meat is beginning to brown.
Use a slotted spoon to take the chorizo out, then add the garlic, onion, carrot, and celery.
Stir well and simmer, covered, until everything is becoming tender—about 10 to 15 minutes.
Add the chopped tomatoes and simmer for around 15 minutes on medium heat, stirring occasionally.
Preheat the oven to 300°F.
Stir in the drained beans, bay leaves, orange zest, chorizo, and the chicken stock.
Submerge the bunch of thyme somewhere in there.
Put the whole pot into the oven, covered with a circle of waxed paper sitting directly on top, and let cook for about $1^{3}/_{4}$ hours.
Check the seasoning, make sure the beans are cooked, and let it rest, preferably till tomorrow, for full flavor effect.

◎See Suppliers, page VI in Appendix.
* See page 95 for our chorizo of choice.

Remi & Agnieszka's Rabbit ✓ *DF* **WF GF**

Agnes is just the smiliest person ever to work in the
numbers bit of a business—even her hair has bounce.
This is great picnic food, and very kid friendly. Simple to
make and simple taste. Despite gentle questioning and
coaxing, though, we're all still a little unclear as to why
this is called rabbit when it's made of pork. What with
her boyfriend Remi working at our Bankside restaurant,
these two are a happy couple of Leon lovers.

Remi, at his grandmother's flat, Kaunas, Lithuania 1984.

MAKES 8 NICE PICNIC-SIZED SLICES

2¹/₄ lb ground pork
1¹/₂ cups minced onion
2 eggs
3 cloves of garlic, chopped
1 tablespoon chopped thyme
a small handful of parsley, chopped

1 cup of chicken bouillon (but if you haven't got
*   it water will do)*
¹/₄ teaspoon caraway seeds
bay leaves
salt and pepper

Preheat the oven to 350°F.
All you need to do is mix everything up together (except the caraway, which will go only on top of a Rabbit).
Pack into the loaf pan and then put on the bay leaves and sprinkle with caraway.
Then put it on a baking pan and bake for about 1 to 1¹/₄ hours till you see that Rabbit become brown
and it comes away from the sides of the pan.

Leon's Family Recipes

Maryte, Remi's mom, is a very kind and
soft person (although sometimes she can
lose her temper). She had a hard time as
a child, losing her parents at the age
of fifteen and had to start her adult
life early because she had a younger
brother to look after. When money is
short you learn how to cook using whatever ingredients you have, so she can
make a wonderful dish having almost nothing in her fridge. As a mom she is very
warm, would do anything for her child,
and never says no if you need her. She's
got probably more friends than me and
Remi together, as she is very sociable,
loves dancing and chatting to people,
meeting and listening to their problems.
She's got a beautiful smile and eyes you
could kill for. She's just great.
    Eat with pickles, bread (good bread,
not fluffy English stuff), and salad.

Kisses, Agnes

Mom was always testing recipes for cookbooks when we were children, which meant Dad didn't get into the kitchen much. If he cooked for us it was inevitably this Spanish omelet. Very simple, delicious, and, for us, always a little exotic—because it was cooked by Dad.

Henry

The great joy of this recipe is that you don't need to worry about the quantities, just do what you think looks best. You cook everything up as described below and then at the end pour the eggs over, allowing them to cook gently until set, making a delicious and filling omelet. Simple to make. Good either hot or cold.   David

David and his daughter Kate, Dordogne, France 1977

David's Spanish Omelet ♥ V DF WF **GF**

David is Henry's Dad, and a right laugh. Sometimes you can catch him with a really naughty little sparkle in his eye, and it takes one to know one.

It's much quicker (and you don't run the risk of it sticking to the bottom of the pan before the eggs have set) if you put it in a medium oven instead of doing it on the stove, but in our minds the result isn't quite so delicious—a bit puffy and less soft.

SERVES 4—(FEEL FREE TO CHANGE THE QUANTITIES DEPENDING ON WHAT IS ON HAND)

3 medium potatoes
olive oil
2 medium onions
1 red or green bell pepper
2 cloves of garlic

2 tomatoes
8 eggs
a handful of cilantro or parsley
salt and pepper

Chop the potatoes into 1-inch cubes. Put them into a saucepan of salted cold water, bring to a boil, and simmer until softened but not completely cooked. Drain.

Now you need a wide, heavy, nonstick skillet. Cover the bottom with olive oil and into it put the chopped onions and chopped pepper (both either fine or thick) and minced garlic.

Put the tomatoes into a basin and cover with boiling water. Remove the skins and chop the tomatoes.

When the onions and pepper have softened, and the onions appear translucent, add the potatoes. When this whole mess is looking nicely browned, add the tomatoes and keep everything simmering until well cooked. Turn the heat down low.

Now break sufficient eggs into a bowl to cover the entire pan. Beat them, season them, pour them into the pan, and give it all a bit of a stir. Cover with a lid until the eggs are just set.

As a last step, scatter the omelet with finely chopped cilantro or parsley. Remove from the heat and serve in cakelike slices.

Sicilian Grilled Vegetables ✓ ❤ V DF **WF GF**

This was a firm family favorite during its summer stay on the menu, so popular in fact that we kept it on through fall. Some time around the end of October the price of bell peppers went through the roof, and as a result our carefully costed dish started losing us money faster than you could say Cosa Nostra. This was our first harsh lesson in staying true to the seasons and learning not to force nature because she'll win.

SHARER FOR 4

1 large zucchini, thickly sliced
1 small eggplant, cut into large chunks
1 green bell pepper, cut into large chunks
1 yellow bell pepper, cut into large chunks
5 tablespoons olive oil, divided
1 large red onion, cut into wedges
1/2 teaspoon crushed red chili flakes

3 cloves of garlic, sliced
1 x 14-oz can of chopped tomatoes
small handful of niçoise olives, roughly chopped
2 tablespoons capers
1/3 cup golden raisins
a small handful of basil, leaves picked
salt and pepper

Preheat the broiler on its highest setting.
In a bowl toss the zucchini, eggplant, and bell peppers with 3 tablespoons of olive oil and some salt and pepper. Spread the vegetables out under the broiler, spacing them out as much as possible. Broil for 20 to 30 minutes, turning them over a couple of times, until browned and softened.
In a heavy skillet big enough to hold everything, fry the onion, chili flakes, and garlic in the rest of the olive oil for a few minutes. Add the tomatoes and simmer for about 5+ minutes to a saucy consistency. Add about 1 cup of water, then stir in the grilled vegetables, olives, capers, and golden raisins. Simmer again for about 15 minutes.
Season, and stir in the basil leaves just before serving.

Pilaf ✓ ❤ V DF **WF GF**

Over the seasons that turn so easily into years, we've tried lots of different rice dishes, and it took us ridiculous amounts of effort to come up with some Really Nice Rice. Sometimes with cooking it's the seemingly simplest things that are the hardest to get right, and cracking the Leon Rice that went with all our big dishes proved a real headbanger.

So I did what any sensible cook would have done and turned to my friends for advice, and I'm lucky to have such great and talented friends as the lovely Sam and Sam Clark from Moro. This recipe is unashamedly based on one of theirs, with the necessary tweaks to make it not only taste a bit different, but be deliverable on a hundreds-of-pounds-a-day basis. Thanks, Sams.

SERVES ABOUT 4

2 tablespoons currants
1/2 teaspoon ground allspice
1 heaping teaspoon chopped dill
1 large scallion, sliced

1 1/2 tablespoons extra virgin olive oil
heaping 1 1/4 cups brown basmati rice
2 cups vegetable stock
salt

Mix together the currants, allspice, dill, and scallion in a bowl until well combined.
Heat the oil in a pan, add the mixture from the bowl, then the rice, and gently fry for a couple of minutes, stirring occasionally. Add the vegetable stock, cover, and cook for 20 to 30 minutes on a medium simmer. Check the seasoning, fluff up the pilaf, and serve with a squeeze of lemon.

SOUPS

SPRING

Cauliflower, Almond, & Turmeric Soup ✓ V WF **GF**

The Spanish do a great cold summer soup of almonds and garlic called *ajo blanco*, and our feeling with this was to build on the creaminess that the almonds bring, backing that up with the sublime (also dairy-free) creaminess that cauliflowers get when cooked soft and puréed. And then, for a triple cream hit, you can always finish it off with a bit of the real stuff too. Should have the consistency of satin.

SERVES 5, OR 4 IF VERY HUNGRY

1 very large cauliflower, weighing about 3¹/4 lb
¹/2 stick butter
1 very large onion, thinly sliced
3 cloves of garlic, minced
1 teaspoon turmeric
¹/2 teaspoon ground (or whole) fenugreek
¹/2 teaspoon ground ginger

³/4 cup ground almonds
2 pints vegetable stock
generous 2¹/2 cups whole milk
a small handful of whole almonds, skin on,
    slightly crushed
lemon wedges
salt and pepper

Cut the florets off the central trunk and very roughly chop them. Quarter the trunk and slice that too. Melt the butter in a pan, add the onion, garlic, turmeric, fenugreek, ground ginger, and sliced cauliflower stalk, and cook until the onion begins to soften.
Stir in the ground almonds, making sure everything is well coated, then add the stock.
Simmer for about 10 minutes, then add the cauliflower florets—not all of the cauliflower may be submerged in the liquid but as it begins to cook stir occasionally and it will all get there. Simmer for a further 20 to 25 minutes, or until all the cauliflower parts are very tender but not mushy—check that the stalks are soft too.
Then stir in the milk and blend with a hand-held immersion blender until completely smooth.
Ben says for the smoothness and look of this rather refined soup you have to finish it with ground white pepper, but I'd still go for freshly ground black pepper.
Either way it needs a good whack of salt.
Top it off with some crushed whole almonds (or sliced), and serve with a wedge of lemon on the side for a bit of last-minute freshness.

Right: Fresh turmeric root in Zanzibar.

Tom (Really) Yum ✓ ❤ V *DF* **WF** **GF**

A Thai classic, this head-clearing broth is very easily made. Pretty much all the love goes into the base paste, and once you've gone to the trouble of getting all those ingredients together, it's worth making double and keeping half, either in a jar in the fridge for a week or in the freezer for a month. (This is what we've suggested in the recipe, so if you're not prepared to commit to a second sitting, halve the ingredients in the first section.) Lime leaves are found in the fridge or freezer of most Asian grocery stores, and are even in some supermarkets now. They can be frozen, and taken out individually as and when required. Worth trying to hunt them down for their perfume and flavor—there's nothing quite like them in the world.

SERVES 4—MORE IF YOU DO IT IN LITTLE ASIAN BOWLS

THE PASTE
1/2 bulb garlic, cloves peeled
3 sticks lemongrass, roughly chopped
2 1/2 oz fresh ginger, sliced
6 lime leaves
2 1/2 oz cilantro, chopped (keep a few sprigs for the end)
2 to 3 red chiles (depending on how hot you like it), roughly chopped
3 to 4 shallots, peeled
1/3 cup sunflower or peanut oil

THE REST
1 x 14-oz can of coconut milk
heaping 1 3/4 cups fresh or frozen peas (if fresh, use 2 1/4 pounds unshelled pods)
3 cups sliced button mushrooms
2 nice tomatoes
2 cups beansprouts
1 lime
1 scallion, thinly sliced on a serious diagonal
a few sprigs of cilantro, to finish
salt and pepper

Put all the paste ingredients into a food processor or blender and blend to a fine purée (because this makes enough for two recipe quantities of soup, divide it in two and put one half away for later).
Put the remaining paste into a hot pan and stir for a few minutes to release the flavors.
Now add 1 3/4 cups of water, the coconut milk, and a pinch of salt. Bring to a gentle simmer.
Turn the heat off and stir in the peas and mushrooms.
Cut the tomatoes into slivery wedges and divide them, along with the beansprouts, between your four warmed bowls. Check the seasoning and finish with a hefty squeeze of lime.
Divide the very hot soup between the bowls, making sure each has an even amount of peas and mushrooms.
Finish with some shards of scallion and a sprig of cilantro.

Above: Cauliflower, Almond & Turmeric Soup
Below: Tom (Really) Yum

Pauper's French Onion Soup ✓ ❤ WF GF

There's really nothing very Pauper's about this, apart from not having to get veal bones in your life, and then spend 8 hours making a stock. I just like the name, and due to swapping a chicken stock for the veal one, it feels decidedly lighter and more springlike, though maybe a bit less luxurious and certainly less brown-tasting than the original. The best way to get that French onion soup hit in the comfort of your own home.

SERVES 4

3/4 cup navy beans
1/2 stick unsalted butter
2 lb onions, sliced
1 teaspoon dried oregano
1 bunch of thyme, tied together with string
1 tablespoon wholegrain mustard

3 tablespoons white wine vinegar
3 pints light chicken stock
1 3/4 oz Parmesan cheese, grated (reserve rind if possible)
a splash of lemon juice
2 tablespoons finely chopped parsley
salt and pepper

First soak the navy beans overnight.
The next day, melt the butter in a pan over low heat and add the sliced onions.
Cook gently for 20 to 30 minutes, or until soft and starting to caramelize, then stir in the oregano, bunch of thyme, mustard, vinegar, and some seasoning.
Simmer until all the vinegar has reduced away—just a few minutes.
Drain the navy beans, tip them into the onions, cover with the stock, and bring to a boil. Toss in the rind of the Parmesan now, if you have it, in one piece, to infuse its flavor.
Once the soup has come to a boil, skim it, reduce the heat to a simmer, and cook until the beans are soft and tender.*
Check the seasoning and make sure you're happy with the thickness (to alter, either simmer it down to thicken or splash in some water to thin).
Stir in half the grated Parmesan, and finish with a light squeeze of lemon juice, and scatter with the chopped parsley and the remaining cheese at the very last.

Bean cooking is a bit of a funny business because the length of time they take to cook can vary enormously. Two identical beans from different sources may differ in up to a couple of hours before they are tender. This is largely down to crop and age, so be sympathetic, not impatient because they will go soft in the end—well, 95% of the time anyway. Whatever happens, keep topping them off with water to maintain a soupy consistency—DON'T let them boil dry because there's no coming back from there and nothing really stinks like badly burned beans.

Chunky Vegetable & Chermoula Soup ✓ ❤ V *DF* **WF GF**

Chermoula—akin to a Moroccan pesto—is a good thing to have hanging around in a jar in the fridge. It brings instant zip and bang to whatever it meets, and can be used to fire up beans, salads, meats, and, in this case, a soup. The nice vegetables in the background are some of the classics that you usually find in tagines (especially the turnips, sadly out of fashion at the moment), and throwing in some dried fruit (like apricots or golden raisins, but in this case prunes) is also true to Levant form. As they soften and melt they bring an unsurprising fruitiness but also a richness to the whole.

SERVES 4 VERY WELL

THE CHERMOULA (MOROCCAN PESTO)
1 big bunch of cilantro, roughly chopped
  (about 1 1/2 oz)
3 cloves of garlic, peeled and smashed
1/2 tablespoon ground cumin
1 teaspoon crushed red chili
1/2 teaspoon paprika
a hefty pinch of saffron threads
3 tablespoons extra virgin olive oil
salt, to taste

THE REST
2 medium turnips, unpeeled, chopped into 3/4-inch dice
1 large carrot, unpeeled, diced
1 medium zucchini, cut into chunky dice
1 stick of celery, sliced
1 small sweet potato, unpeeled, diced
1/2 a 14-oz can of chopped tomatoes
5 prunes, chopped small (the ones from Agen
  are yum)
3 1/4 cups vegetable stock
1/2 a lemon, plus more to taste
a handful of cilantro, roughly chopped
salt and pepper

Put all the chermoula ingredients into a food processor and pulse to a fine purée.
Get your favorite large stockpot hot and add the chermoula.
Gently fry, being careful not to burn, and once you start to smell the spices after about 5 minutes, add all the vegetables and stir to coat. Season.
Adjust the heat to medium and cook the turnips, carrot, zucchini, celery, and sweet potato until very soft—around 20 minutes with a lid on, stirring regularly.
Add the chopped tomatoes and the chopped prunes, then stir for a minute or two until the tomato is all incorporated.
Pour in the hot stock and simmer very gently, covered, for 20 minutes to allow all of the flavors to come together.
Blend one-third of the soup until smooth and stir back into the rest. Rinse the blender out with a mug of water and tip that in too.
Squeeze in some lemon juice, and season very well.
When you are ready to go, scatter with the chopped cilantro.

Roast Chicken & Corn Soup ✓

A souped-up and slightly Westernized version of the standard on Chinese menus, this became the big hit of last summer. Finishing it with flour is optional but does help to give it a smooth, rich texture, which is the role the MSG plays in the original. Goes down well with kids.

SERVES PLENTY... ABOUT 6

THE MARINADE
2 cloves of garlic, chopped
1½ tablespoons wholegrain mustard
1 tablespoon honey, stringy-bark if possible (see page 127)

THE REST
14 oz free-range chicken thighs, cut into medium dice
3 cobs of corn
2 pints chicken stock
½ stick butter

1 tablespoon olive oil
2 sticks celery, cut in half down the middle and diced
1 onion, diced
1 large carrot, cut in half down the middle and sliced
3 tablespoons flour
2 tablespoons marsala or sweet sherry
¾ cup cream
2 tablespoons chopped flat-leaf parsley
salt and pepper

Mix the marinade ingredients together in a bowl. Add the chicken, cover with plastic wrap, and let marinate in the fridge overnight.

Next day, preheat the broiler to very hot.

Shuck the corn by standing the cobs on one end and cutting downward with a knife so the kernels fall off. Put the corn cobs into a saucepan with the chicken stock and any stray vegetables/aromatics you have hanging around.*

Bring to a boil and simmer for 30 minutes.

Meanwhile, arrange the chicken evenly spaced on a broiler rack and place under the broiler. Sear for 5+ minutes, or until well browned, then turn it over and do the same to the other side.

Get your best stockpot on the stove over medium heat and add the butter and the olive oil.

When the butter is sizzling and going brown, add the vegetables and allow them to cook, picking up just a bit of color. Add some salt.

Once the chicken is cooked, tip any chicken juices into the corn stock and set the chicken aside; when it's cooled down a little, shred the chicken by hand.

Add the flour to the vegetables in the pot and stir for a couple of minutes, then splash in the marsala and give it a bit of action with the wooden spoon.

Strain the corn stock slowly into the vegetables, stirring all the time to ensure a smooth complexion, then add the cream.

Bring up to a gentle simmer for 30 minutes.

When all the vegetables are meltingly soft, blend till chunky-smooth, then tip in the shucked corn and shredded chicken, and give it a final season.

See page 90 for a basic lesson on stock.

Clockwise from top right: Roast Chicken & Corn Soup; Chunky Vegetable & Chermoula Soup; Pauper's French Onion Soup.

SUMMER

Pea(ce) & Mint Soup ✓ ❤ V *DF* **WF** **GF**

The joke in the name is because we originally put it on as a special for World Peace Day, but it's now become a summer standard (without the brackets). Every sensible British person has pea and mint soup on a fairly regular basis through the summer months, and, of course, everybody except the very lucky few make theirs with frozen peas. Even though availability-wise and taste-wise you can cook and eat this dish at any time of year (it's not like frozen peas lose their flavor in winter), it still feels wrong once the evenings have turned cool. That's the time to move into pea and ham soup, but then you have to use split or mature, field-ripened peas—never frozen. Marking the changing of the seasons is like an annual game, where the rules are based on an innate sense of what feels right.

PLENTIFUL FOR 4

3 tablespoons olive oil
2 medium onions, sliced
2 small sticks of celery, sliced
3 cloves garlic, smashed
3$^{1}/_{2}$ cups fresh or frozen peas (if fresh, use 4$^{1}/_{2}$ lb pods before shelling)

$^{1}/_{2}$ cup mint (about 1$^{1}/_{2}$ oz) leaves picked and chopped (save the stalks)
1 cup sliced scallions
$^{1}/_{2}$ a romaine lettuce, very finely shredded
salt and freshly ground white pepper

In a nice deep saucepan gently heat the oil and add the onions, celery, and garlic plus some salt and pepper.
Cover and cook gently on low heat for about 20 minutes, or until all is very soft—absolutely no browning, please.
Now add the peas (saving a few for the end), mint stalks (tied together with string), and scallions.
Mix everything together, then add a generous 2$^{1}/_{2}$ cups of boiling water and simmer for 5 minutes.
Stir in the lettuce and, once this is wilted and soft, add the chopped mint leaves.
Bring the soup back up to a boil, remove if from the heat, and pull out and discard the mint stalks.
Blend the soup to a very fine purée—completely smooth—and chill in shallow pans as quickly as possible to keep the color. Season to taste before serving with a few more peas scattered on top.

Spinach Vichysoisse ✓ ❤ V **WF** **GF**

As old summer rivals, Vichysoisse is currently losing out to Gazpacho, maybe on perceived health value, or maybe it's just a color thing. So, this über-green-and-good-for-you version is here to redress the balance. When done right, with a good stock (a light chicken stock also works well), this peasants' soup of leeks and potatoes turns into a dish worthy of any passing Vichy nobleman.

SERVES 5

THE STOCK
2 big or 3 medium leeks
a handful of flat-leaf parsley, plus stalks
1 large carrot

2 sticks of celery
1 large onion
2 cloves of garlic
$^{1}/_{2}$ teaspoon black peppercorns

THE REST
2 medium onions, thinly sliced
2 sticks of celery, thinly sliced
2 cloves of garlic, sliced
1 heaping tablespoon butter
2 tablespoons olive oil

*1 medium-sized floury potato, peeled and diced
(see page 65)*
10 1/2 oz baby spinach
3/4 cup + 2 tablespoons heavy cream
sea salt and freshly ground white pepper

Trim the leeks well and put all the parts you've stripped off, plus the trimmings from the root end, into a pot with the other stock ingredients. Cover with 2 1/2 pints of water and simmer for 40 minutes. Slice the trimmed leeks thinly, and wash really well.

Sweat the leeks, onions, celery, and garlic in a medium saucepan over really low heat with the butter and olive oil until translucent—about 20 to 25 minutes.

Add the potatoes, stir well, then drain the hot leek stock directly into the pot and whack up the heat. Simmer until the potatoes are cooked, around 20 minutes, then blend to a velvety smooth purée. Spread out in a baking pan and place in the fridge or freezer to chill.

Wash the baby spinach and purée in a food processor or blender to a bright green mush.

Once your tray of vichysoisse in the fridge/freezer has cooled, add it to a large bowl, stir in the cream and baby spinach and taste for seasoning.

Gazpacho ✓ ❤ V *DF* **WF** **GF**

There are more ways to make this soup than there are recipes with celery in them in this book, and everyone will tell you theirs is the true Spanish recipe, taught to them by their Spanish friend who was shown it as a child by their great-granny. Truthfully though, they may all be right—even in Spain they have hundreds of regional and artistic differences. Our gazpacho has all the usuals, with some celery and cucumber to keep it cool on the palate, as well as in temperature. This makes ours a bit greener, but on a hot, sticky day in the city, it sure makes you feel a whole load better.

APPETIZER FOR 4

6 tomatoes—must be best of the summer beauties
1/2 cucumber, peeled and cut into rough chunks
a big handful of cilantro, roughly chopped
3 cloves of garlic, smashed
1/2 red chile, roughly chopped
2 scallions, thinly sliced

*1 red bell pepper, seeded and cut into tiny dice—
small as you can*
1 large stick of celery, minced as finely as you can
1 lime
1/4 cup extra virgin olive oil
salt

Core all the tomatoes, make an "X" on their bottoms, and put them into a heatproof bowl. Add boiling water to cover, let sit while you count to 20, then drain and run them all immediately under cold water. Peel and quarter them, and discard the seeds.

Put the tomatoes, cucumbers, cilantro, garlic, and chile into the blender and blitz to a slightly chunky purée. Or, you can use a hand-held immersion blender, if you have one.

Stir the scallions, red bell pepper, and celery into the tomato base. It'll probably be a little thick, so loossen it with a generous 1 1/4 cups of water.

Season with salt and lime juice, then stir in the extra virgin, leaving some to pool on top.

NB: We like to leave this wheat-free, but in España a little bread soaked in vinegar is often added to the blender to give body and innate sharpness. If you're not funny about wheat/gluten you can do this or serve with crunchy croutons on top. Also nice with a bit of crushed ice floating in it, but that would be instead of the croutons, not as well.

ROAST TOMATO, CHILI + CUMIN SOUP

✓ ❤ V *DF* **WF** **GF**

One day I was at the Big Kitchen bulking up the little recipe for this soup, which had just sailed through at our summer menu tasting session. A week before at home I had roasted half a dozen tomatoes, but I was now facing a large wall entirely built of 11-pound boxes of them. It took about half a day for me to ensure that each of forty roasting pans had a ladleful of olive oil, a sprinkling of salt and pepper, some chopped garlic, and a dusting of fructose in it. The next stage involved halving the tomatoes before individually rolling the cut side in the flavored and seasoned oil. As I did this not particularly stimulating (though it was a very important job), I could feel a bit of frustration—or boredom—growing: as my culinary copilot Fred would say, I had a crab rising. But the truth is there's no short-cut to some flavors, and my slight crabbiness was more than made up for when I heard the pleasure this soup had bought to our lads and lasses in the restaurants, not to mention the people who eat with us.

SERVES 4+

5 to 6 vine-ripened tomatoes
1/2 cup extra virgin olive oil
1 heaping tablespoon fructose
3 cloves of garlic, roughly chopped
2 large red onions, thinly sliced

1/2 teaspoon ground cumin
1/2 teaspoon whole cumin seeds
3/4 teaspoon red chili flakes
1 x 14-oz can chopped tomatoes
salt and pepper

Preheat the oven to 375°F. Halve all the tomatoes across the middle. Take a shallow roasting pan and pour in half the olive oil. Add the fructose, the garlic, and some salt and pepper, then give it a bit of a stir so that everything is evenly distributed in the pan.

Pack the tomatoes closely in the oil CUT-SIDE DOWN. Put them into the preheated oven for 20 to 30 minutes, or until the skins have shriveled and the tomatoes are soft to squeeze.

Meanwhile put the rest of the olive oil into a big heavy saucepan and fry the onions, both kinds of cumin, and the chili flakes over medium heat for a few minutes. Cover and cook, stirring occasionally, for 10 to 15 minutes, or until the onions are soft.

Tip in the canned tomatoes, cover, and cook down for about 10 minutes, same temperature, stirring occasionally.

Pour in around 3½ cups water and bring back to a simmer.

When the roasted tomatoes are ready, take them out of the oven and let stand until cool enough to handle. Quickly pick the skins off by hand, then add the tomatoes and all the flavored oil to the saucepan. Simmer everything together gently for about 20 minutes, then you can either leave it chunky or blend to a rough purée in a blender or usng a hand-held immersion blender.

Have a look at the consistency, loosening it with a little hot water if necessary, and have a final seasoning check before serving.

Clockwise from top: Roast Tomato, Chili & Cumin Soup;
Pea(ce) & Mint; Spinach Vichysoisse; Gazpacho

FALL

Chile Pumpkin & Wild Mushroom Soup ✓ ❤ V WF **GF**

This is a great way to use up the inside of your scooped-out Jack'-o-Lantern, and a cup of this when you're standing next to a bonfire with some people you love might just create one of those hilarious "I'm so happy I could explode" moments. Free Leon brownie for anyone who makes it and sends us a postcard with a better name.

FEEDS 4 HUNGRY, SLIGHTLY HIPPY PEOPLE WHO LIKE ITALIAN FOOD (AND CHILES)

1³/₄ lb pumpkin, peeled and diced into roughly
    1-inch chunks
1¹/₂ leeks, sliced and washed well
¹/₄ cup olive oil
¹/₂ teaspoon dried chili flakes
3 cloves of garlic, sliced

a small handful of dried porcini (about ¹/₄ oz)
1 teaspoon chopped marjoram
1 teaspoon thinly sliced red chile
a big nugget of Parmesan cheese, grated
salt and pepper

Over very low heat, in a wide saucepan, cook the pumpkin and the leeks in the olive oil for 45 minutes, covered, or until they have a pleasing braised appearance.

Meanwhile add the dried mushrooms to a bowl and pour in 3¹/₂ cups boiling water. After a few minutes, drain them, keeping the soaking water—the porcini will be soft enough to chop up small.

Stir the chili flakes and garlic into the pumpkin and continue to cook for a further 10 minutes.

Strain the soaking water through a fine sieve into the pumpkin mixture and stir in the chopped mushrooms.

Bring to a simmer and cook until the pumpkin is good and soft—about 20 to 30 minutes.

Stir in the marjoram and chile; check the seasoning, then run a masher haphazardly through the soup a few times, to help the consistency, but don't overdo it.

Finish with a flurry of grated Parmesan and a splosh of good extra virgin.

This one tastes even better the next day.

Clockwise from top: Pinto, Black Bean & Chorizo Soup;
Chile Pumpkin & Wild Mushroom Soup; Lentil, Pancetta & Italian Herb Soup

Soups—FALL   **181**

PINTO, BLACK BEAN & CHORIZO SOUP

✓ *DF* **WF** **GF**

When we first opened we did so with a swathe of Brazilians who were a lot of fun to work with and used to proudly bring in bits of their national cuisine for us to try. I'm not sure if the conquistadores taught the pig and bean thing to the natives or vice versa, but surely the Brazilians and the Iberians are top of the world league. The origins of this soup are in their national dish of feijouada, which involves pork, beans, then more pork and more beans: absolutely delicious, but just don't book yourself in for a power afternoon afterward. Our version doesn't trigger your nap button in quite the same way, which is either a good thing or not, depending on how you see your afternoon going.

SERVES 4, BUT YOU CAN PROBABLY STRETCH IT TO 6 BECAUSE IT'S PRETTY FILLING

SOAK OVERNIGHT

¹/₄ cup + 2 tablespoons dried pinto beans
¹/₄ cup + 3 tablespoons dried black turtle beans
9 oz good-quality raw chorizo sausage⊚
3 tablespoons extra virgin olive oil
1 teaspoon ground coriander
1 teaspoon cayenne pepper
1 red bell pepper, medium diced

3 cloves of garlic, sliced
1 medium red onion, thinly sliced
1 x 14-oz can of tomatoes
2 to 3 pints chicken stock
¹/₅ Savoy cabbage, chopped
a big handful of cilantro, chopped
salt and pepper

Soak the pinto and black turtle beans separately in cold water overnight.
Next day drain them, cover with fresh water, and cook in their own pots with a few bean friends (see page 120 to find out what exactly beans' friends are). Cook all the way through but not to total collapse.
Dice the chorizo into medium cubes and get your oil warming in a deep heavy saucepan.
Sizzle the chorizo until it's browned and that red oil starts to seep out, but beware, the golden brown sausage and lustrous red oil can quickly turn to brown-black in an instant if your heat is too high.
Stir in your spices, red bell pepper, garlic, and onion. Turn the heat up a little and cook until translucent and all well mingled together. Season with sea salt.
Add the tomatoes, let it all burble together for around 10 minutes, then add 2 pints of stock and reduce on a well maintained simmer for 20 minutes.
Drain the beans, keeping about 1 pint of their cooking liquor, and then stir the beans, liquor, and the cabbage in well. Cook for another 20 minutes, letting the soup simmer down to a pleasing thickness.
Turn off the heat and let it rest for 5 minutes, covered, to let the flavors settle.
Check the seasoning and consistency, loosening it with the remaining stock if you like. Stir in the chopped cilantro to serve.

⊚ See Suppliers, page VI in appendix.

Lentil, Pancetta, & Italian Herb Soup ✓ ❤ WF **GF**

The kind of soup that everyone should know about.
All the easies, followed by all the deliciousnesses. A great drawbridge between summer and winter eating.

INSTANT WARMING FOR 4

1 heaping tablespoon butter
1/4 cup olive oil
5 1/2 oz pancetta, cut into small nuggets
2 medium carrots, finely chopped
1 1/2 sticks of celery, finely chopped
1 large onion, roughly chopped
3 bay leaves
1 teaspoon dried oregano

4 cloves of garlic, sliced
1 tablespoon tomato paste
1 tablespoon red wine vinegar
1 cup brown lentils
2 pints chicken stock
a small bunch of basil, chopped
salt and pepper

Heat a big solid saucepan up to high heat and add half the butter and all the oil.
When the oil is hot add the pancetta, making sure you scatter it all over the bottom of the pan.
Once the pancetta is crisp and browned on all sides, add the rest of the butter, followed by all the vegetables.
Cook gently for 15 minutes, until the vegetables are soft and starting to pick up a bit of color.
Stir in the bay leaves, oregano, and garlic and cook for a further 5 minutes.
Now add the tomato paste, mix well, and splosh in the vinegar.
Tip in the lentils, give them a good stir, and then add the chicken stock.
Bring to a boil, then turn the heat down to a simmer for 30 minutes, or until the lentils are very tender.
Take out 2 large ladlefuls of soup, blend to a chunky purée, then stir it back into the soup.
Stir in the basil, check the seasoning, and serve.

Good Soup for a Bad Day ✓ ♥ WF
(Chicken, Pearl Barley, Mushroom, & Tarragon)

This soup may not be the quickest of makes, but as long as you follow the method you're guaranteed to feel better at the end of the day.

RESTORATIVE MEASURES FOR 4*

2 free-range chicken legs
2 large carrots—1 left whole, 1 chopped into
   $^1/_2$-inch dice
2 sticks of celery
2 medium onions, sliced
6 cloves of garlic, peeled
4 bay leaves

a handful of parsley, with stalks
$10^1/_2$ oz sliced closed-cup mushrooms
3 tablespoons extra virgin olive oil
$^3/_4$ cup pearl barley
1 heaping tablespoon butter
1 tablespoon tarragon leaves, chopped
salt and pepper, plus a few whole peppercorns

Put the chicken legs into your favorite winter stockpot, along with the whole carrot, celery, half the sliced onion, half the garlic, two of the bay leaves, the parsley, and the peppercorns.
Prise the stalks from the mushrooms and throw them in too.
Cover with 3 pints of water and bring to a simmer, then skim and turn the heat down until the stock is just steaming. Let cook like this until the chicken meat is coming away from the bone—about an hour.
Go and sit down for half an hour with a nice glass of wine and a newspaper, and put your feet up.
In a different saucepan, when you're ready, over low heat, fry the remaining onions in the oil with the rest of the garlic, chopped, and a bit of salt and pepper for a very gentle half hour or so until softened. (Meanwhile, do a bit more damage to your bottle while stirring your gently goldening onions, smelling the calming aromatherapy of simmering chicken stock and gazing into the middle distance.)
Add the pearl barley, diced carrot, and bay leaves to the onions, then pour in the stock through a strainer and bring to a simmer. Throw the vegetables away (or purée for another day's soup base) and put the chicken aside to cool down.
After an hour (i.e. your luxurious bath), get the butter to the edge of brown in a skillet and fry the mushroom through golden until just coming up to crispy, chuck the tarragon in, give it a quick toss, and then swirl it all into the soup.
Around about now your barley should be tender.
Amuse yourself by picking the meat off the chicken bones, chopping it into little pieces, and adding to the soup.
When you are comfortable with your barley, have a long, hard moment with the salt and pepper and if it seems a bit thick for a soup loosen it with a little hot water.
Eat with crusty bread and a sense of well-being, then sleep the sleep you deserve.

Plus leftovers for tomorrow, which will be a better day.

Above: Indian Parsnip Soup
Below: Good Soup for a Bad Day

Indian Parsnip soup

✓ ❤ V *DF* **WF** **GF**

Roots and the Raj. An easy soup to make, and just right for a blusterous fall day.

SERVES ABOUT 5

3 tablespoons sunflower oil
1 teaspoon cumin seeds
1 teaspoon caraway seeds
2 medium onions, sliced
3 big sticks of celery, sliced
1 fat thumb-sized piece fresh ginger, grated
1/2 teaspoon dried chili flakes
a big pinch of ground cloves
1/2 teaspoon turmeric
1/2 teaspoon garam masala

1 1/2 lb parsnips, peeled and diced
1 x 14-oz can of coconut milk
1 3/4 oz creamed coconut
6 sprigs of thyme and 2 bay leaves, tied together
a small scattering of sumac
just a drizzle of honey, preferably stringy-bark ☺
   (see page 127)
a squeeze of lemon juice
salt and freshly ground white pepper

Heat the oil in a pan and stir in the seeds. When they start to pop add the onions, celery, ginger, chili flakes, and the rest of the spices (except the sumac).
Cook gently until soft (about 15 minutes), then add the parsnips, both kinds of coconut, and some salt and pepper.
Add 2 1/2 pints of warm water—enough to cover, plus a little more—and toss in the thyme and bay, bring to a boil, then turn down to a steady simmer.
Cover and cook for about 40 minutes, until the parsnips are very tender. Check the seasoning, then blend or purée with your favorite soup tool until smooth. Finish with the sumac, a drizzle of honey, and add a squeeze of lemon at the last minute, just before serving.

☺ See Suppliers, page VI in Appendix.

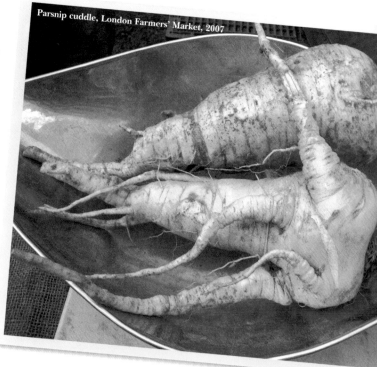

Parsnip cuddle, London Farmers' Market, 2007

Butternut & Bacon Chowder ✓ WF GF

Chowders are usually associated with clams, summertime, and New England, but this is a slightly heartier recipe that gently slides into autumnal eating. Nice as a Saturday lunch soup when you have the time to enjoy making it.

SERVES 4

3 tablespoons butter
7oz bacon slices, diced small
3 cloves of garlic, chopped
1 large onion, diced
1 small butternut squash (about 1^1/$_2$ lb), peeled
    and cut into ^{3}/$_4$-inch dice
2 medium floury potatoes, scrubbed and cut into
    ^{3}/$_4$-inch dice

2 cups chicken stock
scant ^{1}/$_2$ cup heavy cream
2 cups whole milk
3 big handfuls of flat-leaf parsley, leaves picked
    and roughly chopped
1 tablespoon thyme, roughly chopped
salt and pepper

Over medium heat melt the butter in a big heavy saucepan. When it's just about going nutty brown, scatter in the bacon in separate pieces, not a clump.

Keep cooking on medium heat until the bacon starts to crisp and takes on a nicely golden-brown appearance. Once this has happened, stir in the garlic and continue to cook for a further few minutes to allow the flavors to release.

Add the onion and some salt and cook gently for a further 10 minutes or so, covered, until the onion is very soft but not browning. Splosh in a couple of tablespoons of water to get the color and to loosen anything sticking to the bottom of the pan.

Once the onions are super-soft, add the squash and potatoes, turn the heat down a little, and continue to cook, stirring occasionally, for a further 10 minutes.

When they are all well coated, whack the heat up a little and pour in the chicken stock and cream. Simmer the soup for 15 to 20 minutes, or until the squash and potatoes are soft but not collapsing.

Now add the milk and bring to a simmer; as soon as this has happened, turn the heat off:

DO NOT LET IT BOIL OR THE MILK WILL SPLIT.

Using a slotted spoon, take out about half the vegetables, letting the liquid drain back into the pan. Blend the vegetables to a smooth purée and add back to the soup.

Check the seasoning, stir in the chopped parsley, and scatter with thyme just before serving.

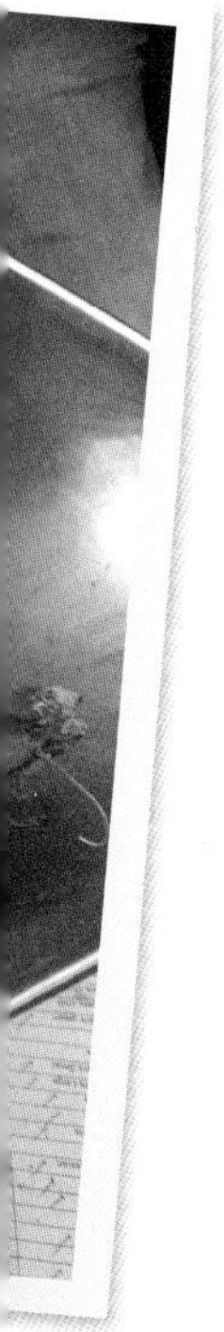

WINTER

Moroccan Harira ✓ ❤ V *DF*

Traditionally this is the soup that Moroccans break their dawn-till-dusk Ramadan fast with, and once you've tried it you'll understand why: it has a triple carb action (chickpeas, lentils, and rice) to get those energy levels back up, and while ours is vegetarian, the ones in Morocco tend to have a lamby base to them. The light floury stir-in is essential to the final silkiness, and there should be a definite fresh sharpness to it from the lemon juice. We've loved making this soup for years, and while the batches are bigger it's still exactly the same recipe, based long, long ago in the mists of Marrakesh on the teachings of one of Leon's food heroines, Claudia Roden. One of our absolute faves, this is a soup that just keeps on giving, both physically and emotionally.

Ramadan is in the ninth month of the Islamic calendar, which is lunar-based, so according to our calendar it can fall in any season. We can truly recommend it at any time of year, but have put it in winter because of the joy it can bring on a bleak winter's day.

MAKES ENOUGH FOR 4 FAMISHED PEOPLE

³/4 cup brown lentils
1 x 14-oz can of chickpeas
1 large red onion, diced
1 x 14-oz can of chopped tomatoes
¹/2 teaspoon ground cumin
¹/2 teaspoon turmeric
2 tablespoons harissa
a large pinch of saffron

1¹/2 tablespoons lemon juice
heaping ¹/4 cup white basmati rice
2 tablespoons all-purpose flour
a big handful of cilantro, leaves picked and
  chopped
a big handful of flat-leaf parsley, leaves picked
  and chopped
salt and pepper

First soak the lentils in cold water for 1 hour, then drain.

Drain the chickpeas, then place them in a large heavy saucepan and cover with 3 pints of water. Add the diced onion and bring to a boil, uncovered.

Tip in the tomatoes and the drained lentils along with the cumin, turmeric, and harissa. Continue to cook until the lentils are tender, about 15 to 20 minutes.

While this is happening, soak the saffron in the lemon juice to release the flavor and color.

Add the rice to the pot and continue to cook until it's ready.

Meanwhile, place the flour in a bowl and slowly add ¹/4 cup of cold water while whisking to a loose paste. Add ¹/4 cup of hot stock from the soup and keeping on whisking, then pour the hot floury mixture into the soup along with the saffrony lemon juice; stir thoroughly and well over medium heat for just a couple of minutes but DO NOT BOIL.

Your soup is now ready, save for an extensive seasoning moment (chickpeas, rice, and lentils all need salt) and stirring in an abundance of chopped herbs.

It really is much better the next day, but didn't want to say that at the beginning in case it discouraged you from making this soup I love.

Clockwise from top: Winter Root Soup with Sage & Chestnuts;
Moroccan Harira; White Bean & Winter Greens Soup

Winter Root Soup with Sage & Chestnuts ✓ ❤ V WF **GF**

Slow cooking is the right way to get the most out of your root vegetables, and matched up here with some chestnuts for sweetness and winter's favorite herb, sage, they really are deserving of their place center stage. Obviously, if you can get them and have the time and inclination, roasting your own chestnuts would be even more rewarding. We felt this was more of a butter kind of soup, but olive oil can always be used instead—better for you, but in this instance maybe a little less yum for the vegans.

SERVES 5+

2/3 stick butter
2 large onions, diced
5 1/2 oz precooked, vacuum-packed chestnuts, chopped
1 good-sized parsnip, cut into chunky dice
1/3 of a small celeriac, cut into chunky dice
2 small or 1 large carrot, cut into chunky dice
1/3 of a rutabaga, cut into chunky dice
3 pints light vegetable stock

a small handful of sage, leaves picked and chopped
a small handful of thyme, leaves picked and chopped
2 bay leaves
a big handful of flat-leaf parsley, leaves picked and chopped
salt and pepper

Melt the butter in a large saucepan and fry the onions and two-thirds of the chestnuts until the onions have softened.

After about 10 minutes add the root vegetables and continue to cook for about half an hour with the lid on, until they are slightly tender .

Now add the stock, sage, thyme, and bay leaves and bring to a boil. Reduce the heat and simmer for 30 to 45 minutes, or until the vegetables are very soft.

Check the seasoning, then take out about 3 large ladlefuls of the vegetables with a slotted spoon and blend to a purée. Add this back to the soup to thicken it, then stir in the parsley.

Slice the rest of the chestnuts and scatter them on top, then season well, my friend.

White Bean & Winter Greens Soup ✓ ❤ V *DF* **WF** **GF**

This is a most uplifting bowl: the chard, one of winter's finest greens (see page 54), sits extremely comfortably within the thick, creamy background of the beans. Finishing it with pistou (roughly speaking a French version of pesto, without the pine nuts and Parmesan) gives it an almost summery lightness, sometimes much needed in the depths of winter. Nice one, Benny.

SERVES 6

1 cup dried cannellini or navy beans or
 1¹/₂ x 18-oz cans, drained
¹/₄ cup olive oil
6 shallots, sliced
4 sticks of celery, sliced
2 carrots, sliced
5 to 6 small waxy potatoes, sliced (see page 65
 for the ideal potatoes)
1 lb Swiss chard
2¹/₂ pints vegetable stock
salt and pepper

THE PISTOU
2 large bunches of basil (about 2³/₄ oz),
 roughly chopped
2 large cloves of garlic, minced
¹/₄ cup extra virgin olive oil
1¹/₂ tablespoons lemon juice
salt and pepper

First soak the beans in cold water overnight or, if you're using canned ones, come straight in at * below.
Next day drain the beans, tip them into a big pan, and cover them with lots of fresh water. Bring to a boil with some helpful aromatics (see page 32), then reduce to a simmer.
Cook the beans until they are well and truly tender, which should take anything between 1 hour and 2.
*While the beans are doing their stuff, heat up the olive oil in a large heavy saucepan on medium heat.
Add all the vegetables except the Swiss chard.
Sauté the vegetables until they are nice and soft, stirring from time to time and keeping the lid on.
This should take roughly 20 to 30 minutes.
Meanwhile, prepare the chard by trimming off the bottom couple of inches from the tough end of the stalk and discarding. Then cut the rest of the stalk away from the green leaf, and thinly slice. Add the stalk slices to the vegetable pot, and thinly slice the green leafy part, setting it aside for now.
Once the beans are cooked, add them to the vegetables (or add the canned beans if using); stir to coat the beans and then add the vegetable stock and some seasoning. Bring to a boil.
The soup is ready once the potatoes are nice and soft—roughly another 15 to 20 minutes.
Make the pistou by mixing together the basil and garlic, then stir in the lemon juice and oil and season well.
Take one-third of the soup out and blend briefly until creamy, then pour it back into the pot.
Check the seasoning, then stir in the sliced green chard leaves and ley simmer for just a couple of minutes.
Finally add the pistou and check the seasoning.
Let sit for 5 minutes with a lid on before serving with crusty bread.

Carter in the garden, USA 2006

Linda sitting on the porch,
Orchard Nebraska 1959

Leon's Family Recipes

I've made Nana's soup for years. My
granddaughter, like many children, doesn't
care for vegetables. She did, however, taste my
soup once when she was quite young and
named it Nana's soup.

Is it my delectable recipe and perfect
combination of flavors and seasoning …
I think not … I think it's the love that goes into
the food we make, and for my granddaughter
Nana's soup spells love.

Takes 20 minutes to prep and ignore for
2½ hours to cook, which is a great time to
read a book or go rake the leaves and come in
to a warm hearty dinner. Have one wonderful
meal of it, then freeze the rest in small
portioned containers for those late-night
snacks and ready dinners after a long day.

Linda's Nana's Soup ✓ ❤ *DF* WF **GF**

Linda has more in common with Wonder Woman than you might
think at first glance. It's not just the name and nationality (the US
of A)—Linda truly is a wonder woman. This little lady from Kansas
has had an illustrious career with Burger King, owning four in
Kansas City, one of which had a waterfall! One day she walked into
one of her restaurants, saw a lot of fat people and decided she didn't want to be a part of that any
more. Through mutual friends of John's she heard about us and has been flying back and forth
helping us get sorted out enough to open Leons in America, which would be pretty cool. She's also
the most amazing person I've met in a while—I might have hinted at that at the beginning—and her
soup truly matches her understated greatness; went down very well with my little nieces and nephew.

MAKES 6 HEARTY SUPPERS

2¼ lb good-quality beef, diced into ½-inch cubes
    (shank works well)
½ a medium onion, chopped
a little light olive oil
2 pints beef stock (you might need as many as
    3 pints because it may boil down)
6 medium potatoes, cut into ½-inch cubes
3 organic carrots, cleaned and cut into ½-inch pieces
3 tablespoons cooking sherry, normal sherry, port,
    or Madeira
2 teaspoons smoked paprika
2 x 14-oz cans of tomatoes

2 shakes of Tabasco sauce, or more to taste
a handful of parsley, chopped
salt and pepper

Brown the meat and onion in oil in a Dutch oven
and add salt and pepper.
Add the stock, potatoes, carrots, cooking sherry,
and smoked paprika. Bring to a boil, then reduce to
low heat and simmer, covered, for 2 hours. May need
to add some water.
Add the tomatoes and Tabasco and continue on low
heat for 30 minutes.
Scatter with the parsley and serve with cheese and
crackers, or a slice of buttered bread.
This is comfort food at its finest.

Ham Hock, Savoy Cabbage, & Rosemary Soup ✓ ❤ WF **GF**

This is a beautiful, calming, very healthy clear winter broth. Ham hocks are an excellent source of flavor and very cheap. Whenever you go to a good butcher just pick one up and stick it in the freezer—very handy standby for soups, casseroles, and pies. This soup takes a bit of time on the stove, but relatively little effort, and is impossible to get wrong. Keeps for days, becoming more and more at one with itself.

SERVES 6

1 ham hock
3 large carrots
3 medium onions
leaves from 2 sprigs of rosemary, chopped
2 bay leaves
2 whole cloves

2 cloves of garlic, sliced
5 to 6 small, waxy potatoes*
1/4 of a Savoy cabbage, very finely shredded
extra virgin olive oil
a nugget of Parmesan cheese
salt and pepper

Put the ham hock into your stockpot with plenty of cold water and bring to a simmer with one whole carrot, one onion cut in half, half the rosemary, 1 bay leaf, and 1 clove.

Simmer for many, many hours with a lid on (about 4, but the Poles, who are pig experts, cook it all day), until the meat is cooked and is coming away from the bone.

Lift the hock out and set aside; strain the stock into a large measuring cup and discard the vegetables: you need 3 pints of stock for this soup, so put any that you have left over into the fridge/freezer for your next porky need.

Halve the remaining carrots and slice thinly and do the same with the remaining onions and add them to the saucepan. Pour the hock stock onto the vegetable, add the remaining aromatics, and set on low heat. Shred/dice small the meat from the bone and slice the new potatoes very thinly.

Once the hock stock and vegetables have come up to a simmer, skim, and add the potatoes and the shredded cabbage.

After 20 minutes stir in the shredded or diced ham and check the seasoning. Add more hot water if necessary, but it should be a clearish lovely winter broth. Great for purists just like that but somewhat richer with a shot of extra virgin poured on top and some grated Parmesan to finish.

* See page 65 for suitable varieties of potatoes.

Karma Soupra (for St. Valentine's Day) ✓ ❤ WF GF

We came up with this one for Valentine's Day one year: it's got beautiful threads of saffron for attractiveness, brown rice to keep your energy levels up, mussels (which really are just plain rude), and chile to make you go like a rocket. Talk about a setup.

FEEDS 2 LOVERS

2¹/₂ tablespoons brown basmati rice
2 tablespoons unsalted butter
3¹/₂ oz banana shallots, sliced
2 cloves of garlic, chopped
¹/₂ a red chile, thinly sliced
1 stick of celery, thinly sliced
a few sprigs of thyme, tied together with string

1 glass of white wine
a few threads of saffron
2 pints fish stock
³/₄ lb mussels, beards removed
lemon juice
a small handful of flat-leaf parsley, chopped
salt and pepper

First soak the rice in cold water, just to get it swelling.

Gently heat the butter in a pan until it starts to fizzle, then toss in the shallots, garlic, chile, celery, and thyme sprigs.

Cover the pan and cook gently for about 10 minutes, stirring occasionally—no browning, please.

Drain the rice and tip it in, making sure it gets a good coating of butter, then add the wine and the saffron and cook until all the liquid has gone.

Add the fish stock and bring up to quite an aggressive simmer with the lid off so the liquid is reducing while the rice is cooking.

Once the grains are done, tip in the mussels. Put the lid on, and, holding onto the pan and the lid tightly, give everything a firm but gentle swirl around.

Don't peek for about 3 minutes, by which time the mussels should have opened up to reveal their pleasure inside.

Season well, and finish with a squeeze of lemon for a final zing. Serve in shallow bowls to show off the best of these *fruits de mer*, with a scattering of parsley on top.

Above: Ham Hock, Savoy Cabbage & Rosemary Soup
Below: Karma Soupra

Panzanella ✓ ❤ *DF*

The most important thing about this is that you only make it with properly good tomatoes. To do anything else would be insulting to this classic Tuscan salad. According to the rules (and when it comes to cooking Italians love rules), this shouldn't have any greenery in it, but ours does because we like leaves. Great way to use up old stale bread.

SERVES 4

$10^1/_2$ oz ciabatta, cut into 1-inch chunks
$^1/_3$ cup extra virgin olive oil
$^1/_2$ cup good black olives, stoned
1 heaping tablespoon capers
a small handful of flat-leaf parsley
$5^1/_2$ oz vine-ripened cherry tomatoes, torn in half
a small handful of basil leaves, torn up
$5^1/_2$ oz arugula
12 boquerones (Spanish escabeched anchovy fillets, the white ones)
salt and pepper

THE DRESSING

$5^1/_2$ oz vine-ripened tomatoes (cherry ones work well)
1 clove of garlic
$^1/_2$ cup tomato juice
1 teaspoon dried oregano
2 tablespoons red wine vinegar
$^1/_3$ + 1 tablespoon extra virgin olive oil
salt and pepper

Preheat the oven to 350°F.

Spread the ciabatta pieces in one layer on a cookie sheet and drizzle with the oil, making sure you give the white parts of the bread a good soaking.

Season well with salt and pepper and bake for 20 minutes on the top rack, shuffling them around halfway through.

Put the olives, capers, and parsley on your cutting board and roughly chop them.

Now get on and make your dressing by washing the tomatoes and sticking them into a blender with the garlic, tomato juice, and oregano.

Pulse for a good minute until you have a smooth, fine liquid—it should be a bit foamy.

Now add the vinegar, pulse again, and add the oil in spurts with a pulse in between until combined, smooth, and emulsified. Season.

When the ciabatta croutons are ready, tip them into a large bowl with the caper and olive mixture.

Add the dressing and give the croutons a really good stir to combine. Stir in the torn cherry tomatoes and basil and let stand for 15 minutes.

When the bread has been softened by the dressing toss the arugula through it, season again, and serve with the anchovy fillets on top.

House Dressing ✓ ❤ V *DF* **WF** **GF**

We really only included this because people always ask us what's in it. So simple, fresh, and versatile.

MAKES A SMALL JAM JAR FULL—ABOUT 1½ CUPS

1 tablespoon Dijon mustard
$^1/_4$ cup lemon juice

1 cup olive oil
salt and pepper

Combine the mustard and lemon juice in a bowl and add some seasoning.
Then beat in the olive oil slowly until all incorporated.

Leon Original Superfood Salad ✓ ❤ V WF **GF**

This is one of only a few dishes that have been on the Leon menu since we first opened our doors in London's Carnaby Street in 2004. Something magical happens when these ingredients get together—this salad really does what it says and keeps you up-and-at-it for hours. When my best friend Bridget was pregnant this salad was her No. 1 craving, and almost every night she would make her boyfriend cycle a mile to their nearest Leon to get it for her. Joseph is a very good, healthy baby. More importantly, of course, this salad is delicious.

SERVES 2

2 tablespoons quinoa, Fair Trade if possible
$2/3$ head of broccoli, cut into bite-sized florets, stalks sliced
scant 1 cup frozen peas (if using fresh, use 1 lb 2 oz unshelled pods)
$1/4$ cucumber, cut into slim batons
$3^1/2$ oz good-quality feta cheese, crumbled
a handful of alfalfa sprouts

2 tablespoons toasted seeds (see page 122) like pumpkin, sesame, and sunflower
$1/2$ an avocado, cut into pieces
a small handful of flat-leaf parsley, roughly chopped
a small handful of mint, roughly chopped
3 tablespoons lemon juice
generous $1/4$ cup extra virgin olive oil
salt and pepper

Put the quinoa into a small pan. Cover with cold water to about an inch above the grain, and let it gently simmer over low heat until the water's gone (about 15 minutes) then let cool to room temperature. Put an inch of hot water into a saucepan on high heat. Add a pinch of salt and cover. Once boiling, drop in the broccoli (and the peas if you're using fresh), and put the lid back on. Drain after 3 minutes, and hold them in a colander under cold running water to take all the heat out and keep them good and green.

Now build your salad in layers: broccoli, peas, cucumber, feta, alfalfa sprouts, seeds, avocado, quinoa, and finally the herbs. Only dress it just before you eat it.

Goat Cheese Pasta Salad with Toasted Almonds & Arugula ✓ V

Those of you who like pasta salads would be hard pressed to find a better one for the same input of effort. However, cold pasta leaves me a bit, well, cold. Thousands proved me wrong, though, by loving it long and hard when it was on the menu. Best eaten within an hour or so of making.

SERVES 4

4 plum tomatoes, cut into quarters
3 tablespoons extra virgin olive oil
$^1/_2$ cup sliced almonds
9 oz conchiglie pasta
$5^1/_2$ oz goat cheese, preferably the one with a skin

$2^3/_4$ oz arugula, chopped twice
a good squeeze of lemon juice (about $^1/_2$ a lemon)
2 tablespoons finely grated Parmesan
salt and pepper

Preheat the oven to 350°F.
Put the tomatoes skin-side down on a lightly oiled baking pan. Season with sea salt and drizzle with a couple of tablespoons of olive oil.
Pop into the preheated oven for around 30 minutes on the middle rack.
At your leisure, toast the almonds until lightly golden—not too dark, please.
Boil a big pot of heavily salted water. Add a good splash of olive oil.
Add the pasta and stir immediately. Boil for the amount of time it says on the side of the package.
Drain and let cool for 5 minutes—do not run the pasta under cold water. Stir in another glug of olive oil to make sure the pasta doesn't stick together as it cools.
Put the warm pasta into a big mixing bowl and crumble over the goat cheese. Gently roll and turn it around with a wooden spoon until all the cheese has melted and every surface of the pasta is coated.
Check the seasoning—plenty of salt and pepper needed for this one—then as soon as the tomatoes are ready, fold them, the arugula, and the almonds into the pasta.
Once it's cooled a little it may all start looking a bit tight, but a couple of tablespoons of warm water will restore the creaminess.
Finish with the lemon juice, a firm hand on the pepper grinder, a splash of your best extra virgin, more salt if necessary, and some Parmesan on top.

Moorish Lentil Salad ✓ ♥ DF WF **GF**

The pleasure of this dish lies in its duplicitous nature: lovely, comforting lentils with the zip and freshness that the greenery brings. Try to get celery with some leaves either at the top of the sticks or wedged in the middle because they add something a bit undefinable to the salad.

SERVES 4 TO 6 AS AN APPETIZER OR SIDE

1 cup Puy lentils
$^1/_2$ a stick celery, cut into $^1/_2$-inch dice, with any
    leaves roughly chopped too
$^1/_2$ a medium carrot, cut into $^1/_2$-inch dice
$^1/_2$ a small onion, chopped
1 small clove of garlic, sliced
1 tablespoon extra virgin olive oil

2 sprigs of thyme
1 bay leaf
2 tablespoons red wine vinegar
scant $^1/_2$ cup chicken stock
1 tablespoon lemon juice
a small handful of parsley, chopped
salt and pepper

Soak the lentils in water for an hour or so.
Heat the oil in a heavy ovenproof pan over medium heat and add the vegetables, garlic, thyme,

and bay leaf. Cook gently with a lid on the pan for 5 to 10 minutes, then stir in the drained lentils. Add the wine vinegar and simmer until all the liquid has evaporated.

Preheat the oven to 325°F.

Add the chicken stock and cover with waxed paper and foil.

Bake in the preheated oven for around 35 to 40 minutes, or until the lentils are tender with a slight bite.

Season to taste, and let cool. Stir in the lemon juice and parsley before serving.

Tuk-Tuk Salad ✓ ❤ V *DF* **WF**

Enter our Tuk-Tuk Salad, so named after the buggies in Thailand that bomb around town in the same way that this salad's flavors motor around your mouth. As zippy as its namesake, this salad just sings of freshness. Brown basmati and wild rice with loads of seasonal greens and a dressing that goes like a rocket—fresh ginger, chile, lime, sesame, cilantro, and soy. Puts the Bang back into Bangkok.

SERVES 4 AS A HEALTHY MAIN, MANY MORE AS A SIDE

1 cup less 2 tablespoons brown basmati rice, Fair Trade and organic if possible
2/3 cup wild rice
1 cup less 2 tablespoons peas, fresh or defrosted
2/3 cup fava beans, fresh or defrosted
2 scallions, thinly sliced
2 plum tomatoes, roughly chopped
a handful of arugula, very roughly chopped
2 tablespoons toasted seeds (we use sunflower, pumpkin, flaxseed, sesame)
2 tablespoons chopped cilantro

1 lime
salt and pepper

THE DRESSING
1 red chile, minced, seeds or not depending on how hot you like it
1 1/4-inch piece fresh ginger, washed and grated
1/2 a large or 1 small clove of garlic, minced
3 tablespoons lime juice
3 tablespoons sesame oil
3 tablespoons soy sauce

Get both kinds of rice on the stove—you have to cook them separately because they take different times—and cook them for the time it says on the packages.

Meanwhile, make your dressing by whisking all the ingredients together, then letting it sit to infuse.

As each batch of rice is ready, drain it into a sieve and hold it under cool running water. Drain again, then combine both kinds of rice together in a bowl. Stir in the peas, fava beans, scallions, and some salt. Add the dressing and stir until all is well coated.

In a little bowl mix together the tomatoes, arugula, seeds, and cilantro and spread them evenly over the top of the rice. Serve with quarters of lime.

Chicken (or Salmon) Superfood Salad ✓ ❤ WF **GF**

Nowadays only the chicken version of this can be found on the menu, but back in the day there was a salmon one too. It's just a perfectly balanced lunch: great, goodie-packed ingredients, some simple cooking, and away you go. We have some wonderful regulars who've been eating this three times a week for years.

SERVES 2

2 tablespoons quinoa
$^1/_2$ a head of broccoli
10$^1/_2$ oz free-range chicken thighs, each cut into
    4 pieces and marinated overnight (see recipe
    below), or 4 x 2$^1/_2$ oz slices of salmon
2 handfuls of arugula
2 handfuls of baby spinach
2 vine-ripened tomatoes, roughly chopped

scant 1 cup frozen peas (if using fresh,
    use 1 lb 2 oz unshelled pods)
1 lemon
2 tablespoons extra virgin olive oil
a light sprinkling of alfalfa sprouts
3 tablespoons aïoli (see page 259)
2 tablespoons toasted seeds (see page 122)
a hefty scattering of chopped mint and parsley
salt and pepper

MARINATE OVERNIGHT

Put $^1/_3$ cup of water into a little pan over high heat and bring to a boil. Stir in the quinoa and boil fast for 5 minutes, then turn the heat down and simmer for 5 minutes more. Turn the heat off, fluff with a fork, and set aside until cool.

Preheat your broiler to very hot, or get your ridged grill pan smoking. Cut the broccoli into small florets and slice the stalks into $^1/_2$-inch thick circles. Drop the broccoli into a pan of rapidly boiling salted water for 3 minutes, then drain in a sieve and hold under cold running water until cold.

Season your protein before you broil or grill it: for chicken, grill for 5 minutes, turn it over, then 5 minutes more; a scant 3 minutes each side for the salmon slices.

While all this is going on, build your salad: toss the leaves, tomatoes, broccoli, and peas in the juice of half a lemon and the olive oil. Lift them onto whatever you're serving them on, be it one big dish or individuals, then scatter with the cooled quinoa and alfalfa. The next layer is the protein (try feta if you're vegetarian), and top it off with the aïoli, seeds, and herbs, with the other half lemon, wedged, on the side.

Chicken Marinade ✓ ❤ V *DF* WF **GF**

Marinating your meat is a really good thing to get into the habit of doing. Instead of just letting it sit in your fridge, shrink-wrapped in man-made packaging, why not give it some space and some friends to mingle with? Our recipe is simple and hasn't changed since we opened; it offers exactly what we want—flavor and tenderness.

MAKES ENOUGH MARINADE FOR 2¼ LB DICED FREE-RANGE CHICKEN

2 tablespoons olive oil
3 tablespoons lemon juice
1 to 2 cloves of garlic, minced

Whisk all the ingredients in a bowl, stir in the chicken to coat. Marinate, covered, overnight in the fridge.

Magic Mackerel ✓ ❤ DF

These days you have to choose your fish carefully: sadly it's no longer just about what we want, and planet-wide considerations have to be taken into account. Beautiful mackerel ticks all our boxes: tastes great, full of good oils that make you think better, from the seas around here, and not endangered.

SERVES 4 FOR A LIGHT LUNCH

1 cup + 2 tablespoons couscous
2¹/₂ tablespoons extra virgin olive oil
1 teaspoon ground cumin
2 juicy lemons
¹/₂ a head of broccoli, cut into florets
5 fillets of undyed smoked mackerel
¹/₂ cup + 2 tablespoons hazelnuts, toasted and
    very roughly chopped

heaping ¹/₂ cup dried apricots, chopped
2 tablespoons toasted seeds (see page 122)
2 tablespoons dill, finely chopped
2 big handfuls of arugula, roughly chopped
¹/₄ cup extra virgin olive oil
salt and pepper

Put the couscous into a large bowl and stir in the oil, cumin, and a hefty pinch of salt, plus the zest and juice of ¹/₂ a lemon. Make sure each granule is well coated.

Add a generous 1¹/₄ cups of boiling water to the couscous, stirring well to make sure there are no dry areas left.

Cover with plastic wrap and let stand for 10 minutes somewhere warm.

Blanch the broccoli for 3 minutes in boiling salted water, drain in a colander, then hold under cold running water until cold.

Once the couscous has done its thing, break it up by gently rubbing it between the palms of your hands. Take the skin off of one of the mackerel fillets and flake it through the couscous in small pieces that you can't really see.

Stir in the nuts, apricots, broccoli, seeds, dill, and lastly the arugula (be gentle).

Adjust the seasoning and dress with lemon juice (you should need about ¹/₂ to 1 lemon (serve the rest in wedges alongside) and extra virgin olive oil.

Gently break each of the remaining fillets into two or three pieces and set them on top of the couscous.

Autumn Slaw ✓ ❤ V *DF* **WF GF**

Full of fall flavors and probably the best of the bunch in terms of nutritional whatnots. If you've never tried a salad of grated beets, this is a good place to start. As well as all the antioxidant action, this one carries bonus fiber points. A perfect packed-lunch salad because it stays crunchy for 2 to 3 days and the flavors continue to improve.

SERVES 4 ON THE SIDE

1/2 medium carrot
1 small raw beet
1/4 of a small celeriac
1/8 of a red cabbage
1/2 a stick of celery
1 small dill pickle
2 tablespoons golden raisins
1/4 cup red wine vinegar
1 apple
extra virgin olive oil
salt and pepper

Peel and grate the carrot, beet, and celeriac.
Slice the cabbage and celery nice and thin.
Chop the dill pickle roughly.
Put the golden raisins into a small saucepan with half the vinegar and simmer for just a few minutes until the liquid has all gone.
Quarter and core the apple and slice.
Mix all the ingredients together, and dress with the remaining vinegar and some seasoning.
Finish with the extra virgin at the end.

Open Sesame Slaw ✓ ❤ V *DF* **WF GF**

This has the appearance of a light mayo dressing but is dairy-free, thanks to the remarkable and versatile workings of soy.

MAKES A PARTY PACK FOR 8

THE DRESSING
3 1/2 tablespoons soy milk
1 teaspoon Dijon mustard
2 tablespoons white wine vinegar
1/4 teaspoon paprika
1 clove of garlic, chopped
1/4 teaspoon fennel seeds, ground or roughly chopped
1/2 cup sunflower or peanut oil
salt and freshly ground white pepper

THE EXTRAS
1 teaspoon black onion seeds
1 teaspoon sesame seeds, toasted
1 teaspoon wholegrain mustard

THE SLAW
scant 1 1/3 cups frozen peas, defrosted
3/4 cup frozen fava beans, defrosted
1/4 of a white cabbage, shredded
2 medium carrots, grated
a small handful of parsley, chopped

Put all the dressing ingredients, except the oil and seasoning, into a bowl and mix together.
Slowly whisk in the oil until it is all emulsified.
Then add 1 1/2 tablespoons of water and stir in all The Extra Ingredients.
We used to roughly chop the peas and beans, but it's up to you if you want to or not.
Tip all the slaw ingredients into a bowl and mix well. Add seasoning, then stir in the dressing.

Happy Carrot ✓ ❤ V *DF* **WF** **GF**

This salad went straight on the menu after we'd just come back from Morocco one time: they had an appetizer there called *Salade Marocaine* that consisted of anything between 8 and 12 little bowls of marvelousness, and a version of this was usually included.

SERVES 4 ON THE SIDE

2 heaping tablespoons golden raisins
3 large carrots, grated
1 clove of garlic, minced
1 heaping tablespoon toasted seeds*
1 scallion, thinly sliced
1 tablespoon roughly chopped cilantro
1 tablespoon roughly chopped mint
1/2 a red chile, minced
2 tablespoons lemon juice
2 tablespoons extra virgin olive oil
salt and pepper

Plump up the golden raisins in hot water for 5 minutes, then drain.
Mix everything else together very thoroughly and season well.
Only put the lemon juice and olive oil on when you're ready to go.

Go to page 122 for our seedy thoughts.

Sumptuous Slaw ✓ ❤ V *DF* **WF** **GF**

Not even sure this qualifies as a slaw, due to all the vegetables being briefly cooked in an *à la Grecque*–type stock: the cooking base is loaded with aromatics, has a good bit of vinegar poke to it, and a healthy dose of extra virgin olive oil so that everything comes out with a built-in dressing.

MAKES A NICE-SIZED BOWL FOR 4

2 1/2 tablespoons white wine vinegar
2 tablespoons extra virgin olive oil
2 cloves of garlic, chopped
5 sprigs of thyme, tied together with string
scant 2/3 cup water or vegetable stock
1/2 a red onion, thinly sliced
3 cups thickly sliced white cabbage
1 small zucchini, halved lengthwise then medium sliced
1 cup less 2 tablespoons frozen peas (if using fresh, use 1 lb 2 oz unshelled pods)
1 teaspoon of dill, finely chopped
a pinch of fennel seeds, ground or chopped
1/2 a lemon
salt and pepper

Put the vinegar, oil, garlic, and thyme into a sizeable pot with the water or vegetable stock and a hefty pinch of salt.
Once the base stock is steaming, but not simmering, tip in the red onion and cabbage and cook for 10 minutes with a lid on, stirring once or twice.
Turn the heat off, add the zucchini, cover, and let cool.
Once cold, drain, then mix in the peas, dill, fennel seeds, seasoning, and lemon juice.

Rainbow Superfood Salad ✓ ❤ V *DF* **WF** **GF**

This salad was based on the thinking that eating a vegetable that's particularly brightly colored is better for you. If your squash is really orange, your broccoli deep dark green, and your tomatoes very ripe and red, research has shown that these contain more beta-carotene (squash), sulforaphane (broccoli), and lycopene (tomatoes) than more insipid models, and those are outstanding antioxidants that our body loves so much. We originally put it on our fall menu, as a gentle way to keep your salad intake up as the days got darker and the urge to eat lots of raw ebbed away. A little time-consuming to make but here's how we did it.

SERVES 6

3 medium raw beets (unpeeled)
6 vine-ripened tomatoes, halved lengthwise
1/2 cup extra virgin olive oil, divided
1 small butternut squash (about 1 lb 5 oz), peeled
     and chopped into 1 1/4-inch dice
2 cloves of garlic, chopped
7 oz cremino mushrooms
2 tablespoons lemon juice

1/2 a head of broccoli
3 tablespoons quinoa
2 cups finely shredded red cabbage
1/2 cup fresh or frozen peas (if fresh, use
     9 oz unshelled pods)
3 tablespoons toasted seeds (see page 122)
heaping 1 cup alfalfa sprouts
salt and pepper

Preheat the oven to 400°F.

Put two of the beets into a small roasting pan with a good sprinkle of salt and a scant 1/2 cup water. Cover with foil, and put them into the oven on a high rack for just over an hour, or until a knife goes in without a lot of resistance.

Lay the cut side of the tomatoes on a baking pan, season with salt, and drizzle liberally with a couple of tablespoons of olive oil. Pop them into the oven for around 1 hour on the lowest oven rack.

Put the cubes of butternut squash on another baking pan and roll them in a little oil and plenty of seasoning. Roast them in the oven on the middle rack for 45 minutes, then stir, moving everything around at least once during the cooking time. Now all three of your oven racks should be cookin' away—tomatoes on the bottom, butternut in the middle, and beets up top.

When the vegetables are all done, let them cool, but peel the beets while they are still warm and then cut them into wedges.

Put another couple tablespoons of oil into a hot skillet and sauté the garlic for a moment, swiftly followed by the mushrooms. Season with salt, pepper, and lemon juice and get them out of the pan in less than 4 minutes.

Put a small pan on to boil with a little salt in it. Cut the broccoli florets off the trunk, blanch them in the boiling water for a couple of minutes with the peas, then drain in a colander and hold them under cold running water until completely cooled.

Stir the quinoa into the broccoli water and simmer for 15 minutes, then drain.

Grate the remaining (raw) beet and mix with the shredded cabbage.

Meanwhile, start building this labor of love, starting with the cabbage/beet mix on the bottom, then the broccoli, peas, tomatoes, mushrooms, and toasted seeds, finishing with the alfalfa sprouts.

All that remains is to season from a height and dress sharply.

MAINS:
MEAT

Pork, Lentil, & Rosemary ✓ *DF WF* **GF**

So there I was in a gas station on a highway in Spain and, although cleanliness wasn't top of their list, the place had proper character, something sadly lacking in its British counterparts. They also had something else we don't have in ours: good food, and this simple bowl was as good as anything else I ate on that trip. They did it with pieces of ribs, like we use in our Braised Pork with Rigatoni recipe (page 235), so if you really want to eat like a true trucker use them instead—they'll take about the same amount of cooking time.

SERVES 4

9 oz diced pork belly
1 lb 2 oz diced stewing pork
2 sprigs of rosemary, leaves chopped
1 teaspoon cayenne pepper
2 tablespoons olive oil
2 pork sausages, cut into bite-sized pieces
1 large Spanish onion, cut into large dice
1/4 celeriac, quartered and sliced

1 large parsnip, cut into small dice
3 sticks of celery, sliced
1 large carrot, sliced
2 cloves of garlic, chopped
1 x 14-oz can of chopped tomatoes
2 pints chicken stock
1 heaping cup brown lentils
salt and pepper

Sprinkle the pork belly and stewing pork with the rosemary and cayenne and let marinate for a few hours, or preferably overnight.

Next day, in a large, heavy saucepan, heat the oil and fry the sausage pieces until they start to brown. Use a slotted spoon to remove the pieces, and reserve them in a bowl.

Tip the other pork bits into the hot fat and keep the pan over medium heat for about 15 minutes, or until the pork bits pick up some color.

Add the onion, celeriac, parsnip, celery, carrot, and garlic and cook everything gently together for about 20 minutes with a lid on, stirring regularly.

Stir in the canned tomatoes and chicken stock.

Bring to a simmer, cover, and let bubble very gently, topping off with water if necessary, or until the pork is beginning to soften. This can take up to 2 hours.

Add the lentils and reserved sausage pieces, giving it all a stir to combine, and top off with 2 cups of water, or enough to cook the lentils.

Once the lentils are cooked (about 30 minutes) and the diced pork is totally tender, have a look at the consistency: lentils and pork both have quite a lot of variance in the amount of water they need, so if you think it looks a little thin, let it bubble away until you have a consistency that appeals, and conversely add a bit more liquid if you think it could do with loosening.

Season and let stand for a few minutes before serving. Some say it's nice with a dollop of Greek yogurt.

Chili con Carne ✓ ❤ *DF* WF **GF**

Our now classic take on the original uses braised-to-the-point-of-falling-apart chunks of beef chuck rather than ground beef, as most people would expect. The benefit is that there's more flavor in the bigger pieces, and if we all had a bit more time in the world I'm sure more people would choose to do it like this. Gives you a little more control about which part of the animal is used too, which is a good thing. Apart from that it's the usual bossanova party on your palate that it's supposed to be. Great with a slug of our Smokin' Chili Sauce (see page 261) on top to really blow your mind.

SATISFIES 4 VERY HUNGRY GRINGOS

1 heaping teaspoon dried chili flakes
2¹/2 teaspoons ground cumin
2 teaspoons dried oregano
1 teaspoon cinnamon
5 sprigs of thyme, tied together with string
5 cloves of garlic, roughly chopped
1 lb 2 oz braising beef, chuck works well, roughly
    chopped into 1¹/2-inch chunks
3 tablespoons olive oil
1 heaping teaspoon cumin seeds

1 heaping teaspoon coriander seeds
¹/2 a red chile (or more, if you like it
    hot), thinly sliced
2 Spanish onions, cut into large dice
2 carrots, cut into small dice
1 x 14-oz can of chopped tomatoes
2 x 14-oz of kidney beans,* drained
1 small red onion, thinly sliced
juice of 1 lime
salt

Put the dried chili flakes, ground cumin, oregano, cinnamon, thyme, and half the garlic into a dish and add the beef. Stir to coat, cover the dish with plastic wrap, and let marinate in the fridge for a few hours or overnight if possible.

Heat the olive oil in a Dutch oven over medium heat and gently fry the cumin and coriander seeds for a few minutes until you start to smell them.

Turn the heat up to high, stir in the beef along with the thyme. Fry on all sides to reach a good brown color. Add some salt, the fresh chile, remaining garlic, Spanish onions, and carrots and keep stirring for about 15 to 20 minutes, or until the onions are transparent and the carrots are soft.

Tip in the chopped tomatoes and simmer for 10 minutes before the kidney beans join in the fun.

Add water just to cover, then simmer, covered, for 1 hour. Then take the lid off and simmer for up to an hour more, or until the meat is very tender and the mixture has become quite thick.

In a little bowl squeeze the lime juice over the thinly sliced red onion. Turn the onion slices over with a spoon a few times, then let macerate for half an hour.

Finish by adding a good pinch of ground cumin to the chili to give fresh flavor to the slow-cook.

Lastly check the seasoning and consistency—if it looks a little dry, just slowly stir in water until it is pleasingly loose.

Have all the necessaries on hand: sour cream (we use good-quality yogurt), macerated onions, and wedges of lime.

If using dried beans, soak about 2 cups overnight in plenty of cold water and add at the same point in the recipe as the canned ones.

Ben's mom and dad at Morley and Kate's wedding, 1978

This little gem came from my dear old Mom—well, not so much of the old, she parties with the best of us. When the weather set in, or Mom had been supporting us kids at our weekly BMX races and we were one cold family, this is what she would rustle up so we were one satisfied warm family. This recipe has gone through some changes since its birth in 1950s Ilkeston, Derbyshire, where Mom was taught it in Home Economics class. Some years later it was her stunning wit and amazing looks that won my dad over, but he always said her sausage and bean pot pie helped. Mom hasn't made it for about ten years now, but I have taken on the tradition, honing it over the last couple of years into a dish my wife and I couldn't be without.

And that is the story of how the Hand-me-down Sausage and Bean Pot Pie was born, or should we say evolved organically. It's a bit like cassoulet meets Lancashire hot-pot.

Ben's Hand-me-down Sausage & Bean Pot Pie ✓

For Ben's credentials look on page 99.

SERVES 4

SOAK OVERNIGHT

$1^1/4$ cups dried navy beans
1 tablespoon olive oil
4 large chunky/coarse pork sausages, or Italian
    fennel and pork sausages (if possible)
$1/2$ a Spanish onion, chopped
a couple of sticks of celery, cut into small dice
1 small carrot, cut into small dice
2 cloves of garlic, crushed and minced

2 bay leaves
2 stalks of rosemary
2 teaspoons tomato paste
$1/2$ a 14-oz can of chopped tomatoes
$2^3/4$ cups to $3^1/4$ cups chicken stock
2 to 3 potatoes (russets would be a winner)
2 tablespoons salted butter, melted
salt and pepper

Soak your beans overnight in plenty of water.

When you're ready to start, preheat your oven to 350°F.

Put a Dutch oven on the stove over medium heat, add the olive oil, and then the sausages.

Gently brown these for 5 minutes on all sides. Then place in the oven to finish, roughly 15 minutes.

Once the sausages have gone a lovely golden color, remove them from the oven, take them out of the pot, and set aside. Reduce the oven temperature to 325°F.

Set the Dutch oven back over medium heat, and add the onion, celery, carrot, and garlic along with the bay leaves and rosemary. Sauté these until nice and soft, roughly 10 minutes.

Now add the tomato paste, cook for a few minutes, and add the canned tomatoes. Cook these down to a thick sauce.

Roughly chop the cooked sausages into chunks and add to the vegetables. Then add the soaked beans. Add 2 cups of the chicken stock and bring to a simmer. Cover with some parchment paper, check the seasoning, put your lid on, and put the pot back into the oven.

Cook the beans for $1^1/2$ to 2 hours, or until they have baked soft. Check them occasionally to make sure they are not becoming too dry, and if they are, add a little more stock.

Peel the potatoes and cut into $1/4$-inch slices.

Uncover the Dutch oven, discard the parchment paper, then lay the potato slices top of the beans and sausages, overlapping each one with the next to create a lid. Keep going around until you have used up all the potato slices. Depending on how wet it looks (beans are funny, unpredictable things), add some more of the stock to the potatoes and baste them with the melted butter. You may not need all the stock. Now put back into the oven for 45 minutes, or until the potatoes are soft and golden.

Serve with a fork—it needs no more than just to relax and eat.

When John and I first moved in together and started doing things like "having friends around for dinner," it soon became very obvious that I didn't know how to cook anything that wasn't a) pasta-based or b) a Victoria spongecake, which I make rather well, but isn't great for a main course.

Then I heard about couscous. I would love to say that I had learned the art of North African cuisine while backpacking in Morocco, but in fact I think I was watching the cookery slot on *This Morning* with Richard and Judy.

I tend to shove some garlicky tomatoes in the oven with it to roast. Or make a salad.

KD x

Katie, aged 4, and her brother Richard, aged 6

John at Broadstairs, in Kent, aged 3ish

John & Katie's (not too) Spicy Chicken Couscous ✓❤

John is one of the three founders of Leon, having bonded with Henry in their previous jobs over the state of fast food in the nation. John does lots for Leon, but by far the best thing he ever did was the stickers. He is married to the very lovely Katie, who is talented in a number of areas including making beautiful children (Natasha and Eleanor) and being a news broadcaster.

SERVES ABOUT 6

4 skinless chicken breasts, *cut into big chunks*
2 teaspoons dried chili flakes
a few hefty pinches of ground cinnamon
8 cloves of garlic, peeled and chopped
about 8 tablespoons of olive oil, divided
1 1/2 tablespoons good curry powder
1 3/4 cups of couscous
2 heaping tablespoons butter
2 handfuls of raisins or golden raisins

2 cups chicken stock
salt
pine nuts, mint leaves, cilantro, and lemon, to serve

GARLICKY TOMATOES
6 ripe plum tomatoes, halved
3 cloves of garlic, minced
2 tablespoons extra virgin olive oil
salt and pepper

Put the chicken pieces into a large ovenproof dish. Mix the chili flakes, cinnamon, garlic, salt, half the olive oil, and the curry powder together. Coat the chicken with it and let stand for 20 minutes or so. Preheat the oven to 430°F. Mix the garlic and oil for the tomatoes together.
Arrange the tomato halves on a heavy baking pan and anoint with the garlic/oil mix. Season liberally and set aside.
Meanwhile, put the couscous and golden raisins into a bowl and stir with the remaining oil to coat the grains. Add the chicken stock. Lay a dish towel over it and let stand for 5 minutes or so.
Mix the couscous well into the chicken, pushing the golden raisins below the surface (they can burn). Dot the top with small pieces of butter and cook on the upper rack in the oven for 25 minutes, putting the tomatoes on another rack underneath them.
Meanwhile I tend to have toasted a few pine nuts (which I am slightly obsessed with) to scatter on the top with chopped mint and cilantro and a squeeze of lemon. Serve with the roasted tomatoes.

Moroccan Meatballs ✓

When you meet a Leon regular, especially blokes, and ask them what they usually have there, more often than not the answer will be "Meatballs!" This recipe was the subject of much hot debate and flowery language among those who were on the scene at the time, and all this passion before we even had a restaurant to cook them in. Time has proved that it was all worth it, not only because they're still on the menu in exactly the same recipe as we started with, but because they are always in our top five year-round best sellers.

However, the "I have created a monster" feeling still rises in our cheeks when we think that all our lovingly made meatballs are still individually hand-rolled (tested doing it by machine but it squashed the meat too much). Since we opened, our guys and gals in the Big Kitchen have individually rolled more than 5 million of the buggers. Side by side they could run the entire length of the Central Line on the London Underground and back again. Which is not only a slightly odd image, but also involves a truckload of patience and a whole lot of balls.

HANDSOME SUPPER FOR 6

THE MEATBALLS
1½ wholemeal flatbreads (the smaller size,
    roughly 8 inches in diameter) or pitta
½ cup milk*
2¼ lb ground lamb
a small bunch of parsley, finely chopped
a small handful of mint, finely chopped
1 teaspoon dried oregano
2 cloves of garlic, chopped

THE SAUCE
2 tablespoons olive oil
3 cloves of garlic, crushed
4 x 14-oz cans of chopped tomatoes
1½ tablespoons harissa ◎
a handful of basil, leaves picked and chopped
a handful of parsley, chopped
salt and pepper

Rip the flatbread into pieces and soak them in the milk for 10 minutes.
Then put the bread into a mixing bowl, add the ground lamb, and stir in the parsley, mint, oregano, garlic, and some seasoning.
Mix well, then roll the mixture into walnut-sized balls.
Either on a ridged grill pan (best) or under a very hot broiler, brown the balls quickly. It's all about coloring them and not cooking them through, so 5 minutes total cooking time, turning each ball about three times.
To make the sauce, heat the olive oil in a large heavy skillet and gently fry the crushed garlic.
Add the chopped tomatoes and harissa. Simmer for 25 to 30 minutes, or until the sauce has reduced.
Add the meatballs and continue to simmer, covered, for a further 20 minutes, or until the sauce looks about right.
Lastly stir in the herbs and have a final seasoning check.

* In the restaurants we make this with water instead of milk to keep this dish dairy-free; I do find they
    turn out a bit softer inside with milk though, but it's not a biggie.
◎ See Suppliers, page VI in Appendix.

Coq au Vin ✓ *DF* *WF* **GF**

I was totally delighted when in the first fall of our Leon life this went on the menu: for six months we'd been cooking and running a fast food restaurant with all the salads, wraps, and juices that come with it, but this classic bit of French peasantry appealed to a part of my cooking that I'd been missing. We were proper chefs making proper food, just served fast. When we decided to add potatoes, thus straying away from the usual recipe but giving it a really welcoming warmness, we did quite a lot of work to find a low GI potato that wouldn't make the dish nap-inducing. We found them: fingerlings. Basically, small waxy potatoes that are not cooked for hours (or fried) retain a reasonably low GI, and big floury ones that are boiled for ages then mashed, are the worst. Shame, though, of course, at home you have the option to ditch the fingerlings and reconnect with a coq's old ally: a creamy, steaming pile of mashed potatoes. (For more on the mighty potato see page 65). When we make this in the restaurants we use diced chicken thighs because the bones can be a little tricky and messy for people, especially at lunchtime, but all food-lovers know that meat on the bone always cooks better.

MAKES SUPPER FOR 4 FRIENDS

4 whole free-range chicken legs, skin on
2 pints red wine
5 bay leaves
a medium handful of thyme, tied with string
6^1/$_4$ oz bacon slices
5^1/$_2$ oz button mushrooms
2^1/$_2$ tablespoons olive oil

8 shallots, peeled and quartered
2 cups chicken stock
14-oz Savoy cabbage, shredded
4 cloves of garlic, chopped
3^1/$_2$ oz small waxy potatoes, sliced
2 tablespoons flat-leaf parsley, finely chopped
salt and pepper

Marinate the chicken with the red wine, bay leaves, and thyme for at least 24 hours.
Next day, drain the wine off the meat, but reserve the wine as well as the thyme and bay.
Cut the bacon into large dice and clean the mushrooms thoroughly.
Heat the olive oil in a suitably French deep pot or Dutch oven until the oil is hot but not smoking.
Fry the bacon first for a few minutes, or until it begins to brown, then add the mushrooms, garlic, and shallots.
Keep stirring and frying until any water has come out of the mushrooms and they are beginning to brown.
Use a slotted spoon to lift them out, leaving the oil in the pot on the heat.
Drain the chicken pieces well (reserve the marinade), season them with sea salt, and arrange them in the pot, skin-side down.
When one side has browned, turn until both sides are nicely colored.
Chuck in the reserved bay, thyme, and red wine marinade and cook until reduced by half.
Pour in the chicken stock, bring up to a gentle simmer, skim well, then stir in the mushrooms, shallots, bacon, cabbage, garlic, and potato slices.
Continue to simmer gently for about another 20 to 30 minutes, giving it a thorough seasoning along the way.
Once the potatoes are cooked but not falling apart and the meat is coming away from the bone, turn the heat off and let the pot rest for 10 minutes. Scatter with the chopped parsley to serve.

Leon's Spaghetti Milanese ✓ DF

A lot of people ask, "Why Leon?" and this here is why. When we were trying to find a name for our idea we invited some helpful people we knew around for a drink and to ask them for a bit of advice. Some said, "You've got to have an '&' in it," others went for the holistic vibe, and a couple just looked confused. As Henry, John, and I left with the depressing word "Nutrilicious" running around in our minds, John mentioned that his dad was called Leon and what about that? We walked around for a few days imagining our fictitious restaurant and saying to no one in particular, "Meet you at Leon for lunch," and "Fancy a Leon?" just to see how it sounded , and we all agreed it sounded just right. So this is the original Leon's recipe in his very own cookbook. It's definitely of the era—not the kind of recipe that you would come across now because we are so spoiled for choice with our ingredients, and people are less likely to cook a pasta sauce that takes this long. And for those reasons we love it even more. The family recipe didn't have any garlic in it—he said it was thought of as an oral contraceptive!

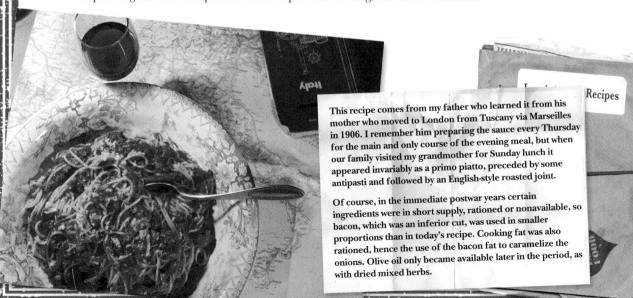

Leon, Praia da Rocha, 1965

SERVES 6

8 thick slices of Canadian bacon, rind on
3 largish onions
1 clove of garlic, chopped (Allegra: seemed wrong without)
2 tablespoons olive oil
2 x 10^1/$_2$ oz jars of tomato paste (Allegra: I found this a scary amount so used 5^1/$_2$ oz concentrated)

1 glass of red wine
1^1/$_2$ tablespoons sugar
a pinch of mixed dried herbs (like oregano, thyme, and bay)
a handful of basil, chopped
Parmesan cheese, grated
1 lb 2 oz dried spaghetti

Cut the band of fat and rind from the outside of the bacon. Cut the rind from the fat and place them both in a large saucepan on medium heat.
Thinly slice the onions and dice the bacon into postage-stamp squares. Remove the rind from the saucepan and sauté the onions and garlic in the rendered fat to a pale brown. Add the olive oil, stir in the bacon squares, and keep stirring for 2 minutes, or until the bacon is firm but not browning.
Stir in the tomato paste with a generous 1 cup of water. Add the wine, sugar, and dried herbs. Stir well and bring to a boil for 5 minutes. Turn down the heat to a slow simmer with the saucepan lid very slightly ajar. Simmer for at least 2 hours, then add the basil.
After straining the cooked pasta, toss in a large serving bowl with half the sauce, using the remainder to place a generous extra portion on the top of each serving, with some Parmesan.

Recipes

This recipe comes from my father who learned it from his mother who moved to London from Tuscany via Marseilles in 1906. I remember him preparing the sauce every Thursday for the main and only course of the evening meal, but when our family visited my grandmother for Sunday lunch it appeared invariably as a primo piatto, preceded by some antipasti and followed by an English-style roasted joint.

Of course, in the immediate postwar years certain ingredients were in short supply, rationed or nonavailable, so bacon, which was an inferior cut, was used in smaller proportions than in today's recipe. Cooking fat was also rationed, hence the use of the bacon fat to caramelize the onions. Olive oil only became available later in the period, as with dried mixed herbs.

(Not very) Kashmiri Rogan Josh ✓ ♥ WF **GF**

One of the things that our slow-cooks have in common is that they fill you up on vegetables and flavor, rather than bad carbs. For that reason, this curry will leave you feeling buoyant and bouncy in a way that you never do when leaving your favorite local Indian restaurant. Apparently the classic Kashmiri version has no onions and no garlic, so flying in the face of tradition, we put two kinds of onions in ours, but behaved more respectfully when it came to the garlic. It isn't spicy either, but offers a rich, almondy backdrop for the meat.

SERVES 6

scant 1 cup plain yogurt
1 heaping teaspoon dried chili flakes or chili powder
1 fat thumb-sized piece of fresh ginger, washed and
    coarsely grated
1/2 heaping teaspoon turmeric
4 cardamom pods
3 bay leaves
1/2 teaspoon ground cinnamon
2 1/4 lb diced lamb or mutton
1/4 cup peanut or sunflower oil
1 1/2 teaspoons mustard seeds

1 medium Spanish onion, chopped
heaping 1 cup ground almonds
about 1 3/4 to 2 cups chicken stock
1 lb 2 oz pumpkin or butternut squash, peeled and
    cut into medium dice
1 cup frozen peas
1 green bell pepper, cut into large dice
4 vine-ripened tomatoes, cut into wedges
a big handful of cilantro
salt and lots of black pepper

Put the yogurt, chili flakes, ginger, chili powder, turmeric, cardamom, bay leaves, and cinnamon into a bowl. Add the meat and stir it to make sure it's well coated (by far the best way to do this is by hand, but wearing latex gloves because turmeric can really get stuck under your fingernails). Let marinate in the fridge for as long as you can, preferably overnight.

Next day, heat the oil in a large heavy saucepan over medium heat and fry the mustard seeds until they begin to pop.

Add the chopped onion and stir for a couple of minutes.

Tip in the meat with its marinade and gently cook on all sides for 5 to 10 minutes in total.

Add the ground almonds and stir well until all the meat is coated in the almonds.

Pour in enough stock to just cover the meat, season with salt and masses of pepper, and bring to a slow simmer.

Simmer, covered, for around 1 hour 30 minutes, stirring regularly to ensure it's not sticking to the bottom of the pan (which the almonds have a tendency to do).

When the lamb is through the tough, teenage stage and beginning to soften (quite a long time if you opted for mutton), add the diced pumpkin and the pepper, and push them all under the surface of the liquid (if this is physically impossible due to lack of liquid then add enough to just cover).

Cook for about 20 to 30 minutes longer, stirring and scraping the bottom of the pan—leave the lid off and let it bubble away nicely—until the pumpkin is just beginning to lose its shape and the meat is good and tender.

Turn off the heat, add the tomatoes and peas, and stir so they are all submerged. Then put the lid back on and let stand for 10 minutes for them to soften up.

Check the seasoning, give it a last good vigorous stir to smash up the tomatoes a little, and then serve with rice, yogurt, and a handful of cilantro on top. Would be nice with a scattering of deep-fried crispy shallots on top, just to really blow the no-onion thing.

Mima's Risi e Bisi ✓ WF **GF**

This is totally delicious—just don't expect the brown rice to turn out like a risotto. This take on it is a different kind of wonderful, better for you, and much easier to get right. Best eaten as soon as you've made it.

THIS MAKES ENOUGH FOR 4 PEOPLE WITH GARGANTUAN APPETITES (THE ONLY KIND I KNOW), OR 6 NORMAL FOLK

From the bottom: Petra, Mima, Samantha, Laura & Hatty

Leon's Family Recipes

In *Italian Food*, all-time Leon food heroine Elizabeth David describes the Venetian dish of *risi e bisi*—rice and peas—as "soothing food for tired stomachs." But such is the power of this ultimate comfort food that it can also soothe a teenage hangover or a broken heart. When Allegra and I were naughty schoolgirls together, we would sometimes spend whole weeks lost in a fug of smoke and debauchery—until, bloodshot and sickly green, I would crawl back home to Mom for a gentle telling off and a restorative plate of *risi e bisi*.

Now I am married to Henry (it's a small world) and a new mother myself. When I was pregnant I craved comfort food, but my rocketing glucose levels meant I was banned from eating any refined carbohydrates, including white rice. So I bastardized *risi e bisi* into a brown rice dish, adding garlic for extra oomph, chicken for baby-growing protein, and (blasphemy!) frozen peas instead of fresh, because when you're toting a cannonball around your waist, life seems much too short for shelling peas.

4 free-range chicken legs
3 smallish onions: 1 whole, 2 minced
1 carrot
1 stick of celery
a few branches of thyme or one of rosemary
2 bay leaves
a generous handful of flat-leaf parsley, chopped
   (but keep the stalks)
1 stick butter
a drop of oil
4 cloves of garlic, minced (optional)
7 oz bacon or pancetta, chopped
1²/₃ cups brown basmati rice, rinsed under cold
   running water
2²/₃ cups peas—or more to taste
3¹/₄ oz Parmesan cheese, finely grated
salt and pepper

Put the chicken, whole onion, carrot, celery, herbs on the branch, bay leaves, and parsley stalks into a saucepan. Cover with 4¹/₄ pints of water, bring to a boil, and very slowly simmer for an hour.

After this time, strain it off, take the legs out, and set them aside to cool. Keep the strained stock on a very low simmer on the stove.

Now melt the butter (plus a drop of oil to stop it from burning) in a heavy saucepan.

Add the minced onions and garlic and the bacon and fry gently over medium heat so the bacon fat melts and the onions turn translucent. Add the rice and stir so that all the grains are coated in fat.

Pour in a cup or large ladle of the simmering stock, and once that has bubbled away add another 2 cups or so. Cook gently, stirring occasionally and adding more stock every time it looks in danger of drying out. Brown rice is very thirsty and can take around 45 minutes to cook. By the time the rice is eventually ready, you should be running out of stock.

Turn the heat off, stir in the peas, cover, and let rest for 5 minutes. Strip the chicken, leaving it in chunky pieces, then stir it into the rice along with the Parmesan, chopped parsley, and salt and pepper to taste. Serve with extra Parmesan sprinkled on top, if you like.

BEEF & GUINNESS

✓

This is really top drawer when it comes to winter slow-cooks. We've upped the Guinness in the recipe from the one we serve in the restaurants, for a richer, deeper, more suppertime than lunch feeling, but if you like it lighter just use one can.

SERVES 4 WITH BIG APPETITES

2^1/$_4$ lb boneless beef chuck or shoulder, diced
2 cans of Guinness
a few sprigs of thyme, tied together with string
2 bay leaves
3 tablespoons butter
1 tablespoon sunflower oil
2 medium carrots, sliced

1 large Spanish onion, cut into large dice
^{1}/$_2$ a rutabaga, cut into 1-inch cubes
1 clove of garlic, chopped
1^1/$_2$ tablespoons tomato paste
^{1}/$_4$ cup flour or besan (gram flour)
generous 2^1/$_2$ cups beef stock, half strength
salt and pepper

MARINATE OVERNIGHT

Marinate the beef in the Guinness with the thyme and bay leaves for 24 hours.

Next day, drain the Guinness from the meat (reserving the Guiness), then heat up a decent sized, heavy overproof saucepan or a Dutch oven.

Preheat the oven to 350°F.

Season the meat, then brown it in two batches in the butter and oil until you get good color on the meat.

Put it all back into the pot, then add the carrots, onion, and rutabaga, cover, and let it all sweat for about 10 to 15 minutes, or until soft.

Stir in the garlic and tomato paste, and cook gently for a further 5 minutes.

Sift the flour into the mixture and stir well.

Now pour in the reserved Guinness marinade and, as it bubbles and reduces by one-quarter, scrape the yummy bits off of the bottom of the pot.

Stir in the light beef stock, then add 2 cups of water and bring gently to a simmer.

Cover and put in the oven and cook for around 2 hours, keeping the lid on for the first hour and a half. After that, take the lid off and keep cooking until the meat comes apart with a push of your finger (if the sauce still looks a bit watery at this point, put it on the stove and give it a good, hard simmer for a few minutes until it coats the back of a spoon).

Check the seasoning and serve with your best winter warmer: rice, colcannon mashed potatoes, or a baked potato come to mind.

Sausage, Kale, & Flageolets ✓

Kale is the new blueberry, which doesn't mean you have to start eating kale ice cream, but just that thanks to its amazing vitamin and mineral count it has muscled its way up to the top of the Superfoods chart. Kale has had to tough it out through some pretty bad press (it's true that it's used to feed livestock, but what's wrong with that?), but its moon (see Brassica Galactica, page 46) is definitely in the ascendancy now. This is one of my favorite slow-cooks—definitely rustic, but the flageolets bring it a touch of class.

SUPPER FOR 4

1 cup dried flageolet beans (or 2 cans of cooked beans)
3 tablespoons extra virgin olive oil
1 lb 2 oz high-quality garlicky pork sausages, cut into 1-inch thick pieces
4 cloves of garlic, thinly sliced
1 heaping tablespoon rosemary, finely chopped

1 large or 2 small red onions, cut into large dice
3^1/$_2$ cups chicken stock
^{1}/$_3$ cup heavy cream
10^1/$_2$ oz kale (woody stalk removed and discarded), chopped roughly into 2-inch pieces
a small handful of flat-leaf parsley, chopped
salt and pepper

Soak the dried flageolets (if using) for 24 hours in cold water.

Drain them, cover with fresh water, and cook until tender but still holding their shape—anything from 1 to 2 hours.

Heat the oil in a Dutch oven and fry the sausage pieces until golden brown.

Add the garlic and rosemary, then turn down the heat and stir in the onions.

Cover and cook gently for about 15 minutes, or until the onions are soft and light brown, giving it the occasional stir.

Pour in the chicken stock, the cooked and drained beans, and some seasoning.

Bring to a relaxed simmer and cook for around 20 minutes, giving it a skim as you feel necessary.

Stir in the cream and kale and mix well, then simmer for 10 minutes with a lid on and 10 without.

Adjust the seasoning and finish with the chopped parsley.

Love Me Tender Ribs ✓ *DF* WF **GF**

There's a new art of cooking that is less instinctive and more technical. Most of Leon's food is definitely made up of the former, but these ribs reach their über-tender state by being cooked for 12 hours at 150°F. That's how we do them: overnight. After careful adaptation for the home cook, we found that you too can tend your ribs as hard and nearly as long as we do with the same result. We just can't help believing that Elvis, both a good Southern lad, would approve.

SERVES 4

Gives you about half a rack each for 4 people—good for a big appetizer, or main with a few sides. For those who like to go the whole hog you'll probably want a rack each, in which case serves 2. And if you don't mind ending up looking like The King did in his twilight years, eat the whole thing yourself. For Breakfast. With a bucket of deep-fried okra (his favorite).

2¼ lb baby back pork ribs
3 heaping tablespoons tomato paste (Italian
    double strength)
1 heaping teaspoon chipotle chili powder*
    or chili powder
¼ cup honey

⅓ cup + 1 tablespoon red wine vinegar
2 tablespoons olive oil (not extra virgin)
½ teaspoon smoked paprika (the sweet one)
½ teaspoon Chinese five-spice
sea salt

Put all the ingredients, except the salt, into a bowl and add the ribs, moving them around until they are coated. Cover the bowl with plastic wrap and let marinate overnight in the fridge.
Next day, season the ribs well with sea salt. Arrange them in a smallish shallow roasting pan and add a generous 1¼ cups of water to come about halfway up the ribs, being careful not to pour it directly onto the meat.
Cover with a lid or foil and cook in the oven on 250°F for around 5 hours. During this time you should visit the ribs now and then, probably once every couple of hours, and turn each one over. (The ribs keep fine in the fridge at this stage for a few days if you want to get the part that takes a long time out of the way in advance.)
Take the ribs out of the oven for a minute while you let the oven heat up to 475°F.
Cook for about 15 minutes, giving them a couple of final roll-arounds in the sauce, then scatter with a little sea salt and give yourself, and the ribs, a round of applause for getting there.

* Or half a can of chipotles in adobo (see page 126).

We both like the Australian/Asian style
of cooking, which is unfussy, healthy,
simple, and very tasty. On our return we
found a Donna Hay recipe that reminded us
of what we had eaten in our magical time
down under around the night when I had
asked Karen to be my wife.

   Over the years we've played with the
recipe and made it our own: we like it
because it has the feeling of comfort food
without being heavy or stodgy—the ginger
gives it a refreshing clean taste. I like
it with rice to soak up the broth, Karen
finds the sweet potato enough starch and
doesn't always have rice. I like mine
almost submerged in the broth, Karen has
hers with a more sensible amount.

Love, Simon

Simon, Panal Primary School, Harrogate, 1971

Karen in the garden, Northwood, 1974

Simon & Karen's Harmony Supper ✓ ♥ DF WF **GF**

One of our best stickers has a massive bull on it against a red background, with the words "Big and Strong." This particular image has been commandeered by our financial team, who have grabbed the bull by the horns to steer Leon forward. Too many analogies and a really long way of saying that Simon takes care of all that, and he does it with a quiet grace and endearing warmth.

   Those words could apply to this dish too, a supper Simon and his wife often make together. As well as the Zen look, feel, and flavors, the name came from Simon talking the dish through with me, and as he did so, his taking for granted the understanding there is between them as they cook it together.

SERVES 2 WITH SOME LEFTOVERS

1 medium sweet potato, peeled and sliced into disks
generous 2^1/2 cups chicken stock (fresh is best, but
   we sometimes make it with stock cubes though
   we use less than recommended on the package,
   because otherwise it makes it too salty)
2 to 3 tablespoons unpeeled grated fresh ginger
   (depending on how fiery you like it),

unpeeled and caringly grated by me (Karen has a
   fear of adding grated knuckle)
2 chicken breasts off the bone, chopped into chunks
^{1}/2 a head of broccoli, cut into pieces
3^1/2 oz green beans, trimmed
a small handful of cilantro, chopped
salt

Put the sweet potato, stock, and
ginger into a deep, wide saucepan
and bring to a rolling boil for
a couple of minutes before turning
down to a simmer for 5 more.
Now add the chicken pieces and
keep cooking for another 5 minutes.
Add the broccoli and beans, stir
well, season, and cook for a final
3 minutes.
Finish with the fresh cilantro.

Chicken, Asparagus, & Fair Trade Lemon Cassoulet ✓♥DF

We did this as a special recipe for "Fairtrade Fortnight," an event to try to get British restaurants, and customers, more aware about this very good cause. Good, light, summery bean action.

SERVES 2, WITH BEANS LEFT OVER FOR TOMORROW

1 Fair Trade lemon, zested and juiced
4 cloves of garlic, roughly chopped
3 tablespoons olive oil (not extra virgin), divided
2 heaping tablespoons chopped thyme leaves
2 free-range chicken supremes (chicken breast with
    wing bone attached), skin on, with the little
    bone left in
1 bunch of asparagus, with thickish stems
1 medium onion, cut into medium dice

1 x 14-oz can of navy beans*
2 bay leaves
1/2 a glass of white wine
scant 1 cup to generous 1 1/4 cups hot chicken stock
    (much better if homemade in this instance)
1/4 cup fresh breadcrumbs
Fair Trade lemon wedges
salt and pepper

Put the lemon juice and zest, half the garlic, two-thirds of the olive oil, the thyme, and plenty of black pepper into a dish. Add the chicken, turn to coat, cover, and let marinate in the fridge overnight.
The next day, break the woody ends off the asparagus, then chop the stalks into 1 1/2-inch pieces, keeping the tips whole: save two whole spears for the top.
In your favorite skillet heat the remaining olive oil.
Take the chicken out of the marinade, but don't discard the marinade.
Season the chicken well, especially on the skin side, and lay it skin-side down in the hot oil.
Once the skin is a nice light golden brown (it shouldn't be in the pan for more than a couple of minutes), take the chicken out of the pan and let rest, skin-side up.
Now tip the onion into the pan and stir for a minute or two.
Keeping the heat up, add the reserved marinade and the rest of the garlic and fry for another couple of minutes to get the flavors moving.
Stir in the drained beans and bay leaves, pour in the wine, and reduce the liquid by half.
Turn the heat off, stir in the asparagus pieces, and season to within an inch of its life.
Preheat the oven to 400°F.
Tip it all into an ovenproof dish so that the beans are filling it pretty much to the brim, then press the supremes in, skin-side up, so that the flesh is just at the same level as the beans.
Pour in the hot stock to the point where you can JUST see it below the beans.
Scatter the breadcrumbs all over the beans but not the chicken, arrange the last two asparagus spears on top of the breasts and give it all a last light drizzle of olive oil.
Bake in the oven for around 30 minutes—you want golden breadcrumbs, bubbling edges.
Serve with a handsome wedge of lemon on the side.

FAIR TRADE USA (www.fairtradeusa.org) helps free trade work for the poor and is the leading third-party certifier of Fair Trade products in the US, providing farmers in developing nations with the tools to thrive as international business people. Instead of creating dependency on aid, they use a market-based approach that gives farmers fair prices, workers safe conditions, and entire communities resources for fair, healthy, and sustainable lives.

*For the purposes of this dish, it actually works better to use canned beans so the chicken doesn't dry out waiting for the beans to finally soften.

Chicken, Pumpkin, & Cranberry Beans ✓ ❤ *DF* *WF* **GF**

Nearly all the work here is done overnight by the busy marinade, so that life is easy the next day. Cranberry beans are a special, chalky kind of bean (see page 120). If you're buying them cooked in cans you'll miss out on the amazing pink Jackson Pollock effect of the fresh ones, undoubtedly the most spellbindingly beautiful thing ever to have popped out of a pod.

Unless you're doing it for Hallowe'en, buying a pumpkin for a single recipe can be a bit daunting, so plan to make yourself Susi's Pumpkin Pie (page 269) this week too.

FOOD FOR 4

2 tablespoons red wine vinegar
1 tablespoon wholegrain mustard
1¹/₂ tablespoons clear honey, stringy-bark© if
    possible (see page 127)
¹/₂ teaspoon dried chili flakes
2 cloves of garlic, chopped
³/₄ teaspoon fennel seeds
1 teaspoon dried oregano
2 bay leaves

3 tablespoons extra virgin olive oil
1 lb 2 oz boneless chicken thighs, cut into large dice
¹/₂ cup + 2 tablespoons dried cranberry beans*
1 x 14-oz can of chopped tomatoes
1 medium leek, thickly sliced and washed well
2 cups chicken stock
1 heaping tablespoon chopped sage
9 oz peeled pumpkin cut into 1¹/₂-inch dice
salt and pepper

MARINATE OVERNIGHT

Put the vinegar, mustard, honey, chili flakes, garlic, fennel seed, oregano, bay leaves, and olive oil into a dish and roll the chicken around in it. Cover and let marinate in the fridge overnight.

At the same time, soak the cranberry beans overnight in plenty of cold water.

Next day drain the beans, cover with fresh water, and simmer for about 1¹/₂ hours, or until cooked.

When the beans are pretty much cooked, place a medium-sized heavy saucepan over high heat. When it is hot, add the chicken with the marinade and fry it. (You don't need any oil because it's already in the marinade.)

Cook for about 10 minutes, stirring occasionally; be careful about it sticking to the bottom of the pan: caramelizing good, burning bad.

Preheat the oven to 410°F.

Add the tomatoes, leek, cooked drained beans, stock, and sage to the chicken, stir well, and simmer gently for about half an hour.

Roll the pumpkin cubes in a little oil and some seasoning, lay them out on a baking pan, and roast in the preheated oven for about 25 minutes, shuffling them once—you want them to have a bit of color.

Once the pumpkin is done turn the chicken off and stir the pumpkin into it.

Add a generous splash of great olive oil to finish. This dish is even better the next day.

*Or 1 x 14-oz can, drained, added at the same point in the recipe as the other ones.

Sweet & Sour Pork with Cashews ✓ *DF* WF

This is nothing like the pork balls fried in batter and coated in neon orange MSG sauce that you might remember from 1973. The term "adobo" is an interesting one, and is used from South America to the Philippines, where it is taken to mean cooked down in vinegar. Over in that beautiful archipelago they will adobo almost anything to within an inch of its life, and being a lover of sharp things (like knives) I became a little obsessed with how it played with the pork, and promptly stuck this on the menu when I got back.

SERVES 4

1/2 cup unroasted, unsalted cashew nuts
2 tablespoons sesame oil
1 1/4 lb diced pork, a little fat left on if possible
1/2 teaspoon Chinese five-spice
1 bird's-eye chile, thinly sliced
3 cloves of garlic, minced
1 thumb-sized piece of fresh ginger, washed and coarsely grated
2 tablespoons fructose
scant 1/2 cup rice wine vinegar, or cashew vinegar if you can find it
2 pints chicken stock

1 tablespoon besan (gram flour)
1 large green bell pepper, seeded and cut into bite-sized pieces
1 large red bell pepper, seeded and cut into bite-size pieces
6 scallions, cut into batons
14 oz button mushrooms, cut in half
a shot of soy sauce
a big handful of cilantro, roughly chopped
1 tablespoon sesame seeds
lime wedges
salt and pepper

Preheat the oven to 325°F and roast the cashews for 20 to 25 minutes, moving them around halfway through.

Heat half the sesame oil in a wide heavy saucepan. When it's really hot, fry the meat until it's nicely browned—about 5 to 10 minutes—all quite ferocious.

Stir in the five-spice, chile, garlic, ginger, some seasoning, and the rest of the sesame oil. Fry for a few minutes more, stirring and scraping because the spices will want to stick to the bottom.

Tip in the fructose and mix it in well. Keep stirring on the same ferocity of heat until the contents of your pan are all well browned (won't take longer than a couple of minutes, less probably).

Pour in 1/4 cup of the vinegar, let this all bubble away, then add the chicken stock and bring back to a simmer.

Simmer now, uncovered, for roughly 45 minutes, or until the meat has become tender.

Skim off a ladleful of the juice and slowly whisk it into the besan, then pour this back into the pot and stir it in well. This serves to thicken the sauce.

Stir in the green and red bell peppers, scallions, mushrooms, and the last of the vinegar. Continue to cook for around 10 minutes, uncovered, over medium heat, until the vegetables have softened but still have some bite. At this point if your sauce is looking a bit watery then just boil it hard until it has reduced to a consistency you like more (shouldn't take more than about 5 minutes).

Turn the heat off and stir in the cashews and soy sauce, then scatter with cilantro and sesame seeds. Serve with basmati rice and lime wedges.

Just imagine a simple, very nice, and intelligent woman with bright little blue eyes, very warm face, beautiful smile, soft hands, who is always full of energy and happiness; terrified of snakes but loves swimming and cooking; a good laugh and adores romantic movies; who is always right (which can be really annoying sometimes), and whose love and care for others are just unconditional. She is an amazing person and I am very proud and happy to be her daughter. Love you so much, Mom.

Mom never had a proper recipe, she is always cooking it by eye, so you don't need to be too precise. This dish has been in my family for a long, long time and we all love it, not only amazing as a soup, but as a stew as well. Enjoy the cooking and bon appetit!

Janka xxx

Janka, her brother Miro, ando her mum Maria. Topolcany, Slovakia, Christmas 1979

Janka's Mom's Goulash ✓ ❤ *DF* WF

Janka's been with us for years and years, starting in the front of house at Carnaby right at the beginning, then as time passed moving into maybe her more natural place at the financial focus matrix in Mission Control, that is to say, the mothership in Waterloo. When it came to shooting her very authentic goulash (she's from Slovakia) it smelled great but looked a little flat for the camera, and I made a judgment call to add carrots to it, knowing it wasn't entirely out of form. But Janka was aghast, saying with narrowed eyes, in the same tone of voice as if I'd just denounced my whole family to the Spanish Inquisition, "My mother would never put carrots in it." She's pretty straight up and down, is our Janka, and her recipe for this book matches that perfectly: it is what it is, and does what it does very well. Janka says eat it with pickles and kneidlach (matzoh balls).

SERVES 4

Put vegetable oil/olive oil just to cover the bottom of a large cooking pot.
Add 2 big onions chopped and 4 cloves of chopped garlic.
Stir in a couple of carrots, sliced [*just don't let Janka see*]—and cook on the stove with a lid on for about 10 minutes.
Then add 1 lb 10 oz of beef, cut it in small cubes (1½ inches) and add it to the above. Increase the temperature. When the meat is grayish, add salt, 1 tablespoon of ground red paprika* and stir it. In order not to burn it, add about 2 pints of beef stock. Put the lid back on and keep on a slow and steady simmer until the meat is softening (after about 1½ hours).
Then add 2¼ pounds of peeled potatoes cut into small pieces as well as 2 sliced green bell peppers and 2 medium tomatoes, chopped large.
Push all the vegetables below the surface of the stock and put the lid back on.
About half an hour later the potoatoes are soft and have started to fall apart and the liquid should have thickened up nicely.
At the end just taste, if necessary add more salt, black pepper, Vegeta™ **, and 2 tablespoons of marjoram (fresh is best but dried will do; just use half the amount).
It's best if you let it sit for a good ½ an hour with a lid on before dinner.

*…and we added half a teaspoon of smoked paprika too.
** You can buy Vegeta™ from Polish delis for that really authentic taste—great packaging, just don't look at the ingredients: we found it's delicious either way.

Braised Pork with Rigatoni ✓

Apart from chickens, pigs are the other livestock that are often bred in intensive farms, so it really is worth having a look at where your pork (or bacon) has come from. It's a flavor thing as well as just wanting the animals to have happier lives (see Pork, page 92). This is an all-in-one supper, easy and delicious. It just takes a bit of cooking time.

SERVES 4+

1 teaspoon smoked paprika
3 tablespoons extra virgin olive oil
1 teaspoon dried oregano
1 teaspoon chopped mint
3 cloves of garlic, chopped
1 lb 2 oz pork ribs, cut into 2-inch pieces
1 medium red onion, cut into 1/2-inch dice
1 1/2 celery sticks, cut into 1/2-inch dice
1 x 14-oz can of chopped tomatoes
2 pints chicken stock

1/4 of a cinnamon stick
3 bay leaves
10 1/2 oz summer squash or 2 medium zucchini
    (we use yellow), cut into 1 1/4-inch pieces
1 tablespoon sherry vinegar
1 tablespoon roughly chopped flat-leaf parsley
7 oz dried rigatoni
Parmesan cheese, for grating
salt and pepper

Preheat the oven to 475°F.

Put the paprika, salt, olive oil, oregano, mint, and garlic into a Dutch oven, then add the meat and roll it around to coat.

Place the Dutch oven (uncovered) in the oven and roast for 20 minutes, moving the meat around occasionally to ensure even browning.

Reduce the oven temperature to 350°F and add the onion and celery to the meat.

After 30 to 40 minutes, when everything's well colored, add the tomatoes, chicken stock, cinnamon, bay leaves, and some seasoning. Move the meat around a little, then cover with the lid and put back into the oven for an hour.

Once the time has passed, add the summer squash or zucchini, sherry vinegar, half the parsley, and the rigatoni. Stir gently but thoroughly. Cover and cook for 15 minutes more.

Gently stir again, and at this point the pasta should be just cooked, or slightly under (it won't take more than another 10 minutes).

Enjoy with grated Parmesan and scattered with the remaining parsley.

Moroccan Chicken Tagine ✓ ❤ DF WF **GF**

Since we started doing a different slow-cook every day this one has been a consistent bestseller. When people ring up to ask what today's specials are and find out it's chicken tagine, you can actually hear the smile in their voice. Tagines have a special Dimbleby connection for me, since it was Henry's mom who first introduced them to the McEvedys. My big sister Floss, at the tender age of 15, tried one at their house and thought, "That looks easy." She bought a clay tagine pot and tried her hand at it. What came out of the oven was so inedible that our Pa was determined never to have to eat anything out of it again: he took the clay pot into the garden and smashed it. Poor Floss had grasped the first of the two tagine principles—that all the ingredients go into the clay dish raw—but not the second: that you therefore have to give them time (and plenty of it) for the magic to happen under the conical lid. I've written this recipe two ways: first on the off-chance that you happen own four tagines (ideal) and secondly as an oven thing. Just thought I'd give you the options.

SERVES 4

4 free-range chicken legs, split into thigh and
   drumstick (we like to leave the skin on, but it's
   up to you)
1 lb 2 oz rutabaga, peeled and cut into
   1-inch chunks
2 medium turnips, peeled and cut into
   1-inch chunks
2 carrots, sliced into thick disks
1/2 a leek, sliced into thick rings
1 or 2 zucchini, thickly sliced
scant 1/2 cup of roughly chopped dried apricots
chicken stock (fresh is best, but cube does the job:
   amounts differ depending on the method used)
2 tablespoons olive oil (not extra virgin—see page
   132 for why)

a few sprigs of thyme, or 1 teaspoon dried
a handful of mint leaves, roughly chopped
salt and pepper

THE MARINADE
scant 1/2 cup lemon juice
3 cloves of garlic, minced
a couple of bay leaves
1 teaspoon ground cinnamon
1 teaspoon ras-el-hanout (see page 107) or mild
   curry powder
1 heaping teaspoon turmeric
1/2 teaspoon cumin seeds

MARINATE OVERNIGHT

Put the chicken into a bowl and add the marinade ingredients, making sure all the flesh is well coated. Let marinate overnight (you can't cheat and rush this part).

If you're using four tagines, split the vegetables between them, nestle a thigh and drumstick in each, along with the apricots. Add the stock to come up to the edge of the lower lip (you'll know what I mean). Season well.

Stick the tagines on a low-to-medium heat for about 2 hours, or until the meat is falling off the bone and the vegetables are soft.

If, as is far more likely and just as delicious, you're using a Dutch oven, preheat your oven to 400°F. On the stove, heat the olive oil in the pot. Sprinkle some salt on the chicken and once the oil is hot put in the legs, skin-side down.

Brown them for a few minutes on both sides, then throw in all the rest of the ingredients except the stock and mint and cook for 10 minutes without a lid. Add enough stock to come about two-thirds of the way up the level of the ingredients and cover with a lid.

Once it comes to a simmer, put the casserole dish into the oven for 1 1/2 hours, then have a peek—the chicken should be coming away from the bone and all the vegetables soft and tender.

At this stage our two methods become one again: taste the stock for seasoning and serve scattered with mint on top.

Couscous would be ideal to have with it but it also works really well with brown basmati rice.

MAINS:
FISH

FISH AS PRESENTS

As those of you who've done your reading on fish in the ingredients book will know, these magnificent sea creatures are becoming something we can't take for granted any more. Choose carefully, don't eat the ones in trouble and start thinking of them as Neptune's gift to us. But that's not the only reason for this headline.

Back when we were littler (and Ben and I were cooking our hearts out in the kitchen at Carnaby Street), we used to do our fish like this (see over page) laying out literally hundreds of pieces of foil all over any flat surface in the kitchen, then loading them up and folding them all individually and meticulously. Labor-intensive as it was, there was a lot of joy and love that went into those little shiny parcels, and it always felt as if we were making presents for the people who ate with us; which was really crazy. Folk never got to see the foil pillows all proud and puffed up as they came out of the oven because the guys in the service kitchen upstairs used to slip the fish+fun out of their parcel (or *papillote* as the French call it or, as their friends over the Alps prefer, *cartuccio*) and straight into the box or plate.

Anyway, we settled on this way of cooking our fish because it was the most fail-safe way to keep the flesh all moist and delicious, letting the flavors inside do all the work. On the next page are a couple of recipes we tried and liked best, but it works with almost anything you have around. Chopped chile-parsley-garlic mixed with a little extra virgin olive oil; pesto with a few slices of lemon and some thyme… The theory is the same all ways and, because the fish is usually quite delicate, serve it with something simple like boiled new potatoes and a salad, or rice is always good.

It's a stupidly simple way for anyone who's a little scared of cooking fish to conquer their phobia.

PRESSIES FOR 4

1. Preheat the oven to 425°F.
2. Lay out four pieces of foil about 12 inches square, shiny-side down.
3. Splash on a bit of olive oil, and some salt and pepper (yes, you're seasoning the foil).
4. If you feel like it, put a little bit of something down next: some sliced fennel, a few slivers of onion, long ribbons of zucchini, some fresh herbs—whatever you have around. Just put it all in the middle of the foil in a flattish pile.
5. Place a fish fillet skin-side down on top of whatever you've laid down and now season the fish (salt is very important in this dish because you can't add any during the cooking).
6. Put your fun on top (see the following recipes or use your imagination), and then fold the bottom edge of the foil over the fish to meet the top.
7. Fold the sides in one at a time until you meet either end of the fillet, pushing down firmly after each fold to secure well (it's usually about three folds on each side).
8. With only the top side now open you have the option of giving it a little liquid to get things moving in there. A splash of white wine or vermouth, a litle fish or light chicken stock, or Saki would be nice, too. This step is not obligatory but depending on the fun you've opted for can really add something.
9. Now seal the top in the same way and repeat with the other three so you have four little parcels.
10. Put them on a baking pan (or split between two) and bake for 15 minutes, by which time (if you did good folding) they should have become very attractive puffed-up pillows. If you use two baking pans, switch them around on the oven racks halfway through.
11. Slip each little present onto a warmed plate, then hand them around IMMEDIATELY because, sadly, these beautiful bags deflate very quickly and with that you loose a little of the wow factor.

Spicy Coconut Fish ✓ ❤ *DF* **WF** **GF**

Coming from the Thai school of thought, the coconut cream melts over the fish and allows the bold flavors to sink in. Eat it with simple rice and steamed greens.

FOR 4

$1^3/4$ oz creamed coconut (fridge cold please),
   coarsely grated
$1/2$ a clove of garlic, minced
2 scallions, 1 minced, 1 sliced obliquely
$1/2$ teaspoon turmeric
2 limes
$1/4$ oz piece of fresh ginger, grated

$1/2$ a red chile, thinly sliced
a small handful of cilantro
4 x $6^1/4$-oz portions of sustainable fish of your
   choice (see page 80)
8 lime leaves (optional, but a good idea)
1 tablespoon toasted sesame oil
salt

In a bowl mix together the coconut, garlic, the minced scallion, turmeric, zest of both limes, ginger, chile, cilantro, lime leaves, and a healthy amount of salt (this recipe takes quite a lot of seasoning). Make sure it's all become one, then share between the fishies.
Prepare your foil, then lay a couple of lime leaves down before placing the fish on top.
Finish with a drizzle of sesame oil and by scattering over the other scallion, then fold up and cook as described on the previous page. It is essential that when the parcels are opened they are hit with a bit of fresh lime juice, half a lime each from the ones you zested.

Mushroom, Shallot, & Tarragon Fish ✓ WF GF

Definitely French-ish, worth doing with a good choice of mushroom. Could put a spot of cream in the bag as well to finish it properly, as they would in France.

FOR 4

9 oz mushrooms, like shiitake, button, oyster, or
* cremino (just avoid field mushrooms—they*
* make everything turn blackish gray)*
3 tablespoons extra virgin olive oil, divided
4 shallots, sliced
2 cloves of garlic, sliced
1 glass of white wine
1 tablespoon capers, whole if small, chopped
* if big 'uns*

a small handful of tarragon, chopped
a big handful of parsley, chopped
4 x 6 1/4-oz portions of sustainable fish of your
* choice (see page 80)*
a shot of Noilly Prat vermouth
2 tablespoons butter
1 lemon, quartered
salt and pepper

Slice or cut up all the mushrooms.

Heat up 2 tablespoons of the olive oil in a skillet and sauté the shallots and garlic for a minute or two. Toss in the mushrooms and some seasoning and flip and stir for a couple of minutes until softened. Pour in the wine and watch it sizzle and reduce for a minute or two; while that's happening, throw in the capers and chopped herbage.

Turn the heat off—you want it to be a little wet—and finish with the last of the oil, checking the seasoning. Divide the mixture between the fish, topping each one with a walnut-sized piece of butter, and put a little splosh of vermouth in the bags before making the final seal. Cook as described on page 239.

Serve the foil pillows with a wedge of lemon on the side and encourage your compadres to reinvigorate with a squeeze of lemon once they have bust their bags.

Crunch-coated Fish Wrap with Red Rice Tartare ✓ ❤

Trying to replace the mainstream was where this came from, the Leon version of the breadcrumbed fish-in-a-bun thing you may be familiar with. To this day, at every menu-change meeting, John still asks for this dish to make a comeback. Strikes me as a perfect Saturday lunch dish.

MAKES 2 FAT WRAPS

heaping $^1/_3$ cup red Camargue rice
$5^1/_2$ oz firm sustainable white fish (see page 82),
   skinned and filleted
2 handfuls of all-purpose flour
$^1/_2$ teaspoon of cayenne or chili powder
1 egg
2 handfuls of coarse ground semolina
6 to 8 cornichons, sliced
1 heaping tablespoon capers, roughly chopped

$^1/_2$ a clove of garlic, minced
a handful of flat-leaf parsley, chopped
a squeeze of lemon juice
2 to 3 tablespoons good-quality thick Greek yogurt
2 whole-what flatbreads (big ones—12-inch
   diameter), the fresher the better
a couple of leaves of romaine/little gem lettuce
2 ripe plum tomatoes, sliced
salt and pepper

First get your rice cooking following the directions on the package (it should take about 30 minutes). Next cut your fish into strips $3^1/_4$ to 4 inches long and about $^3/_4$ inch wide—they should look about the same size as your middle finger—you want to end up with 8 to 10 pieces. Season very thoroughly with salt, pepper, and cayenne.

Get three wide bowls: in the first put the flour and a hefty amount of seasoning; in the second beat the egg well with 2 tablespoons of water; and the last holds the semolina.

Put one-third of the fish strips into the flour and rustle the bowl around until the fish is lightly coated. Move the fish strips along to the bowl containing the egg and roll the strips around so that all their surfaces are wet.

Now lift the fish slices into the semolina and move them around until they have an all-over thin coating. Put this batch on a plate and repeat with the rest, in two batches.

Preheat your broiler to hot.

Somewhere around about now your rice will be cooked. Drain it and let it cool a little, but not completely. In a bowl mix the rice with the cornichons, capers, garlic, parsley, lemon juice, and some seasoning. Fold in the yogurt and season again.

Put an oiled piece of foil onto your broiler rack, arrange the fish pieces on it, and drizzle healthily with olive oil. Broil for 4 minutes, then turn them over and broil for a further 4 minutes; the coating should be browning and fizzing—you'll see what I mean.

Meanwhile start building your wraps: soften the flatbreads under the broiler (underneath the fish) for a couple of minutes, add the lettuce leaves and tomato slices with some seasoning; spoon on half the red rice tartare and as soon as the fish is ready place it on top.

Give it a final and generous squeeze of lemon before wrapping it up (and it's a big wrap) and tucking in.

Henry's Sweet & Sour Mackerel

✓ ❤ *DF* **WF GF**

Henry, John (see recipe on page 215) & I are the Three Original Pillars of Leon. All the fantabulous people who work at Leon adore Henry for his eager energy, charm, and enthusiasm. He works really hard to keep the Good Ship Leon (and all who sail in her) on a direct and true course, and he does it with passion and belief.

SERVES 4 FOR MAINS AND 8 AS AN APPETIZER

1 lb 2 oz carrots
2 large red bell peppers
2 large yellow bell peppers
1 bulb of garlic
1 lb 9 oz red onions
3/4 cup + 2 tablespoons extra virgin olive oil
a bunch of thyme

4 bay leaves
generous 1 1/4 cups white wine vinegar
1 to 2 tablespoons stringy-bark honey © (see page 127)
a big handful of parsley, chopped
4 mackerel (cut into 8 fillets)
salt and pepper

Peel the carrots and chop them lengthwise into strips, then set them on top of each other and chop lengthwise again so they form long batons. Peel and chop the bell peppers in the same shape. Cut the garlic bulb in half across the middle (so that each clove is cut in half but leave the cloves connected). Slice the red onions in half lengthwise and then finely across to give half rings.

Add the olive oil to the pan, then the vegetables, garlic, thyme, and bay leaves. Sweat these for about 15 minutes, or until they have settled into the pan. Add the vinegar and honey and cook down for another 15 minutes or so, or until the vegetables are soft, but the carrots still have a little bite. Add a little water if necessary to create an unctuous coating around the vegetables. Season and add parsley. Season the mackerel on each side and cook under a hot broiler (or you can bake them in the oven at 350°F for 4 minutes). Mix the mackerel into the sweet and sour vegetables.

While you can eat this hot, it is best cooled and left in the fridge overnight. Take out a couple of hours before serving so it returns to room temperature. If you want, you can lay the mackerel daintily on plates and spoon the pepper mixture over in an alluring fashion for an appetizer. Otherwise just serve it in a bowl in the middle of the table, with new potatoes and salad for a great summer lunch.

© See Suppliers, page VI in Appendix.

Henry and his Dad, Lanzarote, Summer '75

Leon's Family Recipes

This is such a simple dish. And mackerel - when fresh - is the king of fish. We used to catch them off the Devon coast when we were children - on strings of brightly colored feathers tied at the end of a long orange line. If you were lucky enough to hit a shoal, the line would start jumping and tugging in your hand. You would pull it up to find six fish sparkling on the line. We had a small pan and a pump-up stove on the boat and we would chop them into small chunks and fry them in butter there and then.

Henry

Fred and his first missing tooth, 1975

Leon's Family Recipes

A very long time ago, a duke fell in love with a dazzling Neapolitan princess. He built her a huge, magnificent palace in the sea on the Bay of Naples. The love despaired and the palazzo fell vacant as its roots grew deep through its grottoes to the sea. Two centuries later, perfumiers from France fled the guillotine to beautiful Naples, bought said palazzo in its crumbling glory, and made it home.

Many years later boy met boy, and the perfumiers' great-grandson and I crossed paths; as my Canadian wildernesses were married with Giovanni's Italian precision this historic house became home.

This recipe is from that house and the blue, blue water that smashes up against it.

Fred's Millennium Octopus

✓ ❤ DF

Our Fred doesn't technically work for Leon, but makes it in here as my best friend, an inspired cook, and a long-time Leon lover. He was in the kitchen with Benny & me at the beginning of Carnaby Street, cooked in the early days of the Big Kitchen, has drunk his share at our Christmas and summer parties and finally helped me build this book. Fred may be without title at Leon, but he is loved by all of us. Built of sunshine held together with his own recipe of eccentricity and fun, life would just be a lot less jolly without him.

SERVES 6 GENEROUSLY

1 large bulb of garlic, cloves peeled and sliced
generous 1¼ cups extra virgin olive oil, divided
3 pints tomato purée (or half that amount of purée
*   and 1 bottle good local red wine—the wine*
*   option makes it meatier and less oceanic, so it's*
*   up to you whether you prefer surf or turf)*

6 dried peperoncini (small whole chiles)
3¼ lb octopus, cleaned and left whole
2 handfuls of flat-leaf parsley, chopped
a handful of basil, roughly chopped
1 lb 6 oz linguine
salt and pepper

In your favorite big slow-cooking pot, simmer the garlic in 1 cup of the extra virgin olive oil, along with a pinch of salt over low heat, until smelling good and lightly golden.

Pour in the purée (or purée and wine). Be careful: it will splash and burble. Turn the heat up until it all warms through, drop in the peperoncini, then turn down the heat and simmer for 30 minutes.

Slowly dip in the octopus, tentacles first. They will curl up. Then slowly bury the octopus in the liquid. Cover and cook for 1 hour, continuing on a low simmer. You will have to have a look at it now and then to make sure the whole beast stays submerged.

Cook for 1½ hours uncovered, then add half the chopped parsley and keep it on a vigorous simmer until it's reduced to a very rich, thick tomato sauce. Take out the octopus and chop it up, leaving as many recognizable octopus-looking pieces as you can enjoy. Return them to the sauce to warm through. Cook the linguine following the instructions on the package.

Check the seasoning. Mix the well drained pasta with as much sauce as you need to make it wet and wonderful (keep any leftover in the fridge) and the rest of the olive oil and herbs, then check the seasoning again.

Fred loving the octopus, Malaga 2007

Yenny's Steamboat ✓ ❤ DF WF

Little Yenny from Singapore has managed to squeeze so much energy, fun, and enthusiasm into that tiny body that it shines out of her very being. When she smiles (which is most of the time), her entire face rearranges into something you can't help smiling back at. It was for that reason, and of course her other talents (such as delighting us all by dressing up as an elf and hopping around at the Christmas party), that we put her in charge of culture and happiness at Leon. Her steamboat is legendary and spectacular. You can also make it in a wok, on a portable gas stove, or even a fondue pot (in which case just keep half the stock in a pan on the stove for the second-stage broth part). On the other hand, if you fall in love with it, go and buy your own proper steamboat boiler in your nearest Chinatown—worth it for years of fun.

Wei, Yenny, and her lovely Mom, Kulai, Johore Bahru, Malaysia

STEAMBOAT FOR 6 TO 8 OF YENNY'S FAMILY, OR 5-ISH WESTERNERS

2¹/₄ lb raw, shelled shrimp, medium-sized (not jumbo), shells and heads reserved for the broth
2¹/₄ lb monkfish tail (reserve the bone for the broth), cut into ¹/₂-inch thick slices
1 lb 2 oz beef tenderloin
2 packs of enoki mushrooms
a handful of shiitake mushrooms, sliced
a head of napa cabbage, cut into very wide ribbons (the best vegetable for steamboat is called tang-oh, and you can get it from Vietnamese grocers)
fishballs (a great kind of processed food)

THE STOCK
the shells and heads from the shrimp
the bone from the monkfish
a thumb-sized piece of fresh ginger, cut in half
2 sticks of lemongrass, fat end split by bashing with a saucepan
2 carrots, cut in half
2 sticks of celery, cut in half
1 onion, cut in half
a good glug of Chinese rice wine

THE DIPS
FOR THE SEAFOOD:
a big bunch of cilantro, finely chopped
8 tablespoons fish sauce, divided
3 bird's-eye chiles (seeded if you want to lower the heat), chopped
juice of 2 limes

FOR THE MEAT:
3 tablespoons soy sauce
4 scallions, minced
¹/₃ cup + 1 tablespoon toasted sesame oil
3 egg yolks

AT THE END
thin egg noodles (or cellophane will do)
quail eggs (allow a couple per person)

The Chinese characters read "fire pot." I imagine families sitting around a charcoal stove with a pot of broth bubbling away above it, using chopsticks to pick up slices of raw meat or fish and cooking them in the broth.

In Singapore where I come from, we call this way of cooking "steamboat." We make a nice big pot of stock and cook the freshest possible ingredients in it. My favorites are melt-in-your-mouth beef tenderloin (sliced so thinly you risk tearing the slice as you pick it up with your chopsticks), juicy shrimp, slices of pork, monkfish, and slivers of pork liver marinated in Chinese wine and sesame oil. My mom always remembers to pick up some tang-oh, a Chinese vegetable with a distinctive peppery flavor for the soup. I am crazy about it and can eat bowls of soup just with that dunked in.

Having "steamboat" is a noisy, celebratory affair at home. I smile when I think of the little dishes of dips made for meat and seafood, my mom unpacking all the raw food, each prepped item swimming in its own marinade. My dad does not like sesame oil too much so he gets his own dips. My sister loves kidney so sometimes there's a little plate for her.

What a brilliant, wonderful way of sharing and cooking food at the table. Sometimes I get so excited I cook (and eat) too quickly and then feel too full but then you can take a breather and start again. It's a lovely drawn-out affair of inhaling aromas and feeling steam cooling off on your cheeks.

Soak the noodles in hot water for a few minutes just to soften up, then rinse under cold water to stop them from sticking together. Drain and set aside for later.

Put the beef tenderloin into the freezer to firm up.

Get all the stock ingredients, except the rice wine, into a large pot and cover with plenty of water (about 5¼ pints). Simmer for an hour with a lid on, then strain the stock into the steamboat/pan on a portable gas stove set in the middle of the table. Finish the stock by adding the wine.

Meanwhile, get your dips ready by mixing each group of ingredients together and dividing them into groups of little dipping bowls so that every 2 to 3 people have one of each.

After about 45 minutes take the beef out of the freezer and slice it as thinly as you can. Arrange all the fish and vegetables on platters.

Once all your bits and pieces are ready, get your steamboat bubbling away and put all the pieces of vegetables and protein around so everyone can get to them. When the stock is on a good simmer, pick what you want and cook it in the stock using little wire baskets, skewers and/or fondue forks. As a rough guide, the beef really only needs about 10 seconds to cook, the fish about 20 seconds, and the shrimp 30 seconds. Then dip your cooked prize into its sauce and savor the flavor.

When you're done with this part, divide the noodles between little soup bowls, one for each person, and ladle in the stock from the steamboat. Crack a quail egg in at the end for the authentic touch, but don't expect it to cook because it's there to finish the broth with texture and richness.

MAINS:
VEGGIE

Jossy's Moorish Vegetable Tagine ✓ ❤ V *DF* **WF** **GF**

Over the course of our second year we got a bunch of postcards from our vociferous vegetarian following, quite rightly taking umbridge at the fact that our best-selling tagine was always chicken. It's well known that lots of chefs are a bit down on vegetarian food, and I was having a bad day when I was asked to come up with something to appease them. No sooner had I rolled my eyes than Henry mentioned that his mom—a very respected cookery writer—had a vegetable tagine recipe in her repertoire, and so Jossy's Moorish Vegetable Tagine came to pass, and very special it is too.

SERVES 4

2 tablespoons olive oil
juice of 1 lemon
1 tablespoon tomato paste
2 teaspoons paprika
2 teaspoons ground cinnamon
4 plum tomatoes, skinned and chopped (you can use canned)
2 red bell peppers, cut into small pieces (grilled and skinned would be nicer, but that is more work)
1/2 cup raw almonds, skin on

scant 1/2 cup pitted prunes, roughly chopped
1/2 a thumb-sized piece of fresh ginger, peeled and chopped
2 to 3 cloves of garlic, peeled and chopped
2 medium zucchini, cut into medium-thin rounds
1 x 14-oz can of chickpeas, drained
1 tablespoon honey
a handful of cilantro, chopped
salt and pepper

Heat the olive oil in a Dutch oven and stir in the lemon juice and tomato paste, along with the paprika and cinnamon, then season with salt and pepper.
Add the chopped tomatoes and bell peppers and cover.
Cook gently over very low heat, stirring occasionally, for about 20 to 30 minutes.
Stir in the almonds, prunes, ginger, and garlic and cook for another 15 minutes.
When the bell peppers are good and soft, add the zucchini and chickpeas, giving them a good nuzzle in the sauce.
Cover the dish again and cook for about 10 minutes, or until zucchini are tender but not too soft.
Finally stir in the honey and throw on the cilantro leaves at the end.

Zucchini flower, Cannwood Farm, Somerset 2007

Leon Gobi ✓ ❤ V *DF* **WF GF**

At Leon we give the vegetarians who eat with us quite a lot of TLC, and this curry took a long time to get absolutely right before it went on the menu. It's all about the balance of spices, sweetness, and making sure you time the vegetables right so it doesn't all fall apart. The Gobi refers to the cauliflower in it, and like the Rogan Josh, it's the addition of ground almonds that provides the wonderful consistency. Our grandmothers were wedded to arrowroot flour to thicken their sauces, and our moms to flour , but ours is the generation to welcome the almond—so much better than any other thickener, both for health and flavor.

GOBI GOOD FOR 6

1 medium onion, halved and thickly sliced
1 carrot, thickly sliced
2 tablespoons sunflower or peanut oil
1 red chile (go for a bird's-eye if you like it hot—
*   some do)*
2 thumb-sized pieces of fresh ginger, washed but
*   not peeled*
5 cloves garlic, peeled
1 large teaspoon Madras curry powder*
1 teaspoon turmeric
1 teaspoon black onion seeds

1 medium sweet potato, washed and cut into
*   1-inch dice*
heaping 1/4 cup ground almonds
a good handful of golden raisins
1/2 a small cauliflower, broken into florets
1 x 14 fl oz can of coconut milk
1 cup frozen peas
juice of 1/2 a lemon
a really big handful of cilantro, roughly chopped
salt
2 heaping tablespoons desiccated coconut, to serve

In a big and well-loved saucepan cook the onion and carrot in the oil over medium to low heat for 15 to 20 minutes, covered, stirring occasionally. Season with salt.

Blend the chile, ginger, and garlic to a paste in a food processor. Stir the paste into the onions once they have begun to soften, along with the spices (including the onion seeds).

After another 5 minutes, season with salt, add the sweet potato chunks and the almonds, and stir thoroughly so that everything is well coated.

Turn the heat up a little and stir in 2 cups of water and the golden raisins.

Bring it up to a simmer and let it bubble away gently for about 10 to 15 minutes with the lid off, stirring occasionally.

Add the cauliflower florets and the coconut milk and simmer for a further 10 to 15 minutes, covered.

Check that the sweet potato and cauliflower are both cooked, then turn the heat off and stir in the peas.

It'll need more salt, plus the lemon juice and chopped cilantro to finish it off right. We serve it with a sprinkling of dried coconut on top.

*See page 105 on the trouble with curry powder.

Egyptian Eggplant & Tamarind Stew ✓ ♥ V *DF* **WF** **GF**

When we were having all our falafel issues (see page 153) I rang up Leon food heroine Claudia Roden, who told me that in Egypt, where she lived for many years, they make their falafel with half chickpeas and half dried fava beans. So I did a bit of research and found out that I could only get them delivered (and as usual I was a little short of time) in 55-pound sacks. I knew it was a little rash, but I was firmly in the weeds with a big tasting the next day, so I placed my order.

We cracked the falafel problem with the ingenious idea of a sweet potato base, and not a dried fava bean in sight. So there I was left to party with my sack, and this dish, and the name, are the results of my playing. Never is there a truer place than the kitchen for the saying "Necessity is the mother of invention." If you can't find dried fava beans, use chickpeas instead.

Pretty intense, so serve with plain rice and a salad.

SERVES 4

1 eggplant
1/4 cup extra virgin olive oil
1 onion, sliced
2 cloves of garlic, chopped
1 big green chile
1 teaspoon ground cumin
1/2 teaspoon ground coriander
1 teaspoon turmeric
1 teaspoon brown mustard seeds

1 x 14-oz can of chopped plum tomatoes
1 large green bell pepper, cut into bite-sized pieces
3 tablespoons fructose
1 heaping tablespoon tamarind paste
1 cup dried fava beans or 1 x 14-oz can of
  chickpeas
10 1/2 oz tomatoes, cut into eighths
a small handful of mint, roughly chopped
salt and pepper

If you are using dried fava beans (and I can't believe you are) soak them overnight in plenty of cold water. The next day change the old water for new and simmer for about an hour, or until soft.

Preheat the oven to 375°F.

Cut the eggplant into fair-sized chunks and roast for 20 to 30 minutes on a lightly oiled baking pan—you want them to be browned and almost cooked through.

Heat the olive oil and gently fry the onion, garlic, and whole chile in it for 10 minutes, or until softened, stirring occasionally.

Stir in the spices including the mustard seeds and cook for a further 5 minutes.

Add the canned tomatoes and simmer for 5 to 10 minutes, stirring occasionally.

Stir in the green bell pepper, fructose, tamarind, and eggplant pieces and lower the heat.

Tip in the cooked fava beans (or chickpeas) and fresh tomatoes and cook for a further 10 to 15 minutes.

Check the seasoning and stir in the mint before serving.

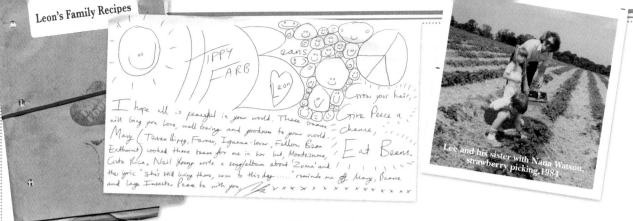

HIPPY FARB Beans

I hope all is peaceful in your world. These beans will bring you love, well being and goodness to your world. Mary (Texan Hippy, Farmer, Iguana-lover, Fellow Bean Enthusiast) cooked these beans for me in her hut, Montezuma, Costa Rica. Neil Young wrote a song/album about 'Zuma' and the lyric "She's still living there, even to this day....." reminds me of Mary, Beans and Large Insects. Peace be with you. Grow your hair, Give Peace a chance, Eat Beans.

Lee and his sister with Nana Watson, strawberry picking, 1984.

Lee's Hippy Farm Beans ✓ ❤ V *DF* **GF**

Our managers are all a wonderfully eclectic lot, but Lee might win the prize as being the most out there of all of them. He loves his food, soccer, and wine, and if you chat to him about his team (Sunderland) it's clear he loves them too. Strong and kind, Lee runs a very happy, hippy ship. Like him, his beans are full of fun, sun, and up for a party; he says he likes them "spleen-meltingly hot."

FEEDS 4 HUNGRY HIPPIES

excellent olive oil
1 large shiny eggplant, cut into rough chunks
3 bell peppers (preferably yellow and orange), cut into rough chunks
ground cumin
1 big onion, coarsely chopped
at least 3 big cloves of garlic, roughly chopped
at least 3 assorted fiery chiles, roughly chopped
³/₄ lb cherry tomatoes
1 can of good-quality diced tomatoes
2 cans of good-quality beans, preferably one mixed and the other kidney, black bean, or pinto (most varieties suit deliciously)

sweet chili sauce
10¹/₂ oz baby spinach, washed well
rock salt

AND ALSO
1 pack of tortillas
3 avocados
a plethora of lime wedges
more chopped chiles
grated cheese, if you feel like some

Right then. Plenty of oil—about ¹/₄ cup. Hot pan, fry the eggplant and bell peppers for 15 minutes, or until golden, crispy, and lovely. Season with salt and cumin (it's my Moroccan part), then take them out, cover, and set to one side.

Get the pan good and hot again. Fry the onion in a little more olive oil for a few minutes (brown it), then the garlic and chiles. Few minutes, hot. Then add the cherry tomatoes. Few minutes. Then add the canned tomatoes and the eggplant and bell peppers.

Bring to a boil and add the drained beans. Now add a good glug of the sauce. Low heat, a gentle simmer, cover for ¹/₂ an hour, uncover for a further hour; stir regularly. You want a gloopy, unky, smooth texture that cries out to be attacked by the mouth. Turn the heat off and stir in the spinach well until wilted.

Heat the tortillas, mash or slice the avocados, wedge the limes, scatter with a few fresh chiles. The colors drive you wild.

Maybe serve with cheese if you have that creamy need.

I just like it with crusty brown bread for dipping.

Green Pea Curry ✓ ♥ V *DF* **WF GF**

This certainly wins the Handy Supper Award. All you need is a can of coconut milk, a couple of onions, and a package of peas to make something that looks like you've really put some effort into it. Great base and would also be nice with some butternut squash or chicken in there too. One of John's additions to the menu.

SERVES 4

2 teaspoons sunflower oil
1 heaping teaspoon mustard seeds
2 large or 3 small onions, thinly sliced
2 thumb-sized pieces of fresh ginger, grated
1 red chile, finely chopped
1¹/₂ teaspoons cumin
1 teaspoon turmeric

4 ripe tomatoes, cut into wedges
2 green bell peppers, cut into large chunks
1 x 14-oz can of coconut milk
2³/₄ cups frozen peas
1 heaping tablespoon creamed coconut
a few sprigs of mint, roughly chopped
salt

In a large wide skillet heat the oil over medium heat and tip in the mustard seeds. Shuffle the pan around until the seeds begin to pop.

Add the onions, ginger, chile, cumin, turmeric, and some salt and cook for a good 10 minutes over high heat until the onion is soft.

Add the tomatoes, bell peppers, and coconut milk and simmer for 15 minutes.

Tip in the peas and cook for 5 to 10 minutes, or until they are soft.

Turn off the heat and crumble the creamed coconut evenly over the top.

Finish with the chopped mint. May like a squeeze of lime.

Ursula and her Mom Jennie, Westwell, summer 1983

Pizza is my fondest memory from childhood. My
Mum used to make pizza bases for me &
all my friends... She would give us bowls of
veggies and cheeses to decorate them with —
and we would create pictures... make a rather
big mess... and then tuck into our very own
customised pizza... Mmmmm,
♡ Scrumdidellyumptious, Yummy ♡ ♡
♡ ♡ ♡
xxx Ursula

Ursula's (Whole-meal) Pizza v

Lovely Ursula is a fairly new addition to the Leon family, winning us all over instantly by exuding a lethal amount of fun. What we hadn't counted on, however, was the business behind the lady—she's a real number-cruncher. Ursula talked about wanting her recipe in this book to be a wholemeal pizza, which made me feel a bit funny in the same way that whole-wheat pasta and pastry do. It's just not quite right. But then she cooked it for me and I was quietly blown away by how tasty it was. Now, having cooked and eaten it with both brown and white doughs, I'm not sure I didn't like it better with whole-wheat because, out of all the pizzas I've eaten in my life, I'll always remember Ursula's, and that memory will make me smile.

MAKES 1 PIZZA

THE DOUGH
$2^1/4$ cups strong bread flour, white or brown
    as preferred
1 teaspoon salt
2 tablespoons olive oil
$1/2$ level tablespoon active dried yeast
$1^1/4$ cups to scant 2 cups warm water

THE TOMATO SAUCE
1 small onion, minced
1 clove of garlic, peeled

2 tablespoons extra virgin olive oil
1 x 14-oz can of tomatoes
2 tablespoons tomato paste
bay leaf, basil, mixed herbs
sugar to taste
salt and pepper

THE TOPPINGS
mozzarella cheese, sharp cheddar cheese
vegetables: mushrooms, bell peppers, red onion,
    zucchini, tomatoes, broccoli

First make the dough. Sift the flour and salt and stir in the oil. Dissolve the yeast in the warm water. Make a well in the flour and add the yeasty water little by little, stirring until the dough comes together. Knead well for 10 minutes, or until smooth, adding extra flour if necessary. Roll the dough out onto an oiled cookie sheet.
Let prove in a warm place, covered with a damp dish towel, for a good couple of hours.
To make the tomato sauce, put the onion and garlic into a large pan and sauté in the oil until soft.

Add the rest of the ingredients. Bring to a boil, then immediately reduce the heat and simmer for an hour or so, stirring occasionally and keeping covered until the taste and consistency are OK.
Spread the tomato sauce on the dough base, evening it out with the back of a spoon. Add your chosen toppings.
Heat the oven to 425°F.
Bake in the oven for around 20 minutes, depending on how you like your cheese.

Black-eyed Peas, Spinach, & Lemon ✓ ❤ V *DF* **WF** **GF**

Compared with the other 3,782 legume recipes in this book, this is a lighter, looser bean dish. Eat it hot immediately, before the spinach all collapses. Tuck in and it's gone in seconds.
Related to its scrumptious factor, this dish suffers from a slightly understated name. Good with yogurt.

MAKES 2 VEGGIES HAPPY (WITH A LITTLE RICE OR A ROTI ON THE SIDE)

1 cup dried black-eyed peas (or beans)
3 tablespoons extra virgin olive oil
3 cloves of garlic, thinly sliced
2 bay leaves
1 red chile, sliced
1 heaping teaspoon ground cumin
1 large red onion, diced
1 heaping teaspoon smoked paprika

1 stick of celery, sliced 1/2-inch thick
1/2 leek, washed and sliced 1/2-inch thick
1 large carrot, peeled, halved lengthwise and sliced 1/2-inch thick
5 1/2 oz baby spinach, washed and drained
juice of 1 lemon
a big bunch of flat-leaf parsley, roughly chopped
salt and pepper

Soak the beans overnight in cold water.
Next day, drain the beans and put them into a saucepan with twice the amount of fresh water to beans, and cook with a few bean friends (I haven't put these in the ingredients because they can be whatever you have around: onion, bay, some garlic, a chile, tomato, herbs, and so on). Cook for about an hour, or until they are beginning to soften.
When the beans are nearly there, warm up a Dutch oven on medium heat, pour in the olive oil, and sizzle the garlic, bay leaves, and chile for a few seconds, or until lightly golden.
Add the cumin, onions, carrots, leeks, celery, and smoked paprika, cover, and let it sizzle away for around 10 to 15 minutes, or until everything is softening nicely and beginning to brown.
Now back to the beans: leave the bay leaves in the pot but discard the rest of the bean friends. Stir the beans with any leftover cooking liquor into the Dutch oven. Add some salt, and if necessary some more hot water to just cover. Simmer, uncovered, on medium heat for 20 to 30 minutes, or until the liquid has reduced right down so that it's coating the beans but they're not swimming.
When it's all come together and is nice and thick, turn off the heat and stir in the parsley and lemon juice, then fold in two-thirds of the spinach so that it half wilts.
Check the seasoning very carefully—it's vital on this one—and serve with the rest of the spinach on top to be stirred in by the happy recipients. We feel it's enhanced with a dollop of yogurt, a final splash of olive oil, and a wedge of lemon on the side.
Contrary to most slow-cooks, this one is never better than when it's just been made.

SAUCES

Salsa Verde for All Seasons

✓ ❤ *DF* **WF** **GF**

Acknowledging and enjoying the passage through the year, paying mind to the seasons just feels right. In California, January may be just like June, but in the UK it's not, and we love that. One of the ways we like to take note is by seasonalizing our salsa verde. In spring we up the mint and onions of that season, whereas in summer we lean more toward basil for that real taste of Med sunshine. Come fall we butch her up a bit by swapping the scallions for shallots, and introducing a little rosemary. And our winter salsa has a taste of a touch of Christmas to it by sneaking in some sage. These are small inflections while the base stays steady, and making more work for ourselves (new recipes, new menus, train the teams, spread the word) is a no-brainer for feeling that little bit closer to nature. This is our summer recipe.

MAKES 6 TO 8 HEALTHY DOLLOPS

a handful of basil
a really big handful of parsley
a small handful of mint
$^1/_2$ a handful of oregano
2 tablespoons capers, roughly chopped
5 fat fillets of anchovies, chopped (the best ones are
  packed in salt and need to be well rinsed)
3 scallions, minced
scant $^1/_2$ cup extra virgin olive oil
juice of $^1/_2$ a lemon or more, to taste
salt and pepper

Pick, wash, and roughly chop the herbs. Put them into a bowl.
Add the capers, anchovies, scallions, oil, and lemon juice, and stir thoroughly so that every little bit is coated.
Check the seasoning and serve.

Our Aïoli

✓ *V* **WF** **GF**

The reason this is called Our Aïoli is because it's a much lighter, fluffier version than the usual, which is generally taken to mean garlic mayo. It's all down to the whipping of the egg whites, and the turning in of the yogurt. This will make far too much for your supper, but keeps for about a week in the fridge and tastes great with almost anything.

MAKES ABOUT 2 CUPS

1 egg + 1 egg white
4 to 5 cloves of garlic, minced and mixed with a
  pinch of sea salt
$^1/_2$ cup sunflower oil
scant 1 cup thick Greek yogurt (not sheep milk)
juice of $^1/_4$ to $^1/_2$ a lemon, to taste
salt to taste (it can take up to a scant teaspoonful)

Using an electric mixer, but not on the highest speed, beat the egg and egg white with the garlic for a few minutes, or until pale and fluffy.
Start drizzling in the oil, as if you were making mayo or hollandaise.
Once all the oil has been incorporated turn the machine off.
Stir/fold the yogurt in gently by hand and finish with the lemon and salt.
Pretty fiery on its own, and great with crudités.

Smokin' Chili Sauce

✓ ❤ V *DF* **WF** **GF**

Of all the recipes we've come up with at Leon, this is the most bankable. When I was a little girl playing soccer on Brook Green I was absolutely convinced that the manager of Queen's Park Rangers was going to drive past and sign me up. Similarly I feel just as sure that some day someone is going to offer us a lot of money for this recipe (but maybe not now it's in our book), and that it'll be in houses up and down the land, or even all over the world. Whether or not that ever happens we'll have to see—it's good to dream.

We make ours with a base of Leon ketchup, so unless you make that recipe too, yours isn't going to taste identical. This one has all the same fire and flavor in there, just comes out a little thicker and is missing the fresh tomato taste at the end. Just saying…

When chili is too hot it's just no fun, but this keeps lingering on your palate and the back of your throat in a memorable and nuclear way.

MAKES 1 BIG JAR

3 red chiles, seeds in
3 bird's-eye chiles, seeds in
2 teaspoons chipotle chili powder©
2 tablespoons red wine vinegar
1³/₄ cups tomato ketchup (any good-quality
  organic one will do)
2 teaspoons dried chili flakes
Maldon sea salt ©, *to taste*

Take the stalks off the chiles.
Put all the ingredients, except the dried chili flakes and ketchup, into a food processor. Add ¹/₄ cup of water and blend.
Once everything has been ground up, pour in the ketchup. Blend again for 10 seconds and finish by stirring in the dried chili flakes.
Gets even better and hotter with time.

Benny's Sweet & Sour

✓ ❤ V *DF* **WF** **GF**

We brought this onto the menu because we thought that our tried-and-tested sauce threesome (chili, aïoli, and salsa verde) might benefit from a bit of competition. It stayed for a couple of seasons, and then it was time for something new. We miss it a lot on our falafel and chicken, and I think it would be superb with duck.

MAKES A MEDIUM-SIZED JAM JAR FULL

1³/₄ oz tamarind
1 tablespoon tomato paste
a large pinch of cayenne pepper
2¹/₂ tablespoons fructose
¹/₂ teaspoon garam masala
a small piece of fresh ginger, grated
2 cloves of garlic, chopped
scant ²/₃ cup tomato juice
2 big teaspoons honey, preferably stringy-bark ©
  (see page 127)
1 heaping teaspoon black onion seeds ©
salt

Put all these bad boys into a pan and bring to a simmer.
Simmer for about 30 minutes to reduce the volume down to a scant 1 cup, then blend until smooth.
Let cool, and check the seasoning once it reaches room temperature.

©See Suppliers, page VI in Appendix.

DESSERTS & CAKES

Apricot Madeira Cake ❤ V *DF* **WF**

Some people are just natural born cake lovers, and watching them tuck into a proper slice of cake, be it Upsidedown Pineapple or Coffee Gateau, is pure pleasure by proxy. This recipe goes out to all the cake lovers out there (you know who you are), and this one's flourless too.

MAKES 8 FAT SLICES

1³/₄ cups dried apricots
scant ²/₃ cup Madeira or sweet sherry
butter or oil for greasing the pan
6 eggs

1 teaspoon baking powder
³/₄ cup fructose
2¹/₂ cups ground almonds
a handful of sliced almonds

Preheat the oven to 325°F.
Put the apricots in a small saucepan and fast simmer in the booze for about 10 minutes, or until there is no liquid left.
Roughly chop eight of the apricots; purée the rest.
Grease an 8-inch cake pan with butter or oil.
Beat the eggs until big and fluffy, preferably with an electric mixer.
In another bowl mix the fructose, ground almonds, and baking powder and then fold the mixture into the eggs.
Add both kinds of apricot to the batter and pour into your prepared pan.
Scatter the surface of the cake with sliced almonds.
Bake for 40 minutes, turning it around halfway through.
Let cool in the pan.

Dittisham Plum Ice Cream V WF **GF**

This recipe comes from Henry's mom, Jossy, and is great
not only because her recipes are, but because it's a proper ice
cream that doesn't need an electric ice-cream maker. My big
sister Floss (who did the drawings in this book) has been
friends with Henry's big sister Liza since aged 11, and she
remembers plum-picking with the Dimblebys.

Jossy, Dartmoor 1978

SERVES 6 TO 8

1 lb plums (not too ripe)
juice of 1 lemon
3/4 cup + 2 tablespoons superfine sugar
the whites of 2 large eggs
a pinch of salt

1 cup turbinado sugar
1/3 cup + 1 tablespoon water
generous 1 1/4 cups whipping cream
fruit liqueur (optional)

Cook the plums in advance. Cut them in half, remove the pits, and put the fruit into a saucepan with
the lemon juice and superfine sugar. Cover the pan and put over fairly low heat, stirring often until
the sugar has dissolved. Cook gently until mushy. Put the plums into a food processor, blend to a
rough purée, and let stand until cold.
Now put the egg whites into a large bowl with the salt and whisk until they begin to stand in soft peaks.
Put the turbinado sugar into a saucepan with the water and stir over low heat until dissolved. Then
increase the heat and boil fiercely, without stirring, for 3 minutes. Pour the syrup immediately onto
the whisked egg whites from above in a thin stream, beating constantly with an electric mixer until the
mixture is thick and looks like uncooked meringue.
In a separate bowl beat the cream until thick but not stiff. Then, using a metal spoon, gently
but thoroughly fold the cream into the egg-white mixture, followed by the plum purée (and
2 to 3 tablespoons of fruity alcohol, if you want, like crème de mur, Armagnac, or Calvados).
Finally, add to a serving bowl—glass looks nicest—and freeze for at least 5 hours before eating.

Leon's Family Recipes

DITTISHAM PLUM ICE CREAM

Illustrated by Jossy

The village of Dittisham, beside the River Dart in Devon, has long been
famous for its unique plums which, it is said, were brought over from
Germany by monks during the Middle Ages. Our holiday cottage was
set in an orchard where, each August, the branches of the trees were
weighed down by great clusters of these plums. Henry, his sisters and
their visiting friends would always ask for my special ice cream as the
plum version was a great favourite.

Dittisham plums have a particularly intense flavour and become deep
scarlet when cooked; you can use Victoria plums as an alternative but
they will taste even better if you include a few damsons. The ice cream
is also delicious made with greengages or apricots, and to make it extra
special stir some fruit liqueur into the mixture before freezing.
Serves 6-8.

For the plums:
450g plums (not too ripe)
Juice of 1 lemon

The whites of 2 large eggs
pinch salt
200g Demerara sugar

Mother Buckle, Rimini, Italy, 1962

Mother Buckle is widely renowned for her experimentation with desserts. Port Jelly or should I say Soup (you can guess the main ingredient of that one) is among those 'still under development'. Raspberry Brûlée cheesecake is by far the best for me, a wonderful creamy comfort food that I remember enjoying as a child, a teenager and that is still a joy to eat today. Thank you Mum for an amazing introduction to the world of desserts; there are none as good as yours.

Lots of love,

Anna xx

Mother Buckle's Raspberry Brûlée Cheesecake

Anna looks after a load of Leons, listening to the people who run and work in them, and making their lives happier. Anna is not Mother Buckle—that's her mom.
You need a 10-inch springform pan and a chef's torch to do it properly.

SERVES 12

THE CRUST
10¹/₂ oz baked plain sugar cookies or ginger
    cookies, if you like ginger
²/₃ stick unsalted butter, melted
1 tablespoon light corn syrup

THE FILLING
1 sachet of gelatin
1¹/₂ cups (about 13 oz) Philadelphia cream cheese
3 egg yolks

¹/₄ cup + 2 tablespoons superfine sugar
2¹/₂ cups heavy cream
2¹/₂ cups of raspberries
3 teaspoons vanilla extract

THE TOP
3 to 4 heaping tablespoons soft light brown sugar,
    or enough to cover the whole top

Whizz the cookies in a food processor until crumbs and place them in a bowl.
Stir in the melted butter and light corn syrup to combine.
Press into the bottom of the pan and let chill in the fridge.
Sprinkle the gelatin over 3 tablespoons of water, let stand until spongy, then microwave to melt. Stir until clear.
Put the cream cheese, egg yolks, and sugar into a food processor and blend until smooth.
Whip the heavy cream until just stiff.
Stir the cheese mixture and vanilla extract into the cream.
Then stir in the gelatin.
Take the crust out of the fridge and sprinkle the whole raspberries evenly onto it, ensuring that you have a healthy number around the edge so they are visible when you come to remove it from the pan.
Pour the cheesecake mixture onto the raspberries, level off the top with a hot metal spatula if necessary, or just let it settle flat. Then let chill for an hour in the fridge.
When the filling has chilled, scatter the top evenly the brown sugar and brown with a chef's torch.
Then, back into the fridge for a few hours to set and it's ready to eat.

Desserts & Cakes   265

Our Chocolate Mousse V WF **GF**

You'd be hard pressed to find a better chocolate book than Helge Rubinstein's, which long ago provided the origin of this recipe. I remember listening to my dad tell a story about how, at the age of 24, he had landed his first book deal and that it turned out he actually had known the great Helge in passing at the time. Food is so evocative and I love that the taste of this mousse always makes me feel warm toward a woman I've never met, muddled in my mind with an intensely focussed young writer getting his first break.

MAKES 4 BIG RAMEKINS (THE ONES THAT ARE ACTUALLY MEANT FOR SOUFFLÉS)

3¹/₂ oz chocolate (70% cocoa solids)
2 tablespoons unsalted butter
2 egg yolks
1 shot of dark espresso

a drop of orange oil (or a little very finely grated orange zest, or a dash of Cointreau/ Grand Marnier, or nothing at all)
3 egg whites
heaping 1 tablespoon fructose

Either in the microwave or over a double boiler, melt the chocolate and butter until smooth.
In another bowl, beat the egg yolks until nearly white and thick in consistency.
Gently stir the beaten yolks into the butter and chocolate, then stir in the coffee and the orange ingredient, if using.
Beat the egg whites to soft peaks, add the fructose, and beat for just a minute more to get that shine.
Now beat one-third of the egg white into the chocolate until nice and smooth, then do the next third more gently, and the last with the strokes of an angel. Neither overmix nor leave white streaks, then put the mousse into pretty ramekins and let stand in the fridge for an hour before serving.

Cardamom Rice Pudding   V WF **GF**

Although we think of rice pudding as being the quintessential children's pudding, this Middle Eastern influenced one tastes really quite sophisticated.

SERVES 4

1 tablespoon butter
³/₄ cup risotto, paella, or pudding rice
1¹/₂ cups whole milk
1³/₄ cups heavy cream

¹/₂ a vanilla bean
3 cardamom pods*
2¹/₂ tablespoons fructose

In a heavy saucepan, melt the butter over medium heat, then stir in the rice, and give it a good roll around in the butter to coat. Add the milk and cream and stir well.
Scrape the seeds out of the vanilla bean and add the seeds and the bean pod to the rice.
Do the same with the cardamom pods, but add just the seeds to the rice and discard the pods.
Continue to cook nice and slowly, uncovered, stirring a few times at the beginning to stop the rice from sticking to the bottom (the dairy will make a steady dome of foam above the rice). Let it cook for 30 minutes like this.
Then turn the heat down to minimum for the final 20 to 25 minutes.
When cooked, stir in the fructose and let the pudding sit for a few minutes with the lid on.
Eat it right there and then or, if you want to be a bit French about your *pot au riz*, put it into the fridge and enjoy it cold.
* We've also done a take on this with rosewater instead of cardamom—just stir in a few drops to taste once it's all cooked.

Cooper

Joey at her Grandma's nursery, Botswana

What-Joey-wants-Joey-gets
Rhubarb Crisp v

Joey, Benny's (see page 99) wife, is the sweetest-looking little lady in the world: wide-eyed, smiley, and very friendly. But behind this there lurks a tough Nottingham lass, and (speaking collectively as folk who love Joey dearly) we can all believe that what Joey wants, Joey gets. Unsurprisingly, because this is one of Benny's recipes, this is a really great crisp.

SERVES 6+

$2^{1}/_{4}$ lb rhubarb, cut into 2-inch batons
$^{1}/_{2}$ cup raw sugar
1 orange, juice and zest

THE CRISP
$^{1}/_{4}$ cup + 2 tablespoons raw sugar
heaping $1^{1}/_{4}$ cups all-purpose flour
$^{3}/_{4}$ stick chilled butter, cut into cubes
$^{3}/_{4}$ cup roasted hazelnuts, roughly chopped

Preheat the oven to 350°F.
Layer the rhubarb batons with the sugar in an ovenproof dish (ours is about 10 inches across and 4 inches deep). Sprinkle with half the orange juice and 2 curls of orange zest.
To make the crisp, place the sugar and flour in a bowl, add the butter cubes and rub with your fingertips until you reach a consistency similar to fine breadcrumbs. Then stir in the nuts to combine. Scatter the crisp mixture evenly onto the fruit, making sure you will have a chunky crisp by pressing some together to create larger pieces.
Bake in the oven for 25 to 35 minutes, or until the crisp is golden brown and the rhubarb juices are beginning to bubble up around the edges.
Serve with custard.

WELL, THIS PUPPY STARTED OUT AS A SIMPLE CRUMBLE COOKED FOR ONE'S WIFE; IT HAS NOT CHANGED MUCH AT ALL REALLY IN ITS SEVEN-YEAR LIFE — THE TIME I'VE BEEN WITH JOEY. THE CHANGING AREA IS ACTUALLY HOW OFTEN I MAKE IT DURING ANY GIVEN MONTH; IN THE SUMMER SHE DOESN'T CALL FOR IT, BUT THEN COME THE CHILLIER MONTHS I MIGHT AS WELL GIVE UP PAID WORK & OPEN A RHUBARB CRUMBLE FACTORY, SUCH IS THE — NEED TO BE ABLE TO MEET HER DEMANDS. OH YEAH, THE HAZELNUTS HAVE BEEN A FAIRLY RECENT INCLUSION, BUT ADD A GREAT — CRUNCH AND NUTTY FLAVOUR.

WARNING: DON'T MAKE FOR A LOVED ONE... THEY WILL JUST WANT IT MORE & MORE.

BENNY WITH KNIVES & POTS + PANS.

Susi, Virginia, Thanksgiving '83

My mom's family is from Virginia, and it was in the Deep South over many a Thanksgiving Dinner where my love of Pumpkin Pie began. As a sweet-toothed child I loved Pecan Pie nearly as much, and in this recipe I've taken the pecans and used them in the pie crust to make a pie that is a meeting of my two favorite American desserts.

Susi's Pumpkin Pie v

Susi is a true ray of sunshine who I am lucky enough to call my wife. Unsurprisingly I tend to do the cooking in the relationship, but for the creation of this pie she dug deep into her Southern heritage and amazed me by pulling this out from far inside her soul.

SERVES 6

2$^{1}/_{4}$ lb pumpkin
scant $^{1}/_{2}$ cup maple syrup
$^{1}/_{3}$ cup turbinado sugar
3 tablespoons whole milk
2 teaspoons butter
a pinch of grated nutmeg
a pinch of ground ginger
$^{1}/_{2}$ teaspoon ground cinnamon
a small pinch of salt
3 eggs (the yolks and 2 whites are for the pumpkin
    mixture, the remaining white is for the seed topping)

THE TOPPING
1 egg white
1 teaspoon turbinado sugar
1 tablespoon pumpkin seeds

THE CRUST
1$^{1}/_{2}$ cups pecans
1$^{2}/_{3}$ cups all-purpose flour
heaping $^{1}/_{3}$ cup turbinado sugar
1 stick butter
2 egg yolks

Preheat your oven to 350°F.

Start by making the crust. Grind up your pecans in a blender and add the flour, sugar, and butter (softened and cubed). Once this is all blended, add the egg yolks and keep blending until it all comes together. Seal the big ball of pastry in plastic wrap and refridgerate for 20 minutes.

Butter your pie pan (roughly 8 inches in diameter and 2$^{1}/_{2}$ inches deep) and grate your pastry into it. Push all the bits together until you have lined the whole pan (the bottom and up the sides) evenly.

Rest for 10 minutes in the fridge, prick the bottom all over with a fork, then bake in the preheated oven for 25 minutes, or until golden brown. Transfer from the oven and set aside.

In the meantime you can start on your pumpkin. Remove and discard the seeds and the stringy parts. Then cut it into 2-inch chunks and chop off the skin.

Arrange it on a roasting pan and brush each chunk with maple syrup (only use half for now).

Bake for 1 hour but after 30 minutes turn the chunks over, brush them with the remaining maple syrup, and return them to the oven.

After another 30 minutes take them out of the oven, add them to a food processor, and blend until smooth. Then add the sugar, milk, butter, nutmeg, ground ginger, cinnamon, salt, the 3 yolks and 2 whites, and blend thoroughly until smooth and frothy.

Pour the mixture into the crust and return it to the oven for 40 minutes.

The last thing that needs to be done is to make the crunchy seed topping: whisk up your remaining egg white, then take out a spoonful of the fluffy white, gently mix it with the teaspoon of turbinado sugar, and use it to lightly coat the tablespoon of pumpkin seeds.

Once your pie has been cooking for 20 minutes, take it out and scatter the pie evenly with the coated seeds, being careful to avoid having big clumps of whipped whites.

Put the whole thing back into the oven for the remaining 20 minutes to finish cooking, then take it out, and let it cool a little. Serve with vanilla ice cream or whipped cream, if you like.

Raspberry & Almond Tart v

Craig is a man with a talent for desserts. We tend to have one of his almond tarts on offer most of the year, moving with the seasons from apricots to berries to plums to prunes, while the frangipane base stays the same. This is a particularly good one, and it would be rude not to take full advantage of the local raspberry season.

Craig and Brett, Weston-super-Mare, 1979

GOOD FOR 8

2 cups raspberries

THE SWEET PASTRY*
1¹/₄ sticks unsalted butter, at room temperature
scant ¹/₂ cup superfine sugar
1 whole egg + 1 yolk
2¹/₄ cups all-purpose flour

THE ALMOND CREAM
1¹/₃ sticks unsalted butter
³/₄ superfine sugar
2 eggs + 2 yolks
1¹/₂ cups ground almonds
3 tablespoons all-purpose flour
zest of 1 lemon

First make the pastry. Using either an electic mixer or a wooden spoon cream the butter and sugar until soft and smooth, then slowly add the egg and yolk, mixing all the time.
Stir in the flour and bring together. Seal in plastic wrap and refrigerate for 30 minutes.
Roll the pastry out on a floured surface to just less than ¹/₄ inch thick and use it to line your tart pan. Preheat the oven to 325°F.
To make the almond cream, beat the butter and sugar until soft and smooth, then add the eggs and yolks slowly until all is combined, making sure the mixture does not split.
Stir in the ground almonds, flour, and lemon zest. Beat for about 30 seconds, or until it is all combined. Prick the bottom of the tart crust and scatter with half the raspberries.
Spoon in the almond cream and level it evenly with a metal spatula. The remaining raspberries are for the top, so deal with them in a way that suits your nature: neat circles or a haphazard scattering.
Bake in the preheated oven for about 40 to 50 minutes, or until the tart has a nice golden color on top.

* This makes enough pastry for 2 x 9¹/₂-inch tart crusts, so freeze half for later; keeps a couple of months in the freezer.

Gooseberry & Elderflower Fool v WF **GF**

Nature gives us gooseberries and elderflowers at the same time of year for a reason.

THIS MAKES 3, A FOOL'S NUMBER

2 cups gooseberries
scant ¹/₂ cup fructose
scant 1 cup good-quality thick Greek yogurt

scant 1 cup heavy cream, lightly whipped
¹/₄ cup elderflower cordial

Put the gooseberries and fructose into a small saucepan add ¹/₂ cup of water, cover, and simmer over low heat for 10 to 15 minutes, or until the fruit is soft and beginning to burst (fresh will take a little longer than frozen). Remove from the heat and let to stand, covered, for 5 minutes.
Stir the yogurt and cream together until smooth, then fold the cooled gooseberries into it. Finish by stirring in the elderflower cordial.
Share between 3 cut-glass goblets and chill in the fridge. Don't panic if it looks a little runny to begin with. It'll soon firm up.

Barn Brac

Grandma would always called Bara-brith, which I think is Welsh, funny as she was born and raised in Sunderland.

Mum said Grandma always said you can tell a good bara-brith if it's able to kill a man from 50 paces. Not the daintiest of cakes these…., but absolutely fan-bloody-tastic with a heap of butter and a strong cup of tea.

Magic woman was my gran!

Dizzy, Justin, and Alison, Coffs Harbour, Australia 1974

Justin's Barn Brac ♥ V DF

At one time or another bold and brassy Justin has looked after nearly all our restaurants, as well as doing a stint at the Big Kitchen. We love his bring-it-on attitude; he's a manager who really manages to get stuff done.

MAKES 1 LOAF—ABOUT 8 TO 10 SLICES

12 oz dried fruit (golden raisins, currants, apricots, prunes, dates, or whatever you have)
1 cup cold tea (made with 1 teabag—Earl Grey if you've got it)
1 large egg

1/2 cup brown sugar, not packed
2 teaspoons baking powder
2 cups all-purpose flour

SOAK OVERNIGHT

Soak the dried fruit in the tea for as long as you like (minimum overnight). Mom said she used to love making a pot of Earl Grey in the afternoon and would leave the last of it thinking she would make a barn brac for us kids.

Stir in the egg and brown sugar. Sift the flour and baking powder together and add to the mixture a spoonful at a time, beating all the while so the batter is as smooth as possible.

Bake at around 325°F for 1 hour (or in our house the measure is "cook until you can smell it").

Some of the more interesting barn bracs seemed to get tastier the more crispy and burnt they were. That's it!

John Hinde
ORIGINAL

BARN BRACK

Recipe
12 ozs dried fruit
3 ozs brown sugar
8 ozs cold tea
1 large-ish egg
8 ozs S.R. flour

HEDGEHOGS
from an original painting by David Teague

Prune & Chestnut Flop with Hazelnut Crunch ✓ V WF **GF**

Thanks to the fact that we made it very hard for the people who eat with us to know that we did any desserts at all, this was kind of a flop. I promise you it's three kinds of yummy though.

SERVES 4

THE HAZELNUT CRUNCH
⅓ cup fructose
¾ cup hazelnuts (filberts), skinned and whole

THE PRUNE–CHESTNUT MIX
2 egg whites
2 tablespoons fructose
scant 1 cup Greek yogurt
1 x 9-oz can chestnut purée—the French stuff
6 small pitted prunes (about 3½ oz), roughly chopped

First make the hazelnut crunch. Preheat the oven to 425°F. Put the fructose into a small heavy saucepan and add a tablespoon of water. Let stand for 5 minutes so the fructose can dissolve.
Toast the hazelnuts in the preheated oven for about 10 minutes, or until lightly golden brown.
Lightly oil a sheet of waxed paper and place it on a baking pan.
Place the pan of fructose water on high heat. This is a case of stand by your pan. Do not stir. Just swirl the pan a little if you see the edges darkening. Keep cooking until you have a golden-brown caramel, then add the hazelnuts.
Tilt the pan to roll the nuts around so they are well coated in the caramel, then pour them onto the oiled waxed paper and let harden and grow cool.
When totally cold and hardened, bring to your cutting board and carefully cut through, slowly now, until roughly chopped.
Now make the chestnut–prune mixture. Whisk the egg whites and the fructose to soft peaks (think of a meringue).
Gently fold in the yogurt and chestnut purée, then the prunes and two-thirds of the hazelnut crunch.
Split between four whatevers (looks nice in glass) and put into the fridge until well chilled.
When you're ready to serve, scatter the tops with the rest of the hazelnut crunch.
Fast, easy, yummy, and light.

Alex's Henry the Hedgehog v

Alex used to work at Leon and, even though she had
technically left, I managed to persuade her to help with the
look of this book because she has such an innate
understanding of what Leon is, and I needed the book to
feel properly Leon-y, not just another cookbook on the
shelf. Undaunted at having never designed a book before,
she threw herself into it mind, body, and most importantly soul, and when I was
bored silly by looking at all the millions of words I'd written, I'd look at some of her page layouts and
my sense of fun would be restored. She's also one of the kindest people you'll ever meet.

SERVES ENOUGH FOR ABOUT 12

12 oz graham crackers, or plain baked sugar cookies
6 oz semisweet chocolate
6 oz milk chocolate
1 stick butter

3 eggs, beaten
heaping $^1/_3$ cup fructose
$1^1/_4$ cup sliced almonds
3 shiny brown candy-coated chocolates

Break up the cookies into small pieces in your hands.
Melt the chocolate in a heatproof bowl placed over barely simmering water.
Melt the butter in a separate pan.
Beat the eggs and fructose until pale then beat in the melted butter.
Stir in the melted chocolate (it should look good and bouncy), then add the cookies.
Line a springform cake pan with plastic wrap. Pour the chocolate mixture in to a depth of 2 inches
(so use a smaller pan) and let stand in the fridge until it's almost set.
Take it out of the pan, cut it in half across the diameter and bring the two halves together like a
butterfly closing its wings. This is messy but just go with it. Gently shape it into a hedgehog, pulling a
little of it out to make his nose.
Stick the flaked almonds in to form his spikes. Then add the brown candy-coated chocolates as his
eyes and nose and you have a hedgehog.

Georgie and Alex in the bath at Wolverton, aged 5

's Family Recipes

Edna was an amazing woman from the village who used to look after us when we were little and Georgie, my twin, and I loved watching her bake... crumbles and pies using fruit from our garden. She was built of strong stuff raising nine children mostly on her own, and had about thirty-six grandchildren – we're still counting on the greats. The baking gene was passed down to her granddaughter Juliette, and this chocolate biscuit cake recipe comes from her.

This was our favourite birthday cake; it was all about making the cake into a hedgehog... cut the round in half, get really messy sticking the two together and shaping Henry. Then have fun with all the spiking and sticking on his beady little eyes. Henry the Hedgehog gives me lots of happy memories and warm fuzzies.

Alex x

RECIPE
TESTED BY
ALFIE

Allegra's Big Kitchen Cake v

Me and Mama, Bryce Canyon, Utah 1985

There's a certain irony to the fact that in a book of Leon recipes written by me, the only one that actually bears my name is somebody else's. And to make it worse, I've already put this recipe in both my other books in some guise. It's that good. But the truth remains, this was the first thing I ever remember making as a youngster, in the kitchen standing next to my brilliant mom, of whom we were robbed at far too young an age. She'd cut it out of the paper and so we'll never know who to thank for this simple and pleasing recipe for "Never Fail Victoria Sponge."

The guys and gals over in the Big Kitchen had had a hard old time of it, so I baked them this cake to say thank you. When I pulled up they were all outside having a break, so we had it right there and then off the hood of my car. We piped on the names of all the people at the Big Kitchen to make it a more personal show of thanks, which they found as hilarious as I do our blue hairnets. And really all I'd done was bake a cake I've baked a thousand times and slather it with strawberries and cream.

MAKES 12 NICE SLICES

$^1/_2$ stick butter
1 tablespoon milk
2 eggs
$^1/_2$ cup + 2 tablespoons superfine sugar

1 cup all-purpose flour
2 teaspoons baking powder
pinch of salt

Preheat the oven to 375°F.

Melt the butter over very low heat: don't let it boil.

Beat the milk and eggs (which must be at room temperature and not straight from the refrigerator) well together and add the sugar, beating hard for several minutes.

Sift the flour with the baking powder and the salt and fold it into the egg mixture. Lastly, very gently, stir in the melted butter.

Divide the batter between two well-buttered 7- or 8-inch round cake pans. Bake them side by side in the middle of the preheated oven for 12 to 15 minutes. Let cool in the pan for 10 minute before turning them out and transferring them to a wire rack.

Layer the two cakes together with a butter-cream filling, or with jam and lightly whipped cream or, best of all, with equal quantities of buttercream filling and homemade lemon curd, beaten together.

Unorthodox but unfailing.

Desserts & Cakes

The Leon Better Brownie v **WF GF**

This is the lovely Emma's recipe, which she's been making for us down in Dorset since day one and which has won many admirers. As you can tell, she's a bit particular about the way it's done. But all power to her. It's the best brownie in the world.

Emma, mom, and Duncan, The Old Vicarage, Humberstone

MAKES 12 BIG 'UNS

THE MELTING

$1^2/3$ sticks unsalted butter

7 oz semisweet chocolate (Belgian 54% cocoa solids)

2 teaspoons espresso at room temperature, or other very strong coffee

THE MIXING

1 teaspoon organic cold-pressed sweet orange oil© or finely grated zest of 1 orange

heaping $^1/2$ cup sweet Spanish almonds (skin on), toasted and chopped

4 free-range eggs

heaping 1 cup ground sweet Spanish almonds

$5^3/4$ oz semisweet chocolate chunks (Belgian 54% cocoa solids)

$5^3/4$ oz bittersweet chocolate chunks (Belgian 72% cocoa solids)

$^3/4$ cup fructose

pinch of sea salt

3 to 4 drops of Madagascan bourbon vanilla extract

Preheat the oven to 350°F.

Melt the butter on full power in a microwave for 1 minute (this can also be done in a little pan on the stove) and separately melt the semisweet chocolate in a bowl over a pan of hot water on the stove. Stir the chocolate well, ensure it's completely melted, and be careful not to burn it.

Once the butter is melted and has cooled slightly, add the coffee and stir well, then add whichever orange flavoring you're using (if you add anything too hot or too cold to the mixture it can cause it to shrink, so have your ingredients ready at room temperature and not straight from the fridge).

Roughly chop the skin-on almonds, toast them for 10 minutes, and then let cool.

(When it comes to this next part take special care to place the ingredients into the mixing bowl in the order stated. This ensures a nice even mix of all ingredients and the eggs don't come into contact with the warmed butter.)

Put the eggs in first, then all the ground almonds, then the semisweet chocolate and unsweetened chocolate chunks, and lastly the fructose. Stir in the salt and vanilla, followed by the melted butter and chocolate ornage mixture. Mix well until creamy and thickened but be careful not to overmix because too much air will cause the brownie to crumble when baked.

Spoon the batter into a well buttered 12 x 12-inch baking pan, or something with a similar volume. Take extreme care not to overbake. The brownie is ready after about 20 to 25 minutes, or when the edges are slightly crusty and the middle is still soft. (The middle should be very moist but should have a firmish feel to it.) Remember that fructose goes much darker when baked than sugar. The brownie also develops a glossy sheen and does not look baked even when it is. I'll say it again: You need to be very careful not to overbake these.

© See Suppliers, page VI in Appendix.

DRINKS

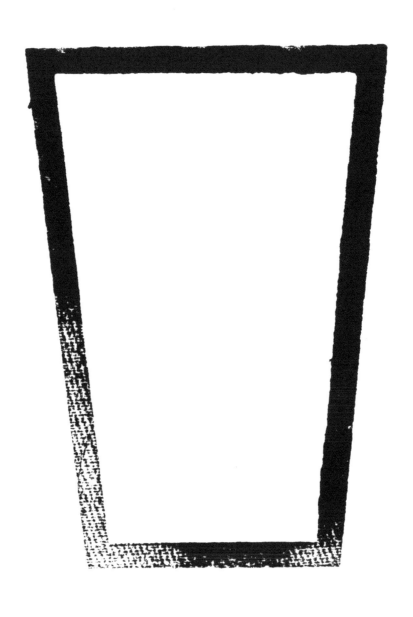

Summer Berry Smoothie ✓ ❤ V WF GF

Emmy is like a country girl stuck in the city. I remembered having a drunken love-in with her about this smoothie, so I asked her to write a little about berries and what they mean to her, because this winner is all about summer's finest fruit. "Summers in Dorset were always about berry-picking, and being slightly competitive I always felt I had to gather the most. So off I went with my basket, down to the local ladies who grew them in the village and who had fantastic redcurrants, raspberries, blackberries, blackcurrants, and strawberries. I remember going nuts in their gardens…gorging myself on them as I picked and ending up with such a red mouth that my mom thought I had been borrowing her lipstick."

MAKES A SMALL PITCHER—ABOUT RIGHT FOR 4

heaping ¹/2 cup blackberries
heaping 1 cup strawberries
scant 1 cup raspberries
scant 1 cup thick plain Greek or
    Turkish yogurt
1¹/2 bananas
generous ¹/2 cup apple juice
a handful of ice

Chuck it all in the blender and off you go.

Rhubarb & Vanilla Smoothie ❤ V WF **GF**

This is so yummy it could almost be a dessert.

MAKES 4 BIG SMOOTHIES

1 x recipe of Rhubarb Compote (see page 149)
*   but take the vanilla beans out*
scant 2 cups whole milk
¹/₂ a banana
generous 1¹/₄ cups Greek yogurt

Put everything in the blender and turn it on.
Serve with ice or fridge cold.

Date & Banana Smoothie ❤ V WF **GF**

With about six dates per glass, this is a good way to get your winter fruit quota for times when the soft fruit season is not upon us.

MAKES 4

9oz dates, preferably fresh like Medjool
1 banana
1¹/₂ cups Greek yogurt
2 cups whole milk
honey, preferably stringy bark©, to taste

Take the pits out of the dates and discard them.
Add the dates to a pan and half cover with water (if you have very fresh, squishy, fudgey Medjool dates you will need fewer).
Bring to a simmer for about 5 to 10 minutes (the fresher they are the less cooking time they'll need), then let them cool.
Drain off any excess water (how much they absorb depends on how dried your dates are) and blend the dates with the banana, yogurt, and milk, either in the blender or using a hand-held immersion blender. Taste and add honey if you like.
If you're drinking it now, chuck a bit of ice in the blender too. If it's for later, just let it get cold in the fridge.

©See Suppliers, page VI in Appendix.

Lemon, Ginger, & Mint Quencher ✓ ❤ V *DF* **WF GF**

Alex, who with Jonathan designed this book, came back from seeing her twin sister in Sydney and told tales of a drink like this that she'd had in a café over there. Seeing as the Aussies are rather good at refreshing drinks, we decided to take a leaf out of their book and whacked it on the menu, where it's been sitting pretty ever since. An ideal big-pitcher drink: plenty of ice, hot summer's day, perfection.

SERVES 4

²/₃ cup fructose
2 fat thumb-sized pieces (about 2 oz) fresh ginger, unpeeled and coarsely grated
3 leafy sprigs of mint, plus a few extra leaves, torn
juice of 3 lemons (about a scant ²/₃ cup)

Put the fructose, ¹/₂ cup water, and mint into a pan and bring to a boil, then turn down until just steaming, no bubbles, for 5 minutes and no more. Stir in the ginger, let steep for 5 minutes, then turn off the heat and let cool.
Pour the syrup and lemon juice into a pitcher with your remaining mint leaves.
Chuck in a load of ice, top off with around 2 pints of water and stir well (we thought it was exceptional with sparkling mineral water).

English Cucumber & Orange Quencher ✓ ❤ V *DF* **WF GF**

Freaky-sounding but super-refreshing and a step away from the norm. Can't help thinking it would work well with Hendrick's gin (which would be less good for you).

MAKES 2 GLASSES

1 cucumber, peeled
2 to 3 oranges (Blood oranges make for a special kind of sunrise.)

Juice* the cucumber—the amount of juice a cucumber produces can vary enormously.
Juice the oranges to the same volume.
Mix together and chill before drinking.

*If you don't have a juicer, just put the cucumber in chunks in a blender with the juice of 2 to 3 oranges.

Sheila's Lurve Potion ❤ V *DF* **WF** **GF**

Sheila (pronounced Shay-la) has more energy than a Superfood Salad, and a shine in her eyes that you've gotta love. As well as all her natural attributes, we're lucky that she's good at running a Leon too. While recipe-testing, Fred and I found this a very useful working drink—made us love the food lots.

PARTY POTION FOR 6

1 bottle of white wine
1½ cups of Sprite
2 pints pineapple juice
1 teaspoon Tabasco
1 peach, chopped
1 orange, cut into chunks
a handful of mint leaves
a couple of handfuls of white grapes

Just mix it all up together and serve over ice to put you in the mood for *lurve*. Best served ice cold.

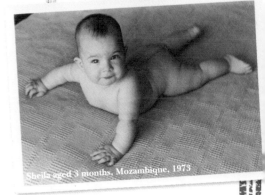

Sheila aged 3 months, Mozambique, 1973

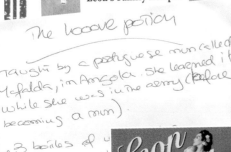

Leon's Family Recipes

THE MILKSHAKES

Not one for the lactose intolerant but really fun for the rest of us. For the full effect, don't skimp on the quality of the ice cream.

Blackberry V WF **GF**   MAKES 4 SHAKES

1 heaping cup blackberries*
heaping $^1/_3$ cup fructose, to taste
$1^3/_4$ cups whole milk, preferably organic
1 pint of vanilla ice cream, softened
*   (preferably organic—good quality really matters)*
squeeze of lemon

Put the blackberries and fructose into a pan with $^1/_3$ cup of water and bring to a boil. As soon as it starts to bubble furiously, take it off the heat, blend to a fine syrup, and let cool. Once the syrup is at room temperature, put it into the blender with the other ingredients— you'll probably have to do it in two loads or face a big mess. Blend for a while to get it really good and frothy, then pour into suitable glasses. Straws are essential.

Chocolate V WF **GF**   MAKES 3 BIG 'UNS

Just change the vanilla ice cream to chocolate (organic and top notch please) and ditch the berries. Whizz it up in a blender with milk.

Vanilla V WF **GF**   MAKES 3 BIG 'UNS

Made using just the ice cream and milk. Did we mention it has to be the best ice cream though?

* Change your blacks for strawbs or blueberries earlier in summer.

Leon Lemonade ♥ V *DF* **WF** **GF**

They always say you can test great chefs by their omelets, and this was our omelet moment. If you have good ingredients, all you have to do as a cook, whether at home or professionally, is not muck it up. This simple drink has been on the menu from the very beginning, quietly setting a standard and becoming a bestseller.

MAKES 4 HIGH-BALL GLASSES

3/4 cup + 2 tablespoons fructose*
juice of 5 lemons (about 1 cup)
3^1/2 oz ice

Make a syrup by dissolving the fructose in ^{2}/3 cup of water over low heat for about 5 minutes.
Cool completely, then mix with the lemon juice, ice, and 2 pints of water.

* If using sugar, increase the amount by one-third because fructose is sweeter.

Allegra's Beautiful Juice ✓ ♥ V *DF* **WF** **GF**

This extraordinary colored juice has massive amounts of goodness in it, specifically vitamins A and C, with a hit of pure ginger power (see page 43). It earned the name because it's made with almond milk, which is especially good for keeping skin supple and well. A really good one for looking after yourself all through the winter.

MAKES 2 OLD-FASHIONED GLASSES FULL OF GOODNESS

14 oz carrots, good to get organic for this one   *juice of 1 orange*
1/2 a thumb-size piece of fresh ginger, unpeeled   *1/2 cup almond milk*

Wash the carrots and ginger and put through the juicer—you should have a generous 1^1/4 cups of juice. Add the orange juice and finish by stirring in the almond milk. Dazzling.

Blackberry & Apple Juice ✓ ❤ V *DF* **WF GF**

If gooseberries and elderflowers mark the start of
the British summer, the far side is bookended with apples and
blackberries. This familiar and comforting couple are
usually met in a fruit crisp, sweetened up to the
hilt, and having been well and truly cooked. It's nice
to see them here in the raw, as Nature intended.

MAKES 2

2 small handfuls of blackberries in season
1³/₄ lb apples
ice cubes

Put the blackberries in the bottom of your glass and, as they say in the bar-tending world, muddle
them (i.e. pound them with the end of a rolling pin).
Juice the apples, pour into the glass with a few ice cubes, and stir well.
If your berries aren't the sweetest, a touch of honey works wonders.

Melon & Mint Juice ✓ ❤ V *DF* **WF GF**

The joy of this is that it doesn't involve a juicer, but you really do need a good ripe melon. More
refreshing than a dip in the Mediterranean.

SERVES 4

1 melon of the musk melon size, or half a
honeydew (which is what they use in the
Middle East), flesh only, seeds discarded
2 handfuls ice cubes

a few sprigs of mint, leaves picked
juice of 1 to 2 limes, to taste
2 tablespoons honey

Chuck everything into the blender with around ¹/₂ cup water and blend for about a minute; it's nice if
it's still got a bit of texture to it and isn't just mushy.

Apple, Ginger, & Goji Juice ✓ ❤ V *DF* **WF GF**

It'll keep your liver clear—The Doctor will stay away,
And the Gojis of Tibet will get you spiritually through your day!

MAKES ENOUGH FOR 1

14 oz apples
a nugget of fresh ginger, unpeeled

a squeeze of lemon juice
1 tablespoon goji berries, roughly chopped

Juice the apples with the ginger, zap with vitamin C (the lemon juice), and stir in your gojis.
All power to you.

Hot Apple Mull ✓ ❤ V *DF* **WF GF**

We tend to bring this and/or the Coldbuster back every winter and, just like old friends, I'm always pleased to see them. This is the spicier one, rich in layers while also being light to drink.

MAKES 6 WINTER WARMERS

1/2 a vanilla bean
2 pints apple juice
scant 1/4 cup fructose
1/2 a cinnamon stick

3 cloves
1 1/2 star anise
2 blades of mace
a few gratings of nutmeg

Split the vanilla bean in half and scrape out the seeds.
Pour the apple juice into a saucepan and add the fructose and all the spices.
Bring to a boil and then simmer for 30 to 40 minutes, or until it has reduced by just over half.
Pour into a sterilized bottle and let stand overnight to allow the flavors to mingle.
When you feel in need of a warmer, pour about 1/4 cup into a mug and top off with boiling water.
Really good with a splash of dark rum.

Lemon & Ginger Coldbuster ✓ ❤ V *DF* **WF GF**

Power-packed with things to keep you well in winter, at home we keep a bottle of this by the kettle from November through to daffodil season and self-medicate in a very cozy way.

ENOUGH FOR 6 COLDBUSTERS

scant 1 cup lemon juice
2 fat thumbs (about 1 3/4 oz) of fresh ginger, grated

1 big branch of rosemary
1/3 cup honey, stringy-bark ® if possible

Heat the lemon juice with the ginger and rosemary.
Once warm, stir in the honey until dissolved.
Remove from the heat.
Let cool, then pour, including the rosemary, into a sterilized bottle.
To make a coldbuster, pour 1/4 cup of lemony love into a mug and top off with boiling water.
I like to stir an extra teaspoon of honey into my mug, but some like it sharp.

®See Suppliers, page VI in Appendix.

LEON COCKTAILS

Having fun is a central part of feeling alive, and there's something intrinsically jolly about cocktails. When planning Leon in Ludgate Circus, in London, it didn't take us long to work out that what we really wanted was a proper bar. Ludgate is still one of my favorite bars in London; it's just fun there, like these cocktails. Tom is the third of our cocktail chefs: first came Joe who set the tone, then Uncle Ian who we all miss, and now Tom. The feeling of our list has always been the same: fun, natural good ingredients, and more fun.

Apple Jack Rabbit ♥ V *DF* **WF** **GF**

FOR 1

If you have a cocktail shaker, great. If not, then a large jam jar will do. Basically you need a receptacle that can seal in and hold liquid while being shaken. This drink has a frosted rim and comes in a martini glass or champagne coupe.

2 tablespoons sugar
1 tablespoon ground cinnamon
$^1/_2$ a lemon
cubed ice
1 oz Calvados
1 oz orange juice
1 oz maple syrup
1 oz lemon juice

Mix some sugar and cinnamon (a ratio of about $^2/_3$: $^1/_3$, but don't have sleepless nights about it) on a saucer. Run the cut side of a half lemon around the top $^1/_2$-inch of the glass, then set the glass upside down in the cinnamon and sugar and rotate to give you a cinnamon rim. Put the glasses into the freezer (20 minutes will probably do it to stop the sugar from tracing into the drink—and it also looks a lot nicer. Fill the shaker or resealable jar, or whatever receptacle you've chosen, with ice and add the rest of the ingredients. Give a good strong shake while counting to 10; you're diluting the drink and chilling it at the same time. Strain into the prepared glass. You'll most likely get shards of ice in the drink, but don't worry.

Bramble ♥ V *DF* **WF** **GF**

FOR 1

A favorite of discerning London cocktail drinkers over the past decade, and us. Serve in an old-fashioned glass or looks quite cool in a jam jar.

cubed ice
generous $1^1/_2$ oz gin
1 tablespoon freshly squeezed lemon juice
(or $^1/_4$ of a lemon)
scant 1 tablespoon sugar syrup
generous $^1/_4$ oz crème de mûres
a lemon wedge and blackberry to sit pretty on the top

First of all put some cubed ice into a freezer bag and smash the living daylights out of it to give you crushed ice. Fill your glass with the ice and add the gin, followed by the lemon juice and sugar syrup. Give a little stir, add a bit more ice, then drizzle the crème de mûres over the top in a similar fashion to a Tequila Sunrise. Garnish with a lemon wedge and a blackberry.

Tip: Contary to popular opinion, sugar syrup is stupidly easy to make. Get an empty bottle, half fill with superfine sugar, and top off with water. Seal and shake until all the sugar is dissolved. Let stand for about 20 minutes to settle and then you'll have sugar syrup.
If you want to get really technical, then $2^1/_4$ lb of sugar + 2 pints water = perfect sugar syrup.

Dark & Stormy ♥ V *DF*

This one's easy and tastes sublime; nice one to impress the guests.

FOR 1

generous 1¹/₂ oz dark rum
juice of ¹/₂ a lime
2 dashes of angostura bitters
ginger beer
lime wedge, to complete

Pour the rum into an ice-filled high-ball glass, followed by the lime and bitters. Top off with ginger beer. The bitters aren't essential, but always a pleasure.

Tip: Substitute vodka for the rum and you have yourself a Moscow Mule.

Tequila Sunrise ♥ V *DF* **WF GF**

We love this version; it's more like the original than the ones you find in cocktail bars these days, and a whole lot tastier. Best use 100% Agave tequila and a young one at that—plata or silver tequilas carry more of the rugged Agave flavors.

FOR 1

1¹/₄ oz 100% Agave tequila
1 oz freshly squeezed lime juice (or lemon)
1 oz sugar syrup (see recipe back a page)
generous 1¹/₂ oz sparkling mineral water
generous ¹/₄ oz crème de cassis
ice and lime wedges, to serve

In a high-ball glass or old-fashioned glass, add the tequila, lime juice, sugar syrup, and plenty of ice.
Stir the ingredients together in the glass and add the sparkling water; taste and add more if you like. Pour in the cassis; it will sink to the bottom and give you a beautiful sunrise effect. Garnish with a lime wedge or wheel.

Rangoon ♥ V *DF* **WF** **GF**

This is a great apéritif for any party. It tastes amazing and looks really impressive.

FOR 1

summer fruit, such as berries, cherries, lemon, lime, (and a piece of cucumber)
a few leaves of mint
generous 1 1/2 oz Pimm's or Plymouth fruit cup
ginger ale
cubed ice

Put the chopped fruit and mint into a high-ball glass, followed by the Pimm's. Fill with ice, lots of ice, and top off with ginger ale.

Leon Rum Punch ♥ V *DF* **WF** **GF**

This is a Leon twist on a traditional Rum Punch, a drink that is all about fun. The ratio of ingredients gives you a great structure but play around with the recipe. For example, try using freshly squeezed grapefruit or guava juice instead of orange and pineapple. Or grenadine or passion fruit syrup instead of orgeat. But most of all enjoy, and have fun.

SERVES 6

4 1/4 oz white rum
4 1/4 oz dark or navy rum
2 1/2 oz orange Curaçao or Cointreau
1 1/2 cups orange juice
1/2 cups pineapple juice
2 1/2 oz lime juice
2 1/2 oz monin orgeat (almond syrup)
2 1/2 oz sugar syrup
1 teaspoon angostura bitters

TIPS FOR GARNISHES
maraschino cherries, lime wedges, orange slices, pineapple wedges, and pineapple leaves

Mix all the ingredients together (without ice) in a large pitcher. When you're ready to serve, either ladle into an ice-filled old-fashioned glass or shake in a cocktail shaker with some ice, then strain into a cocktail glass: "on the rocks" or "straight up." Give it a little stir and garnish.

Bourbon Smash ♥ V *DF*

FOR 1

3 lemon wedges
generous 1 tablespoon sugar syrup
4 to 5 mint leaves
generous 1 1/2 oz bourbon
cubed and crushed ice
a mint sprig, to garnish

Put the lemon wedges, sugar syrup, and mint leaves into a cocktail shaker (or whatever you've chosen previously). Using a muddle (technical barman's tool similar to a wooden pestle) or the end of a thin rolling pin, pound the ingredients together, trying to work the oil out of the lemon skins. Add the bourbon and fill up with cubed ice. Seal and shake hard. Put some crushed ice into an old-fashioned glass and strain the rest of the ingredients into it. Finish with a mint sprig.

Note: Once you've finished shaking, the drink is ready. Do not leave it around to dilute further. In other words, get your glass and all your ingredients ready before you shake.

Tip: Bourbons can differ in flavor quite a lot, so try to taste yours before you make the drink. Decide which you prefer and adjust the recipe accordingly.

THE AWAY WEEKENDS

Sometimes a group of us all go away for the weekend to talk about how we can make our restaurants better and after a day or two of hardcore chat we like to do something that keeps us close to the things that are important to us—like fun and food.

The Pig Weekend—Chilley Farm

Earlier this year, we all headed to Chilley Farm© in West Sussex to learn how to break down a pig or two. While some had a crash course in how to make salamis and chorizos, others had an advanced butchery lesson featuring the art of tunnel boning. And once the pigs were in pieces we went on to make bacon, gammon (cured, uncooked ham), and ham, as well as leaving the superior cuts for a good roasting. Henry was particularly keen on his brawn (headcheese), Benny made some seriously good pork, apple, and sage sausages, while for my part I gave a pork pie masterclass. © See Suppliers, page VI in Appendix.

Blind Tasting—David's House

Another time I did a tasting menu where everybody wore blindfolds, and they had to guess what they were eating. I based my choices of ten courses on things they might find surprising and interesting, and would have to use their palates as well as their brains to try to guess what was in their mouth. All went well apart from the jellied eels…

The Menu

Jellied eels

Flying fish roe (the mad colored green & red ones)

Grilled chicken hearts

Umeboshi (very sharp pickled Japanese apricot)

A salt & vinegar potato chip with a squeeze of lime under the nose—guess the flavor of the potato chip—sensory confusion

Crunchy granita (spearmint, green tea & vodka)

Two cheeses (Mont Enebro from Spain and Stinking Bishop from UK)—guess which animal's milk and from which country

Three oils: grapefruit, brazil nut, pumpkin seed

A shot of frangelico, guess the nut (hazel)

Leaf of gold, straight on the tongue

…and at midnight a few of us stumbled up the hill, through the undergrowth toward the church where Elizabeth David is buried, to pay homage to the great lady and nicely round off the weekend. Unfortunately it was a little too dark and we were a little too merry to see the large step at the entrance to the graveyard, so what was intended to be a quiet moment of respectful reverie was transformed in a nanosecond to the kind of childish giggles that we didn't know we had in us any more. As one, we had fallen headfirst toward the headstone, and as we lifted our bruised bodies, covered in mud and bathed in moonlight, there she was, and just then everything was right in the world: a special, magical moment that I'll never forget.

BUYING GUIDE

FRUIT

Apple Firm, no bruising, should look like you want to eat it.

Apricot Soft downy flesh, deep cheeky split.

Banana All the goodness happens when they are soft not hard.

Blackberry Irregular balls to make up the whole—anyone who's picked them off a bush knows.

Blood orange Should look a bit like an oil painting—good to see a range of red to orange swathes coming through the skin.

Cherry Lots of stems, good and plump, soft but not bruised.

Clementine Come with leaves and eat 'em by the pound. Markets sell great 2$\frac{1}{4}$-lb boxes.

Fig Dark and matt for the purples and soft, almost squishy, for the green. Sticky to touch.

Grapefruit Not spongy when you squeeze it.

Gooseberry Really spiky, and you should be able to see the seeds inside; bold stripes stretched to bursting.

Grape Must is always good to see, and a certain stickiness is also encouraging.

Kiwi Sexy to squeeze, not mealy soft.

Lemon Leafy, knobbly, matt, and pale yellow.

Lime Puckered, firm, and dark green—if not very juicy, pop them into the microwave for 20 seconds.

Mango Fragrance and a bit of give.

Melon Sniff the end where they were attached; should have a good, sweet, melony scent.

Nectarine Smooth, full, and pretty natural blush.

Peach Soft down and softer flesh.

Pear No wrinkling at the stem end; when very soft they can be unpleasantly grainy.

Pineapple Ripe when you tug a leaf and it comes out easily.

Plum Season, season, season, and a little must like on a red cabbage or grapes.

Raspberry A little soft down/fur is nice to see.

Rhubarb Crisp, not bendy. Pinkness is not an indicator of flavor or sharpness.

Strawberry Vivid seeds, no white tops or bottoms, deep red, and glossy. Wild strawberries (yum).

VEGETABLES

Artichoke Nice, firm, pert, and not shriveled, fresh to the tips of the petals. Firm stem. Like a flower.

Arugula Not all stalk, good green; smaller means more pepper.

Asparagus Local only! In season. Taut stalks.

Avocado You just have to give them a gentle squeeze—only a little bit of give.

Beet With tops, please.

Belgian endive Tight bulb, no brown tips, has to be firm, no flimsy parts.

Bell pepper Look at our shot on page 58. A few colors on each one.

Broccoli Never select one that yellowing or sprouting—make sure it's nice and firm. Avoid broccoli with hollow stalks.

Brussels sprouts Very nice on the stalk. No brown bottoms. Dark green leaves should be still tight together, not starting to open.

Carrot Dirty, tops on.

Cauliflower Lots of leaves on the outside, nice bright white, and not in a bag, please.

Celeriac Gnarly dude.

Celery Dark green, deep ridges; lots of leaves at the top not rudely chopped off, yellow hearts.

Chard Deep green and a bright white, not yellowing, stalk.

Chiles Firm, and not with seeds rattling around inside like in a brown paper bag.

Corn on the cob Husks and silk.

Cucumber Not shrink-wrapped in a "condom." Knobbly, firm, and glossy.

Eggplant No brown parts, nice and firm.

Fennel Males that are frondy, frilly, and fat are good and juicy. No hints of brown.

Fresh Ginger Get it from an Asian grocery store, smoother and more plump. Taut skin.

Galangal Look for that pinky hue.

Garlic Not much give, seasonal pink skin.

Green pointed cabbage Tightly twisted head, good variation of color from stem to tip.

Greens With veins: stalk should have strength. The main stalk might look limp but it'll firm up with cooking; bountiful.

Jerusalem artichoke Little bit of yellow and

'mornin leon'

FREE RANGE CHICKEN

LEON

Full of Sun
35 GT. MARLBOROUGH ST.
LONDON

Leon

DANCE WITH ME

BIG AND STRONG

LEON

35-36 GREAT MARLBOROUGH STREET LONDON W1F 7JE

LEON-HOTEL
CASABLANCA

PACKED WITH LOVE

FROM FARMS WE TRUST

LONDON U.K   LE·ON   JUST MADE

35 GREAT MARLBOROUGH STREET LONDON   LEON   BIG AND STRONG

LEON

CHEERS

LEON
LONDON UK

FLAVORS FROM NATURE

LE·ON

35/36
Gt. Marlborough St.
London
W1F 7JE
020 7437 5280

some dark brown; they should bounce.

Kale Not chopped, whole heads—should look like something you found growing wild.

Leek Bushy, dirty roots. No yellow tops. Avoid old ones, when the outer skin comes away and you get a slippery membrane (yuck); the white should be smooth.

Lemongrass Light, not brown, doesn't sound like a snare drum when you tap it. Should have an exciting zingy aroma when scratched.

Lime leaves Buy, freeze, and use as needed.

Mushrooms (*cultivated*) Healthy woodland colors, aside from buttons, which should be white. Slightly moist.

Mushrooms (*wild*) A little like a sponge, so when you squeeze you feel the wet and when you release your fingers, they're damp. A bit of forestry and earth is always a good sign.

Parsnip Dirt is where they live and should still have a touch of it around. No trimmed ends.

Potatoes Dirty, hard.Choose based on variety, not the cooking term.

Pumpkin They are designed to last through fall and early winter, but best to avoid from early in the new year.

Purple broccoli rabe Woody stem means they are old. Subject of much debate. Good purple.

Radicchio Should have a bit of give; avoid those with a brown base.

Radish Green fluffy tops and firm; with the root. Not prepped in bags. Buy from Middle Eastern grocery stores because they really know their radishes.

Red cabbage Real musty.

Red onion Not squishy, because a rotten onion is a truly gross thing. Small and tight.

Rutabaga Fairly indestructible, but at the end of the season they are woody and unpleasant.

Savoy cabbage Dark, loose-leaved, and puckered.

Scallion Really long, lots of green, pert, with roots if you can.

Spinach Still joined at the root, not in bags.

Sprouts Avoid damp in the bag/carton. No translucency.

Tomato Should smell of green vine, with some sweetness; go for irregularity; only cherries from November to May.

Turnip White, not yellow. Tops on.

Watercress Bunches, not bags; thicker stalks have more kick and little white flowers, almost dark bluey green, still on the root.

White cabbage Fineall year round, but never as good as in late winter/early spring.

Zucchini Flower on in season, with slightly spiky down on the skin.

HERBS

Avoid buying from a supermarket(waste of money and packaging). Do buy bunches of herbs from Middle Eastern or Asian stores or from farm stands. Or grow your own.

FISH

Shiny eyes. Dark red gills. Firm flesh. Slimy is good. Check the Ocean Conservancy site to find a sustainable-fish dealer. When you find good fish, buy in bulk and freeze.

SEAFOOD

Still twitching. Shells snap shut when you squeeze them or tap them on a hard surface. Should smell of the sea.

MEAT

Ideally all the meat you buy for one purpose should be from the same animal. Healthy color. Find a source you can trust. Free-range, drug-free. Happy lives, good feed. No nasties like growth-promoting hormones, pesticides on the land, antibiotics, or intensive farming methods.

LEGUMES AND NUTS

Legumes: look for a long shelf-life, then you should know they are sort of fresh. On nuts: the fresher the nut, the clearer and cleaner the aroma. Avoid any with old, lingering oily odors. Fresh nuts are also crisp, not softened by age or moisture.

SOME FRUIT & VEG FAMILY TREES

Brassicaceae

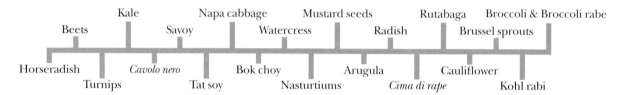

Beets · Kale · Savoy · Napa cabbage · Watercress · Mustard seeds · Radish · Rutabaga · Broccoli & Broccoli rabe · Brussel sprouts

Horseradish · Turnips · *Cavolo nero* · Tat soy · Bok choy · Nasturtiums · Arugula · *Cima di rape* · Cauliflower · Kohl rabi

Solanaceae

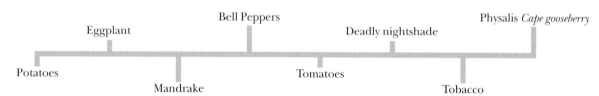

Eggplant · Bell Peppers · Deadly nightshade · Physalis *Cape gooseberry*

Potatoes · Mandrake · Tomatoes · Tobacco

Asteraceae

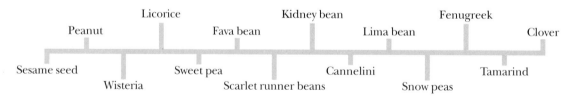

Chrysanthemums · Echinacea · Chamomile · Jerusalem artichoke · Burdock · Belgian endive

Lettuce · Globe artichoke · Thistles · Tarragon · Sunflower · Dandelion

Fabaceae

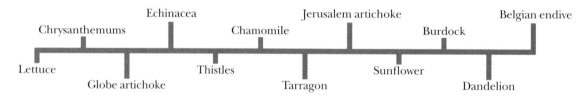

Peanut · Licorice · Fava bean · Kidney bean · Lima bean · Fenugreek · Clover

Sesame seed · Wisteria · Sweet pea · Scarlet runner beans · Cannelini · Snow peas · Tamarind

Roseaceae

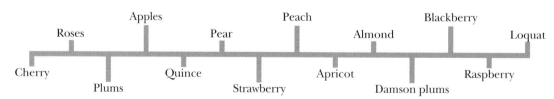

Roses · Apples · Pear · Peach · Almond · Blackberry · Loquat

Cherry · Plums · Quince · Strawberry · Apricot · Damson plums · Raspberry

SUPPLIERS

**Neal's Yard Remedies
(NYR Organic)**
For organic orange oil.
Visit nyrorganic.com to shop online, to order a catalog, or to find an NYR Organic supplier near you.

Olive Oil Merchants
To find telephone numbers and websites of olive oil suppliers near you, visit The Olive Source.
www.oliveoilsource.com/companies-profiles/retailers

Organic Nuts
Braga Organic Farms
Since 2000, all products from this 40-acre farm in Madera, California, have been certified organic by California Certified Organic Farmers. Braga offer a range of products including nuts, seeds, raisins, jumbo dates, and cranberries, all available online.
Braga Organic Farms
10668 Road 26 ½
Madera, California 93637
Toll free: (855) 661 2101 or
www.buyorganicnuts.com

**Organic Chiles
and Chili Powder**
Sorted by hand to ensure high quality, Los Chileros de Nuevo Mexico offer whole, powdered, or frozen chiles along with a wide range of organic chili powders, all available online.
Los Chileros de Nuevo Mexico Gourmet Southwestern Cuisine
P.O. Box 6215 Santa Fe
NM 87502
Toll free: 888 EAT CHILE
www.loschileros.com

Fair Trade Organic Spices
Frontier sells all-natural Fair Trade spices and seasonings. You can purchase the entire range of Frontier products online or refer to their website to find their products at retailers near you.
Frontier Natural Products Co-op
P.O. Box 299 3021 78th St.
Norway IA 52318
www.frontiercoop.com

Miscellaneous
Taylor's Market is a specialty food and beverage market and café located in Sacramento, California. Online, they supply such specialty foods as Spanish chorizo, capers, Madagascar bourbon vanilla beans, olive oil, and a range of organic groceries.
Taylors Market
2900 Freeport Boulevard
Sacramento, California 95818
Toll Free: 1 (877) 770 6077
www.taylorsmarket.com

Chilley Farm Shop
All meat is reared on the farm (all old-fashioned breeds of pigs; Kent ewes). Good farmhouse foods, such as chutneys, pies, and cakes and they also have their own smokery. Full organic status. Excellent pig bits. You will have to pay them a visit next time you are in the UK because they supply from the door only.
Tel: 01323 768836
www.chilleyfarmshop.co.uk

Maldon Crystal Salt Co. Ltd
This company is based in Maldon, in Essex, in the UK (www.maldonsalt.co.uk). However, you can obtain Maldon sea salt online using the Grocery

and Gourmet Department of Amazon or from
SaltWorks®, Inc.
16240 Wood-Red Rd NE
Woodinville, WA 98072
Toll free: (800) 353 7258
www.saltworks.us

Stringy Bark Honey
It's quite hard to get this here in the UK, however these folks say they will ship it (may take a while but lasts ages so bulk buying would be smart). The website allows you to obtain a quote for shipping to the US before you buy.
Email: abaco@access-downunder.com.au
www.access-downunder.com.au

Organic Meat and Poultry
For a state by state listing of suppliers of anything organic from beef, chicken, and lamb through to seafood, visit the website of the Organic Consumers Association. (Also lists suppliers in Canadian provinces.) Products are available directly from the farm as well as through retailers.
www.organicconsumers.org/state/OrganicMeat.html

Amazon.com
Many retailers of high-quality organic foods sell their products on Amazon.
A search through the Grocery & Gourmet Food Department may help you locate specialty food items you are looking for.

THE INDEX

Janet, 1st generation of E. Oldroyd & Sons— she is also the rhubarb queen.

David Hodson-Whittle—for on-hand chicken support and beautiful birds.

Mums & Dads, family & friends for scouring their hearts for the right recipe.

Ben Peverelli, Stuart Burke, Fabrice Berenguer, Yenny Chong, Marlene Oliveira, Carmelita Le Cordier, Henrique Nakano De Souza, Alex Berardinelli, Janka Bielikova, Juliana Zachi, Alexander Martin Ehmcke, Naznin Chowdhury, Andra Simons, Gabriela Putnoki, Marina Vatina, Shabeqal Islam, Brahim Abdallah, Rafal Zuchowski, Jose Rocha, Maciej Zielinski, Marcos Menezes, Marci oDos Santos, Fabiano Teixeira, Helton De Freitas, Claudia Flaim, Eric Lopez, Giulia Giovannelli, Sandra de Borthole Braga, Otavio Augusto, Malin Scanavino, Cyril Rubaine, Adara Scanavino, Marc Rogers, Anna Olsson, Tom Hiney, Dean Parker, Mauricio Lopez, Ola Juszczak, Anna Sandstedt, Belinda Adamson, Alicja Ramotowska, Carmelo Pelligrini, Karim Bouchaker, Ohalia Dos Santos, Claire Nadauld, Magdalena Kozik, Amie Hooper, Peter Gartside, Altair Simonceles, Paulo Roberto De Almeida, Rodrigo Borrero, Shannon Simons, Stephane Roul, Kamal Makram, Jeronimo Fernandes Silva, Rodger Beukes, Fred Dickieson, Jose Miranda da Silva, Vladislav Nastavsevs, Jose Ricardo Zim Nunez, Aristotle Gbaguidi, Joanna Wyrwicz, Alex Maynard, Pauline Heinrich, Katarzyna Karlowska, Brother Ian, Marcello Da Silva, Marta Bezubka, James Backhouse,

Rodrigo Borrero, Mercedes Duch, Alberto Rayado, Uncle Ian, Anne-Marie Gittens, Maria Rickblad, Sarah Robinson, Claudemir Esteuam de Nogueira, Debrah Jones, Olivia McMillan, Laura Kenny, Carla Almeida, Carolina Almeida, Vinicius Vinicius, Giuslan Oliveira Andade, Ailton Albertoni, Ben Tran, Silvia Rueda, Albert Brittz, Annie Jonasson, Joseph Shansky, Jessica Walker, Heber Oliveira, Giancarlo Lanzillo, Houtan Obadai Daniella Guimaraes, Guillermo Hernandez, Pricilla Dresch, Marta Wojcik, Marco Meijide, Kate Sullivan, Emma Greeff, Tahsin Kucuk, Marques Christian, Ben George, Victoria O' May, Leandro Nascimento Loi, Marzena Radwan, Sarunas Kizys, Bertus Bertus, Frida

Alderin, Magdalena Czyzowska, Nick Braxton-Abery, Valdamar Lioti, Edesio Firmino da Silva, Jonathan Pillay, Leandro Eleuterio, Rafal Szarmacher, Tony, Thomas Carey, Jennifer Freeman, Rodrigo Luis Pereira, Cressie, Joe Stokoe Marcos Bernardes da Silva, Daria

Verpritzky, Edson Tocchio, Wyllian Jorge, Kathryn Hughes, Luciano de Lima Fiho, Anna Monika Tkaczyk, Joci Pereira Da Silva, Michael Kancian, Junior Da Silva, Michael Carabot, Michelle Byrne, Jefferson Alves De Oliveira, Damian Thorpe, Sirle Oder, Slawek Malocha, Doroto Musiat, Maria Bernal, Roger Beukes, Peter Kancian, Maria Correa De Barros, Fabiano Teixeira, David Roumagere, Bruno Massaccesi, Olga Geremias, Natalie Bish, Freddie Quartey, Manuela Oliveira, Rafael Barao, Maciej Zielinski, Lucas Sawicki, Leon Joseph, O'Leary Malgorzata Klamut, Patricia Ferreira Martines, Luca Giampieri, Jose Thiago, Santos, Claudia Sampaio, Michaelle Anna Knappstein, Melissa Miani, Justine Issacson, Roee

Holtzkaner, Jorge Giraldo, Edisson Perrez, Luciana Matos, Joas Souza, Mariana Camiloti, Karolina Wojas, Marie Makaya, Francisco Barbosa, Rogerio Monteiro Alex Chaudhary, Heber Emidio Zardiole, Nicolau Da Silva Junior, Johanna Rooth, Antonia Prang, Joao Victor Santos, Alexandre Oliveira, Rafael Pereira Silva, Luciana Bitterncourt, Kay Browne, Luciana Bitterncourt, Patrick Furness, Kimberly Davies, May-Yamna Benbady, Jesse Kropf, Klaudia Szendzielarz, RobertaS Boravskis, Veronica Skantz, Chia-Tzu Hsu, Carlos Alberto Barbosa, Siobhan Davey, Sarah Szymanski, Johanna Maarit Varmo, Jeverson Chaiben, Michelle Anne Bestwick, Fred Henrique Gold Poovan Devasagayam, Oliveira, Davi Coacci, Stephanie Combeer, Kali Gentil Silva, William Hamm, Daisy Barber, Jacobs Dorney, Rogerio Gideon Ferreira, Viodie Barbosa, Ruslanas Spreeth, Elina Ribacenko, Louise Young, Paul (Kwame) Yankson, Ben Oliver, Laetitia Deguy, Jose Pereira, Edivanio Fereira, Emmy Catherine Elsmore, Elton Rognigo Silva,

To my big sister Floss, whose brilliant drawings have made this book so much more for me, and painting the best cheese map ever.

Clive Osbourne @ Maldon—for the salt we couldn't live without.

Jane Sherrard-Smith—for her unswerving nutritional guidance.

Donna Hay for inspiring our Simon to cook

US Meat brochure.

Danny Craze for cooking and doing the dishes.

Krogulec, Charmaine Sylvia Lowe, Lee Hay, Gemma Louise Hunt, Patche Mendy, Mateosz Warpas, Roswita Taylor, Olivier Le Mire, Fabio Constabile, Janet Taylor, Sebastian Nemcek, Denise Vilela, Siaro Isse, Wioletta Woloszyn, Simon Drysdale, Tom Ward, David Baker, Miguel Fontalvo, Milda Zakyte, Sagar Varun Sharma, Norma Sughy Romero, Manana Bouzas Casal, Pietro Verde, Seth David Bradley, Radoslaw Zemsta, Anna Buckle, Sandra Okoye, Pawel Garlicki, Louis Mourlan, Pam Leung, Cedric Montella, Hedi Putallaz, Claudia Barbarotto, Ewa Socha, Lukasz Milak, Piers Harrisson, Floriane Miletic, Diego Oliveira, Chloe Hignett, Agata Szczerecka, Michaela Smazakova, Vikas Kumar, Joe Lynam, Marielle Anguis, Marine Guichard, Javier Lavin, Mubina Fattoum, Ramone Stewart, Chloe

Taylor, Nina Kaczkowska, Carlos Gonzales, Efemena Okogbal, Daniella Guimaraes, Johanna Rooth, Claire O'Keeffe, Gabriela Nicola, Zeyana Al-Mahrizy, Asher Michael Dresner, Magdalena Myskow, Ingrid Chopard-Lallier, Davi Borges, Carolina Sierra Romero, Agota Solyomi, Beatrice

Ray, Marek Malyszko, Reginaldo Matos, Paulina Jonasson, Paula Andrade, Svetlana Poole, Erika Sjoberg, Anna Lipska, Peter McCarthy, Andre Putzier, Egle Narbutaite, Gerda Viljastu, Dilan Kotan, Candy Alderson, Natallia Paulava, Wioletta Jamrozek, Edivanio Ferreira, Julia Karimzanova, Simon Joe Portal, Zhuola Lu, James McCormack, Sebastian Grebos, Piia Vilja, Kaori Tsuchiida, Karina Reyes, Kate Middlemiss, Marta Karcz, Juliana Martins Silva, Viktor Lenken, Lawrence Bowen, Cristina Castro, Mazarra Mazerati, Audrey Colonna, Inah Lee, Mayo Cimarra, Celine Weber, Nishantha Pallawatta, Juraj Mastihuba, Ivana Bednarova, Anna Kalinska,

Richard at Devon Rose—for his help with our four-legged friends—lovely meat.

Kent Murnaghan—for the peaches and bless your pedantry.

The sparkling Tim at Baldwins for all his straighforward nutritional knowledge.

Margaret Rooke for being a true Fairtrade friend.

Ceri from liberation nuts **liberat!on**

Stephanie Garcia-Brazzalotto, Laila Vaziralli, Remigijus Chmieliauskas, Maria Okanrende, Evelyn Ferek, Justyna Rezler, Melody Grelat, Marcos Garrido, Chiara Scipioni,

Persia Aitken-Edwards, Cristian Causa Cecere, Laurence Breva, Otoalse, Claudio Ramin, Maria Zywicka, Yunus Khaydarov, Fabiano Texeira, Crispim Jose Dos Santos, Anna

Freijlich, Shirley Cussi, Maurycy Maciejewicz, Justyna Konca, Erika Kubesova, Yumi Kaneko, John Peter Vespa, Anna Sobczak, Florent Genon-Catalot, Tameira McLean, Hannah Jean La Palombara, Theodore Lestrade, Zuzana Krojidlova, Orlan Masilu-Lokubike, Jon Lopez, Dominik Poczekala, Marta Majewska, Jean-Noel Hardelin, Teja Hudson, Mohamed Ait Ahmed Ouali, Dorota Barczynska, Joost Pronk, Agnes Czolnowska, Maciej Marek, Catherine Elizabeth Neeson, John Cole, Wairunu Mburathi, Piotr Jablonski, Jurga Stackeviciute, Cesar Sandrin, Pedro Francisque, Mariusz Janicki, Charlotte Olsson, Vagner Bustamante, Malgorzata Smiejkowska, Kamila

Helen & Mary at the Trout at Tadpole Bridge—for looking after the worker

Camilla for godmotherly love and peerless internet searching…

M, Fi, and Jigger for shoot props and all our friends and families for more emotional ones.

To Vivian, Robbie, Vincent, Tim, David, and Jacques, thank you for giving us the opportunity to open our first restaurant in Carnaby Street and for your support since. And to Gavyn, Spencer, James, Ian, Michele, Gabby, Kenny, Leon, Mark, Susie, Adam, Susannah, Xander, and Wally for helping us grow. We know we owe you. Literally.

All of the recipe testers, including goddaughter Pillie doo (left), Fred's Mom, and Liz, next door.

John & Perry at Stentons for their brilliant butchery knowledge, and letting us take over their shop.

Fred's sister's intended, Dr. Marc Leger, Assistant Professor of Chemistry, St. Francis Xavier University (Canada)—for the chemical analysis—just like talking to Harold McGee himself.

Rev. Dawn Dickieson MA.—Fred's sis—for all things biblical.

Sarah Smither & Polly & Andy Garnett for the quiet places that got this book written.

Smorgonskis, Nicholas Boyce, Noemie Lehoulleur, Naira Tristao, Rebecca Bish, Bryan John Slaven, Monica Sheila Ventura, Bruno Carvalho, Pedro Da Silva, Claudio Terzoli, Polly Brunt, Stephane Roul, Saffren Pineger, Dianna Hernandez Lopez, Amana Khan, Vitor Vilela Reboucas, David Littlejohn, Kurt Pascoe, Kamil Pajda, Alina Kirgiannaki, Pietro Nughes, Max Cornwall, Vanessa Healy, Beth Amber Delsey, Marlene Dolle, Melissa Ottaviano, Mathieu Johansson, Helen Hacault, Ildiko Tanacs, Leandro Cezar Paiva, Ronaldo Alves, Vanderson Franco, Jackson Freitas, Matheus Begas, Rebecca Neary, Evanildo Fereira, Nicholas Child, Clinette Basden-Tucker, Rodger Beukes, Fernardes Robson,

Jacek Gladysz, Gabriella Heygi, Roberta Pizeli, Callie Rogers, Kinga Jakubowska, Frederic Felix Addey-Mensah, Sofie Maj Thomsen, Conor Irwin, Sophia Geoffrey, Arthurworrey, Leigh Yourell, Danilo Franco Patrick Furness, Carlos Jose Maciel, Pedro Araujo, Alexandre Silva, Luiz Campos, Imogen Eveson, May Benbady, JefersonQuimentoni, Glauco Junior Felicio, Claire Suyang Chang, Bryan Ponza, Frederico Balbi Amatto, Slaven, Ozeias Da Silva, Daria Verpitzky, Camila Nazaret Pereira Macedo, Beltrame, Nicola Bartsch, Sophie Hooper, Kinga Szczypta, Agnieszka Piaskowa, Charlotte Monika Wawrzak, Axelsson, Thiago Pazold, Vanessa Lorenzato, Giuliano Lazzarine, Monteiro Rogerio, Dorota Cavalcante, Alexandra Groszek, Ellie Sylvio Kelly, Luis De Majtas, Rytis Abakumas, Maciej Marly Da Cruz Silva, Lorena Pablo, Marcin Dawicki, Lukasz Zielinski, Paulo Roberto De Garcia-Vila, Alessandra Fortes Grabowski, Luca Genco, Almeida, Ellie Sylvio Kelly, Silva, Jose Andres Riveros, Rodolfo Amaral De Souza, Andrzej Szarmacher, Luiz Vagner Santos, Emilie Alberto Bissaco, Frederico Eduardo, Bruschi Bortol Assi, Marchal, Liza Lindmark, Balbi Amatto, Nurten Canas, Jefferson Freitas, Junior Santos, Naila Broisler, Anne- Kleber Santos, Piotr Luiz Carlos Oliveira, Daniel Cecile Laboure, Smakowski, Sarah Stewart, Fereira Viera, Joseph Spencer, Cedric Magda Teles, Sarah Marcante, Emilia Halayova, Robert Montella, Adriano Machado, Aline Goodchild, Anna Prizio, Daniel Riberio Das Virgens, Jair A Chomiczuk, Lilly Beckett, Fabio Hernandez Mourillo, Brynna Rodrigues, Coarlie Hennen, Jourden, Patricia Parado Lourido, Julie Perignon,

Francesco Cembe-Termex, Virginia Otero, Gregoire Bedoret, Kaisa Palo, Katarzyna Walicka, Emma Home, M Christina Binder, Nina Jaffres, Gavin Williams, Ricardo Martins Da Silva, Jose Aparecido Gomes, Vinisius Mendes, Melanie Kirton, Bruno Massaccesi, Annabel Callum, Alberto Ventin, Shanta Lahiri, Vanessa Soraya Tofano, Michal Kancian, Tatiana Alves

Robson Pizeli, Maria Jose Ruiz, Maria Holubcova, Alex Hamilton, Valdemar Gomes, Krystian Wilegosz, Martin Tchum, Omotola B Alade, Jakub Matusiak, Peter Trojanovic, Krzysztof Zajac, Laila M Vaziralli, Jarod Santana, Angela Longo, Adulai Sabali, Pamela Patricia Campos, Alexandra Di Folco, Terreasha Baker, Niko Nicotera, Malgorzata Jozwicka, Guri Hyustyna, Ali Amjad, Sebastian Bock, Pawel Chryszczanowicz, Piotr Czyzewski, Mariusz Janecki, Ashok Kumar, Wilhelm Menir, Ronaldo Nascimento, Malgorzata Nowicka, Michal Wiech, Robyn B Grundy, Paolo Peretti, Justin Ovenden, Carolina Lopez Garcia, Patricia Kwok, Cristina Castro, Navina Senivassen, Sonia Darbois, Marta Klaudia Holubcova, Zoe Jacobs, Lauren Burris, Alice Gray,

Clara Ostman, Edes Dutra Toreli, Slawomir Dominik, Deborah Lockwood, Anna Sophie Gabriel, Annalisa Ferriano, Benjamin Sparks, Claire Newlands, Beatriz Carvalho, Eustaquio CD Neto, Imanol Plazaola Oyazabel, Ana Carolina Magalhaes, Antoine Serres, Giovana Petry, Malgorzata Adamczyk, Athina Delimara, Elizabeth Okogba, Natalia Juriene, Agnes Von Gegerfelt, Gaelle Citharel, Bana Emmanuel, Nadia Rezguli, Basia Cummings, Placida Di Crescenzo, Regis Kelly, Juliana Rodrigues, Kwame Yankson, Ben Rider, Cristina Carolina Sachs, Ursula Bowerman, Lee Watson, Daisy Barber, Maxine Haher, Charlotte Whelan, Kei Tanaka, Maciej Zielinski, Laura Walcot, Guilherme Turibio Da Silva, Joanna Przytarska, Diana Yekinni, Carlos Gonzales, Olivia Taussig-Moore, Malgorzata

To Georgia Glynn Smith for showing her love of Leon through her mind-blowingly sharp photography, whilst embracing her (and our) madder side.

Sue for helping Georgia, which helps us.

Ellie – the best gofer on a shoot.

The other PHOTOGRAPHERS:
Cousin Henry Simpson, Alex, Allegra, Fred, Susi, Luke and Martin.

Kurasinska, Piotr Glabicki, Carlos Rabanillo, Gregory Rosamont, Vanessa Jarrin, Mayuko Sugimitsu, Nicola Sutcliffe, Anna Marczenko, David Smit, Isabel Merino, Kevin Gendron, Rodrigo Luis Ferreira, Piotr Slabonski, Stanley John Hornsey, Krystian Wilegosz, Marcin Dawicki, Krzysztof Borkowski, Jolita Cekaviciute, Anne- Charlotte Lataste, Joanna Klimczak, Queralt Torrent Llamas, Remy Orciac, Arran O`Neill, Marcio Gonzales Silva, Giovanni Luca Cucurachi, Edyta Plawecka, Stephen Oakley, Maciej Zuchowski, Haoyi Wang, Afonso Padras, Efemena Okogba, Daniele Massino Ciprian, Imogen Hamilton, Jorg Jauernig, Cesar Guerrero, Marina Falabella, Kazimierz Mazur, Ellie Richold, Peter Ternai, Dariusz Lamecki, Fabio Rodrigues, Sagarvarum Sharma, Tereza Sera, Sandra Cieslak, Sarah Lever, Samuel Sallah, David Sandoval Garcia, Robert Malicin, Miguel Torres, David Febrero Lopez, Tero Saavalainen, Daniele Meus, Henry

Hryn Acosta, Nathalia Franco, Alicja Merska, Agata Cyminska, Edward Bocanegra, Pedro Carvalho, Cerys Bowen, Ralev Dimitar, Karolina Jurga, Mitchell Kardon, Tomasz Kolakowski, Dauron Boltaev, Bing Xia, Lorena Ponte, Laura Power, Laure Darcel, Miriam Gontijo, Jose Luis. Merino Garcia, Adulai Sabali, Fiona Tang. Tita Cvetkovic, Robert Doka, Cong Fu, Alex Thirlwell, Pedro Miguel Camargo Da Cunha Reg, Ann Jorgensen, Hector Palacios Jose Antonio Moreno, Aneta Jurkowlanie, Julia Karimzanova, Kassandra Kay, Lindsay Boucher Allegra McEvedy, Henry Dimbleby, John Vincent.

Nicky & Ben at Ludgate for letting us shoot a book in their restaurant, and being oh so gracious about it.

Charles Carey—for oily assistance.

Aunty Sophie for the bean collage that set the tone, not to mention this mad button self-portrait.

Birgit / Carly & all the bakers at Frankonia.

Helge Rubinstein for the chocolate mousse that launched our restaurants.

All those at www.eattheseasons.co.uk for seasonality help.

Golly—for all matters Iranian.

Roger Aldons and Rosalie Archibald for their sweet honey facts.

Sandra, Dave in Soho, Nigel, Alice for their designs, past, present, and future.

Lisa—picture desk at the *Guardian* for help with our worries.

Susi for a year of support (her) and increased crabbiness (me), not to mention her bean jewelry.

To Lorraine, Sybella, Jonathan, and Katherine at Conran Octopus: all examples of people at the top of their game. Thank you for making it everything we hoped, and so much more.

Nick at Cape Clear for fishy facts.

Ben Woodcraft at Ben's Fish.

Laura at MSC—for hand holding through fishy waters.

Stuart and Chef's connection—for all the vegetables, and random vegetable identification.

An Hachette UK Company
www.hachette.co.uk

First published in Great Britain in 2008 by Conran Octopus Limited,
a part of Octopus Publishing Group,
Endeavour House, 189 Shaftesbury Avenue, London WC2H 8JY
www.octopusbooksusa.com

Distributed in the US by Hachette Book Group USA
237 Park Avenue, New York NY 10017 USA

Distributed in Canada by Canadian Manda Group
165 Dufferin Street, Toronto, Ontario, Canada M6K 3H6

This edition published in 2014

ISBN: 978 1 84091 656 0
Printed in China on 100% recycled paper

Publisher: Lorraine Dickey
Managing Editor: Sybella Marlow
Researcher and Co-cooker: Fred Dickieson
Art Director (for Leon): Alex Maynard
Art Director (for Conran Octopus): Jonathan Christie
Illustrator: Flora McEvedy
Special Photography: Georgia Glynn Smith
Production Manager: Katherine Hockley

XIX Acknowledgments

LAROUSSE GASTRONOMIQUE

alian Food
Penguin Handbook 5/-
zabeth David

SECTION THREE
DAINTIES FOR
TEA-TIME

John, James, Brother Ian, our financial friends Spencer & James, Alex & Allegra, Big Kitchen, February 2006

MY CORNERS
FLATTEN ME

Henry, Allegra & John 2004